CAVING BASICS

A Comprehensive Guide for Beginning Cavers
Third Revised Edition

Editor
G. Thomas Rea

Produced by the NSS Special Publications Committee
David McClurg, Chairman

Layout and design by G. Thomas Rea
Cover design by David McClurg

NATIONAL SPELEOLOGICAL SOCIETY
2813 Cave Avenue
Huntsville, Alabama 35810-4431
USA

CAVING BASICS, THIRD EDITION

Published by
National Speleological Society, Inc.
2813 Cave Avenue
Huntsville, Alabama 35810-4431

Library of Congress Catalog Card No. 92-80953

ISBN No. 1-879961-00-8

Front cover photograph by Scott Fee: *"Canyon Climbin'," the 1989 NSS Photo Salon Merit Award Winner. Ray Sira exploring an undeveloped portion of Jewel Cave, South Dakota, that is shown on the "Wild Cave Tour."*

Back cover photograph by David and Janet McClurg: *The entrance to Schoharie Caverns, Schoharie County, New York.*

Printed in the United States of America

CONTENTS

Warning!

Caving involves the risk of serious injury or death. A commitment to safe caving practices, a thorough understanding of the equipment used, and mastery of the techniques involved can greatly reduce, but will never eliminate the risks inherent in the sport.

The techniques and practices described in this manual must be discussed and practiced with knowledgeable, experienced cavers above ground, and must be thoroughly understood and mastered, before you attempt to use them in caving. The place to make your mistakes and discover any misunderstandings is with qualified instructors before you enter a cave. Even after you have achieved a basic mastery of these techniques and practices, your first cave trips should be in the company of competent, experienced cavers who can help you to further sharpen and refine your skills.

Disclaimer of Liability:

Serious injury or death could result from use of the techniques, practices, or equipment described in this book. It is your responsibility to obtain qualified instruction in safe caving for yourself, understanding that even the best training only reduces and does not eliminate the risks of death or injury.

YOU ASSUME THE RISK OF INJURY OR DEATH BY USING THE TECHNIQUES, PRACTICES, OR EQUIPMENT DESCRIBED IN THIS BOOK.

THIS BOOK IS SOLD WITHOUT ANY WARRANTY WHATSOEVER, EXPRESSED OR IMPLIED, BY THE AUTHORS, THE EDITORS, OR THE NATIONAL SPELEOLOGICAL SOCIETY.

FOREWORD

In 1976 the Board of Governors of the National Speleological Society decided to develop course material to be used by its local chapters (called grottos) to train new members. They intended that the new members should be provided with the necessary basic information on caves and caving. This would make it possible for them to gain experience safely with older members of the grotto. The combination of information and experience should help to make it possible for them to explore caves in safety and comfort.

This book is the result of that directive. It is written primarily for the beginning caver and can serve as the basis for a grotto training course or as individual reading for more informal training. It provides a standardized, authoritative guide to the basic information needed to safely explore the typical cave. Each chapter has been authored by an "expert" in that field. In addition to the basics of caving, references have been included to sources of more advanced information.

The first edition, published in 1982, was edited by Jerry Hassemer. The second edition was revised by Tom Rea and appeared in 1987.

This third edition is extensively revised and includes much new and updated material. There are four completely new chapters and five chapters have been completely rewritten by new authors. Most of the remaining chapters have been updated by their existing authors or the editor. An extensive index has been added. Sample release forms (in Appendix B), which may be used as examples to design your form, are also new in this edition.

G. Thomas Rea,   Editor
NSS Executive Vice-President
NSS President 1978-1981
March 25, 1992

PREFACE

This Manual

Caving is the sport of exploring and studying caves. It is a growing sport, not only in the United States, but around the world. People who explore caves are cavers. There are proper and safe caving methods and there are improper and unsafe methods of caving. This manual explains how to cave properly. From it you will be able to learn about lights, helmets, packs, conservation, and much more.

Twenty-three experienced cavers contributed the material which follows. Their combined experience totals about 450 years. Many of the authors are recognized authorities in their field and are constantly developing new theories and improving techniques to make caving safer and more enjoyable for the rest of us. A short section following this preface gives information about these people.

Each chapter of this manual was written independently. The chapter sequence was arranged in an order that the editor felt coincides with the natural way a person becomes comfortable in the cave environment. First, one needs a light, not just one, but at least three of them. Then one needs a helmet, cave clothing, and a pack. He needs to know how to handle himself and his equipment in the cave and while searching for one. A caver will then develop a greater respect for the cave itself, the things he finds there, the land above it and its owner. Finally he will want to satisfy his curiousity about why the cave is there and where the strange animals and objects he finds there came from.

What is included here is only an introduction for a beginning caver or one who does not care to become a specialist in any one aspect of caving. Topics such as cave photography and cave surveying are not addressed. This, then, is a "basic" manual intended only to develop the basis for further exploration by the reader.

The techniques and practices described in this manual must be discussed and practiced with knowledgeable, experienced cavers above ground, before you attempt to use them in caving. The place to make mistakes and discover misunderstanding is before you enter a cave.

The NSS

The National Speleological Society (NSS) is the only national caving organization whose membership is made up not only of sport cavers (those who cave for the fun of it) but also cave conservationists and speleologists (those who study caves). Many members fall into two or more of these categories at the same time. The present membership is over 10,000. The purpose of the National Speleological Society is "to promote interest in and to advance in any and all ways the study and science of speleology, the protection of caves and their natural contents, and to promote fellowship among those interested in them." The Society has a permanent office in Huntsville, Alabama, and also owns several caves. The address of the Society office is:

National Speleological Society
2813 Cave Avenue
Huntsville, Alabama 35810-4431
Phone: (205) 852-1300

Members of the National Speleological Society in the same area generally form a cave club and apply to become a chapter of the Society. Such a group is usually called a grotto; currently there are about 140. Several grottos may join together to form a region. Functions of grottos and regions vary greatly, but each provides an organization in which the novice caver can learn about caving and can find others with whom to go caving. If you do not know of a grotto in your area, write to the national office for the address of the grottos near you.

Any person interested in caves should join the National Speleological Society as well as the local grotto. Membership in the Society provides you with the monthly *NSS News* and the quarterly *NSS Bulletin*. The *NSS News* usually contains one or two cave trip reports on some outstanding cave or cave system, a calendar of caving events around the country, notes on the meetings and actions of the Society, book reviews, reports of equipment testing, accident reports and analysis thereof, and much more.

The *NSS Bulletin* is the scientific publication of the Society. It is the only journal in the United States devoted to speleology. Current ideas on cave development, cave minerals, the evolution of cave life, and other topics are reported.

Just how valuable these are to you depends on how you use them. They can go from the mail to the files. Or you can dig into them to see how the articles in the *News* and *Bulletin* relate to your type of caving and how these ideas can be used to broaden your caving experience. To be a caver is to be flexible in your ideas, equipment, techniques, and practices.

Brand Names

The use of specific brand names of various products in this manual is for clarity and convenience only. For instance, it would be very hard to talk about underground lights without using their names. However, the use of these names does not imply any endorsement of the use of these products by the National Speleological Society, the particular author, or the editor.

ACKNOWLEDGEMENTS

The authors of the following chapters and the artists and photographers who provided the illustrations are the ones who made this book possible. It is sometimes more difficult to review and revise work you have already done, and many of the authors have done their duty in this newly revised and updated edition.

Larry Reece and Scott Fee read the entire book for consistency and style. Noel E. Sloan, MD, reviewed the First Aid chapter. Suggestions have also been accepted from Wayne Marshall and Paul Stevens. Scott Fee provided many new photographs. Susan Sweeney produced the new cartoons on pages 3, 78, and 87.

Linda Heslop provided the drawings on pages 32 and 118. The drawing on page 44, also by Susan Sweeney, is from *Caving in America* ©National Speleological Society. The drawing of a bat on page 140 was given to the National Speleological Society by Mike Hayton in 1984. It has been used on the "Bats Need Friends" brochure.

Without the cooperation and hard work of my Compaq computer and Ventura Publisher software that together did the grunt work involved in layout and typesetting, this edition would not be in your hands today.

G. Thomas Rea, Editor

ABOUT THE AUTHORS

Langford G. Brod, Jr.
Tucson, Arizona

Reading Cave Maps

Lang joined the Middle Mississippi Valley Grotto in 1959. He has served as chairman of the Missouri Speleological Survey and as a director of the National Speleological Society. Lang maps small caves as well as large ones. He is well-known for his efforts in Missouri's 16-mile-long Berome-Moore Cave System. Lang moved to Arizona in 1969 and he is currently a member of the Esrabrosa Grotto and the Arizona Speleological Association.

Roger W. Brucker
Dayton, Ohio

Moving Through A Cave

Roger is an Honorary Member of the National Speleological Society. He was a founder and later president, of the Cave Research Foundation. Roger helped organize the week-long 1954 C-3 Expedition and National Speleological Society project in Floyd Collins Crystal Cave, Kentucky. He is co-author of three books on caves: *The Caves Beyond* and *The Longest Cave* (both about the Mammoth Cave System), and *Trapped!* (a biography of Floyd Collins). He has taught *Speleology* at Western Kentucky University since 1980.

Eileen Carol
Santa Rosa, California

First Aid

Eileen joined the Southern California Grotto in 1969 and the National Speleological Society in 1971. In 1982 she received the National Speleological Society President's Appreciation Award for service to the Society and became a Fellow of the Society in 1984. She has taught courses on caving first aid, conducted rabies immunization programs for cavers, and helped develop a spine board for cave rescue. Her contributions include numerous presentations for the National Speleological Society and various caving groups on caving first aid and safety as well as on the infectious diseases cavers may encounter. In addition to cave exploration in Mexico in the 1970s, she most recently conducted studies on the occurrence of histoplas-mosis in the caves of the Chillagoe Karst and Undarrah lava tubes of north Queensland, Australia. She is also a Fellow of the Explorers Club and a member of the Society of Woman Geographers.

Ray Cole
Alexandria, Virginia

Cave Lamp Battery Charging
Caving Safety

Ray joined the District of Columbia Grotto in 1970 when he moved from West Virginia to Virginia. He was Grotto Chairman in 1972 and 1973. He has been co-chairman of the Organ Cave System Project since 1973. Ray was one of the founders of the Appalachian Search and Rescue Conference. Now with three small children, Ray and Susan are busy with scouting and caving with the next generation. Ray is currently a member of FUN Grotto, DC Grotto, and WVACS.

George M. Crothers
St Louis, Missouri

The Archaeology of Caves

George Crothers has studied caves in Georgia, Kentucky, Tennessee, Virginia, and elsewhere in the eastern United States. He is a member of the National Speleological Society and has been caving since 1979. He is a PhD student at Washington University in St Louis and has authored and co-authored several articles on cave archaeology. His masters thesis was on the prehistoric archaeological remains in Big Bone Cave, Tennessee.

Donald Davis
Parachute, Colorado

Carbide or Electric Lighting?
The Carbide Lamp

Donald discovered the connection passage in Spanish Cave, Colorado, in 1959. He has explored and studied caves throughout the western U.S. He worked as a naturalist at Carlsbad Caverns National Park and has been a carbide lamp collector and dealer. He has recently been active on multi-day exploration trips into Lechuguilla Cave, New Mexico.

William R. Elliott
Austin, Texas

An Introduction to Biospeleology

Bill joined the University of Texas Grotto in 1967. He received an MS and PhD in Biology from Texas Tech. His graduate research was on topics related to cave biology. Bill has studied and described cave life from caves in Texas, New Mexico, California, and Mexico. During 1977 and 1978 Bill conducted an ecological transplant of harvestmen from a cave to a mine for the U.S. Army Corps of Engineers at the New Melones Lake project in California. He has served as chairman of the Texas Speleological Association and chaired the biology session at annual conventions of the National Speleological Society.

Louise Hose
Colorado Springs, Colorado

Fitness and Nutrition

Louise has a BA in Physical Education, an MS and PhD in Geology, and is an assistant professor of geology at the University of Colorado. She is also a former national masters cycling champion and has competed for the national team. She wrote her master's thesis on the geology of the Sistema Purificacion, Mexico's longest cave, and is presently active in the exploration of Sistema Cuicateco, the deepest known cave in the New World.

Kyle Isenhart
Little Hocking, Ohio

The Selection, Use, and Care
of Ropes for Vertical Caving

Kyle joined the National Speleological Society in 1970. He is a charter member of the Vertical Section of the Society and served as its chairman for two years. Kyle is active in developing vertical equipment and new types of rope. He does most of his vertical caving in the tri-state area of Tennessee, Alabama, and Georgia (TAG).

Tom Kaye
Alexandria, Virginia

Electric Light Systems for Caving

Tom began caving in 1975. His caving interests include surveying, photography, the mathematics of cave survey error propagation, cave survey computer programs, the statistical analysis of reasons for becoming a caver, and electric light system technology. He has served the Society as editor of both the *Caving Information Series* and the *Compass and Tape* newsletter of the Surveying and Cartography section. He has also served as the chairman of two caving clubs. Tom particularly enjoys surveying maze caves.

Mark Laing
Indianapolis, Indiana

Cave Conservation

Mark has been caving in Indiana and Florida since 1981 and has been a member of the National Speleological Society since 1986. He has been both Chairman and Vice Chairman of the Central Indiana Grotto. He is currently the chairman of the Society's Conservation Committee.

Ed LaRock
Denver, Colorado

General Equipment for Each Caver

Ed joined the Philadelphia Grotto in 1970. He served as chairman of the Commander Cody Caving Club, a chapter of the National Speleological Society in Newark, Delaware. He is the author of *Caves of Snyder County, Pennsylvania* (MAR Bulletin 10). Ed was active in mapping efforts in the Friars Hole System, West Virginia.

David McClurg
Carlsbad, New Mexico

Why You Should Join an
Organized Caving Club

A member of the National Speleological Society since 1958 and still a very active caver, David has written three books on caving techniques, the latest being Adventure of Caving. He has also served the National Speleological Society as Administrative Vice President; Board Member; Chairman of Public Relations, Program and Activities, and the Vertical Section; and Chairman and Co-chairman of two Society conventions, Sequoia, California (1966) and Angels Camp, California (1975). He is currently chairman of the Special Publications Committee.

Thomas E. Miller
Grand Canyon, Arizona

Caver's Clothing and Insulation

Tom has caved in many climates, from the Andes to the Canadian Rockies and Europe to New Zealand. He was Exploration Editor of the *NSS Bulletin* from 1985 through 1991. He received the Lew Bicking Award, awarded by the National Speleological Society for dedication to thorough exploration of a cave or group of caves, in 1985. His doctorate was completed in 1982 after fieldwork in the Caves Branch Karst of Belize. He left time in his schedule for the Great Expectations connection in 1980, then led the 1984 through 1988 Chiquibul expeditions to Belize and Guatemala. He currently works for Grand Canyon National Park and advises about cave protection.

John E. Mylroie
Mississippi State, Mississippi

The Geology of Caves

John has been a member of the National Speleological Society since 1970 and has caved throughout the United States and overseas. He has done most of his caving in New York, Kentucky, and the Bahama Islands. John is a professor of geology at Mississippi State University, and has written many articles on the origin and development of caves.

Jim Pisarowicz
Denver, Colorado

Additional Light Sources
Caving Helmets

Jim joined Colorado Grotto in 1974. He has served as Chairman of both Colorado Grotto and Colorado Mines Grotto. He is a former editor of *Depths of the Rockies* and *CINTHER*. Jim is an active cave diver and dove Spring Cave's fourth sump in 1978.

Tom Rea
Danville, Indiana

Driving to the Cave
Reading Topographic Maps
Locating Caves on Topographic Maps

Tom joined the National Speleological Society in 1961. He served as President of the Society from 1978 to 1981. He has also served as Secretary-Treasurer and both Executive and Administrative Vice-President. He is the editor of the second and third editions of *Caving Basics*. He holds a Bachelor of Science in Electrical Engineering and a Master of Business Administration in Management. He is retired from Indiana Bell Telephone Company where he served for 33 years in outside plant engineering, right of way acquisition, and computer applications.

Frank Reid
Bloomington, Indiana

Electronics in Caving

Frank began caving in Kentucky in 1961. He is a specialist in cave radio and cave rescue communications and a co-founder of the Electronics and Communications Section of the National Speleological Society. He holds a Bachelor of Science in Electrical Engineering and has amateur radio and commercial pilot's licences.

Joel B. Stevenson
Asheville, North Carolina

Risk Management for
Cavers and Cave Owners

Joel has been an active caver since 1972. A member of the North Carolina Bar, he is senior partner in the Asheville, North Carolina, law firm of Swain, Stevenson and Moore, P.A. His practice is litigation oriented and is primarily concerned with plaintiff's personal injury and criminal defense cases.

He has been chairman of the Society's Legal Committee since 1983, has served as a director of the American Cave Conservation Association and has spoken at numerous cave management seminars on the subject of risk management for cavers and cave managers. He was selected a Fellow of the National Speleological Society in 1988, he is also a trustee of the National Speleological Foundation and a member of the Vertical, Rescue, and Cave Diving Sections of the Society.

William Storage
Long Beach, California

Single Rope Techniques

Bill chairs the Safety & Techniques Committee of the National Speleological Society and is a director of the Society. In 1970 he began caving in the cold, wet caves of West Virginia. He is involved with a number of exploration and survey projects in Appalachia and in Mexico. He is a professional design safety analyst and enjoys engineering analysis of caving equipment and techniques.

William F. Tozer
Pendleton, Indiana

Landowner Relations

Bill has been an member of the National Speleological Society since 1960 and a member of the Central Indiana Grotto since 1963. He has worked with landowners as a grotto officer and as a caver. His caving has been throughout the midwest, TAG, and east to Massachusetts; west in Texas, Utah, and New Mexico; and south in Old Mexico. He is still actively caving and still "talking to land owners."

William B. White
University Park, Pennsylvania

The Geology of Caves

Will has studied caves in Pennsylvania, Virginia, West Virginia, and elsewhere for almost 30 years.

He has served as Executive Vice-President of the National Speleological Society and as Earth Sciences Editor of the *NSS Bulletin*. Will is a professor of geology at Penn State. He is the author of many articles on cave geology.

Alan Williams
Arvada, Colorado

Cave Packs

Alan started caving in 1966 in Arizona. He has explored caves in the USA, Canada, and Mexico. Alan served as an officer in grottos of the National Speleological Society in Arizona, Utah, and Colorado. Recently he has been active in mapping Groaning Cave in Colorado. He is also an accomplished cave photographer and cartoonist.

Equipment

Coulter Miller removes his vertical gear after descending the 70-foot entrance pit to Bighorn Cave, Wyoming. The rest of the cave is strictly horizontal so everyone leaves his vertical gear here. (photo Scott Fee)

Chapter 1

CARBIDE OR ELECTRIC LIGHTING?

Donald G. Davis
NSS 4956

Carbide lamps came into use just before 1900 and were used extensively in mines by 1915. Portable electric lamps were not used to any extent before 1908, but soon thereafter improved models of essentially modern design appeared (Pilley in 1911, General Electric in 1912, Edison in 1913). In spite of the fact that efficiency was low by present standards, electric lighting steadily gained adherents. By the mid-1930s carbide was losing its position as the standard miner's light, and by the mid-1940s its use was considered obsolete except in small operations, prospecting, and exploration (Young, 1946). Acetylene lighting seems to have reached its peak of efficiency long ago, while there is still great potential for improvement in electric lighting, particularly in regard to more compact energy sources.

Why, then, do many American cavers still use carbide lamps as their primary light source? Caving is an aesthetic pursuit; and there is certain atavistic pleasure in lighting one's way underground by fire—even so sophisticated a fire as the acetylene flame. There are, however, more concrete reasons: caving is not mining and neither method of lighting has yet been established as superior under all conditions. Most mining is systematic and relatively predictable; in such a case, procedures can be tailored to take full advantage of the convenience of electric lights—they are clean, safe, and need little routine attention. And the brilliant spot-beam obtainable with electric

point-source light cannot be duplicated by the line-source light of acetylene. Electric lights are also better adapted for intermittent use, as carbide lamps do not switch on and off instantly. An electric headpiece, where the battery is carried elsewhere, is lighter on the helmet than a self-contained carbide lamp.

Carbide lighting, however, tends to be more versatile under the varied demands of caving (except in cave diving or climbing under waterfalls). The lamp and fuel, in the usual form, are lighter and less cumbersome that most electric assemblies, and need no vulnerable cord. The light is even and diffuse, minimizing the hazard of stepping into unseen holes. Fuel supply can be determined at a glance, and consumption regulated as needed. Carbide light has a special advantage for expeditions in remote areas, since it does not depend on the availability of chargers or expensive sets of extra batteries. The lamp can serve as a heat source in emergencies, or the carbide itself can be dampened to make an open fire. The lamp may warn of dangerous CO_2 concentrations by burning poorly or going out. Perhaps most important, their simple mechanical functioning makes them less apt to develop malfunctions that cannot be repaired underground, although even good quality carbide lamps have minor operating problems more often. Electric lights that are as reliable under the mud, dust, wetness, and hard knocks of caving are still much more expensive.

Total costs are lower with carbide than electric lighting except perhaps on a very long-term basis.

An actual example of the performance obtainable with a good carbide system and careful management occurred on a two-day trip several years ago. Using an Auto-Lite with a four-inch parabolic Justrite reflector, I averaged about seven and a half hours per charge of carbide. The lamp was in actual use for 38 hours. The flame was kept at one half to one inch (adequate with a parabolic reflector in normal passages) and only five 2½-ounce charges were used. Weights involved were as follows:

Empty Lamp	8 oz
Carbide Used	12 ½ oz
Water Used	16 oz

Total weight was about two and a half pounds. Carbide containers and spare parts were of negligible weight; canteen weight is not counted since the canteen was necessary for drinking water in any case. (Weight of the lamp water itself could have been neglected as it was freely available in this as in many other caves.) Carbide was obtained in bulk for about 50¢ per pound (1986) for an operating cost of about one cent per hour of light. Since most people seem to get only about three hours from a charge of carbide, the operating cost then would be about 2⅝¢ per hour and the weight of the carbide used would be nearly two pounds.

It is not easy to compare carbide and electric light directly in terms of brightness and burning time per unit weight as most electric lights are focused to a spot beam, much brighter than carbide directly ahead but dimmer to the sides. It is possible, however, to alter an electric light reflector to give a light pattern resembling carbide's (Plummer, 1961; 1962). An electric light using a PR-2 flashlight bulb (1.2 watt, 2.4 volt, 0.5 ampere), is roughly comparable in light output to a carbide lamp with a one half-inch flame. With four nickel-cadmium cells (eight ampere-hour size) this electric light weighs about 2½ pounds and should burn 32 hours (Plummer, per. comm., 1970). This is performance somewhat inferior to the carbide example. Using fresh alkaline cells of the same bulk, however, this same electric light should burn two or three times as long as with the nickel-cadmium cells. This is considerably longer than a carbide flame of similar intensity on a fuel supply of equal weight. In actual practice electric assemblies often weigh more and burn for a shorter time than carbide lamps; but this is because brighter bulbs (up to six watts or more) or inefficient batteries or heavy casings are commonly used. As a source of light energy, carbide (including the weight of the water required) has some efficiency advantage over nickel-cadmium batteries in terms of watt-hours per pound but is considerably inferior to alkaline batteries of modern design.

My experience suggests the following generalizations: for trips less than a day long, in small- to medium-sized passage, and especially where a long hike is involved, a carbide cap lamp will give good light at the best cost/weight ratio. For trips of similar length but in larger passage and/or close to your vehicle, a rechargable electric (Wheat, MSA, FX-2, or NiCd) is best. For greatest efficiency, convert the system to use a halogen bulb if it does not come with one. For multi-day trips, where weight becomes critical, use a halogen bulb with alkaline batteries, which can burn several times as long as any currently available rechargeable system of the same weight. Lithium cells are even more efficient but much more costly. In cold caves, alkaline batteries lose significant power unless the case is carried inside one's clothing; lithium cells are much less affected.

I do not advocate total reliance on any one mode of lighting. A caver should diversify his light sources (at least three) to meet the unexpected; a carbide caver will be wise to carry a waterproof electric light with a lamp bracket for helmet mounting as a secondary light source. And an electric caver would often be wise to carry a backup carbide lamp.

Some technically advanced cavers use a twin carbide/electric system involving two helmet brackets—one with a carbide lamp, used in routine caving to conserve power, and the other with an electric headpiece to be used for swimming, waterfall work, lead spotting, or route finding.

References

Plummer, B. (1961) "Electric Cave Lamp Reflector," *Baltimore Grotto News*, Vol 4, pp 94-96 and Speleo Digest 1961: Section 3, pp 1821.

_____ (1962) "Quantitative Comparison of Cave Lamps," *Baltimore Grotto News*, Vol 5, pp 184-188 and Speleo Digest 1962, Section 3, pp 1-5.

Young, G.J. (1946), *Elements of Mining*: McGraw Hill, New York and London, 755 p.

Chapter 2

THE CARBIDE LAMP

Donald G. Davis
NSS 4956

Introduction

The acetylene lamp was introduced into mine use about 1897 and had become standard for mining by 1915. By about 1940 electric headlamps had supplanted carbide lighting in most mines. Yet today the main light source used by many cavers is the carbide lamp. Carbide lamps afford versatility and ruggedness at low expense under most cave conditions. The advantages and disadvantages that led to these generalizations are analyzed; and the merits of different carbide lamp styles are discussed and the five most common makes compared. Practical aspects of techniques, parts, accessories, and maintenance are considered in detail.

How Acetylene Lamps Function

Miners' or cavers' carbide lamps (Figure 1) normally consist of two chambers, a water tank above and a removable calcium carbide canister below, with a connection valve to permit controlled seepage of water into the carbide. The carbide and water react to generate calcium hydroxide and acetylene gas. This reaction is usually written as follows:

$$CaC_2 + 2H_2O \rightarrow Ca(OH)_2 + C_2H_2 + heat$$

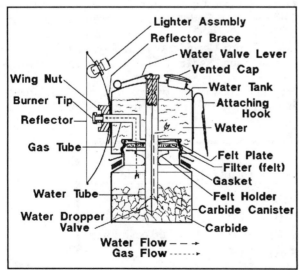

Figure 1—A generalized carbide lamp suitable for mounting on a helmet. Shown are the main parts and the water and gas flows.

The gas passes through a filter into a tube and through a tiny burner-tip orifice designed for the optimum mixture of air with acetylene. When ignited, it burns with a brilliant yellow-white flame. (The unusual brightness of the flame is due to incandescence of tiny carbon particles released from the carbon-rich acetylene.) A reflector concentrates the light in the desired direction.

History of the Carbide Miner's Lamp

The invention of the carbide lamp, a great advance in underground illumination, was not as early as many people assume. Acetylene was first produced by Edmond Davy in 1836, but it long remained an academic curiosity, as early methods of production were costly. Practical use of the intense light of the acetylene flame was accomplished only through the manufacture of calcium carbide. This compound was described by Wohler in 1862, but its commercial history began in 1892, when it was first made in quantity in the electric furnace. By 1897, portable carbide-fueled acetylene lamps had been devised chiefly for use on bicycles, and the first experiments with their use underground had been made.

During the next ten years the new lamps were widely adopted in European mines. In the United States they were slower to displace the traditional candles and oil lamps, but a start was made in 1900 with the patenting and marketing of the early Baldwin lamps. Most carbide lamps of this period had various inadequacies, such as flimsy construction, small and weak reflectors without lighters, nonadjustable water feeds, and easily-broken "lava" (steatite) burner tips. By 1906 they were rarely used in American mines except by bosses and engineers. During the period from about 1912 to 1916, however, several manufacturers had entered the field, the worst defects had been overcome, and the carbide lamp had become popular. In 1919, Justrite alone advertised more than 40 models. By the 1930s, over 40 trade names by more than a dozen makers had appeared.

Carbide lamps were widely used by farmers and outdoorsmen, as well as miners. It may be assumed that cavers were among the early users, though there is little evidence for this other than the appearance of smoked signatures on cave walls in positions where earlier lights could not have placed them!

Carbide Lamp Styles

Carbide lamps are of three standard styles: hand lamps, head lamps with separate generator, and cap lamps. Large hand lamps were frequently used in mining and are used by cavers today in places having predominantly horizontal caves (notably Australia). They have the virtue of burning for up to 20 or more hours without changing carbide, but generally have been found impractical in American caving since the hands must often be free for climbing and crawling.

Hat-mounted acetylene burners, connected by a tube to a large generator carried at the caver's waist, are widely used in Europe but were formerly rare in America. In past editions I dismissed this carbide lamp style for combining the open-flame hazard of acetylene lamps with the inconvenience more typical of belt-battery electric lamps. However, lamps of this style are now stocked by U.S. caving equipment dealers, and are being used in significant numbers in American caving. Increasing experience with them has made my evaluation even more negative.

Belt-generator lamps are presently offered by Premier (British) and Petzl (French), the latter being most popular. The Petzl lamp has a fan-flame burner with a very poor reflector, a brute-force approach to lighting that requires carbide and water consumption at several times the rate of a cap lamp. The burner carries a big piezoelectric lighter, which is often needed because the flame is frequently put out when the generator is bumped or the gas hose is pinched in tight spots. Not only is this extinguishment dangerous in the middle of a delicate move, it pours undesirable raw acetylene into the cave air. Furthermore, the lamps have been nicknamed "ceiling-burners" because the headpiece design lets the flame impinge directly on low ceilings, leaving soot trails. Even when not touching anything, the fan flame burns inefficiently and often smokes visibly.

The belt-generator lamp is best adapted to cold, wet, multi-day expeditionary caving where it can be used for a camp light and for cooking and heating if desired. If you must use one in a clean cave, I strongly recommend fitting it with a cap-lamp single-jet burner tip and reflector, which will burn cleanly with better focus and greatly reduced carbide use (one Premier model comes with this option). Better still, substitute a good electric headlamp on long trips; it will give brighter light for a longer time at equivalent weight.

Only standard cap lamps (Figure 1) will be discussed in detail here. They are self-contained and easily removed from the hat as a unit—a valuable feature, especially for work in tight crawlways. They weigh about three quarters of a pound when fully charged and are made with two types of attachment—flat-hook or wire round-hook. The latter kind is generally furnished with a wire spring-clip for lateral bracing. For some obscure historical reason, round-hook styles have traditionally been advertised for use with soft caps as coal-miners' or hunters' lamps and flat-hook styles for use with hard hats as metal-miners' lamps. The flat-hook type should always be obtained when possible. Many hard hat brackets are not adapted for round-hooks and round-hooks are harder to handle, more easily knocked loose, and more likely to have their side clips damaged.

Characteristics of Available Makes

Carbide cap lamps were once made under many trade names. Some early ones were American Lamp & Splty Co., Arrow, Baldwin, Brite-Lite, Buddy, Defender, Dewar (ITP & Sun-Ray), Elkhorn, Ever-Ready, Fulton, Gee Bee (or Grier Bros.), Gem, Hansen, Lu-Mi-Num, Maple City, Maumee, Milburn, Pathfinder, Pioneer, Scranton, Shanklin Metal Products Co., Squarelite, Springfield, Sure-Light, Union Carbide, Wolf, X-Ray, and Zar. Some of these, such as Grier, Hansen, and Lu-Mi-Num, were superior in some ways to any now available but their good points were combined with defects in such ways that anyone interested only in good

Lamp	Weight	Capacities	
		Usable H$_2$O	Carbide
Flat-hook Premier	180 g (6.3 oz)	47 cc	94 cc
Flat-hook Justrite, brass	171 g (6.0 oz)	49 cc	80 cc
Flat-hook Justrite, plastic	140 g (4.9 oz)	70 cc	80 cc (approx)
Flat-hook Auto-Lite	160 g (5.6 oz)	53.5 cc	87.5 cc
Flat-hook Guy's Dropper	160 g (5.6 oz)	48 cc	82.5 cc
Round-hook Butterfly	150 g (5.3 oz)	52 cc	95 cc

Table 1—Comparison of weights and volumes of carbide lamps

performance need not rush to antique shops looking for any of them. Today only five brands – Premier, Justrite, Auto-Lite, Guy's Dropper, and Butterfly – survive in sufficient numbers to be in regular American caving use. Of these only Premier is still in production. Table 1 provides some measurements on these five lamps taken from representative lamps, clean and free of dents, with reflectors and rubber grips removed.

Premier. Premier is an English brand produced in several models. Their products were not marketed in this country until about 1970. Most users have found the Premier quite satisfactory. The carbide capacity is greater than that of the Justrite or Auto-Lite and I have averaged over six hours per charge at a flame level of two thirds to one inch. The lamp comes with a flat-hook which fits American hard hat brackets. The bottom has a bumpergrip. Premier bottoms are often interchangeable with the old-style Justrite, although in some cases the Premier bottom will be a little too tight for a Justrite top. Justrite gaskets and old-style felt assemblies, lighters, and reflectors will also interchange with Premiers. Justrite tips can be used in Premiers, but may not hold well unless an adhesive such as gasket cement is used. Some Premier reflectors are of non-magnetic aluminum alloy, a point of possible interest to cave surveyors.

The Premier does have some drawbacks. The felt assembly was poor on the older model but in 1977 improvements were made with a better three-piece felt assembly to reduce tip clogging. I recommend buying the Premier with a four-inch reflector or four-inch parabolic reflector as offered by some suppliers.

The hook sometimes works loose along the solder joint. This possibility is easily forestalled by reinforcing the attachment with a small brass bolt sealed with epoxy or pipe dope. The water valve seems somewhat insensitive, though not so much

Figure 2—A Premier lamp (without reflector) on the left and a Justrite No. 2-844 on the right with the standard four-inch reflector.

so as to be seriously troublesome. The wing nut and reflector-brace are not interchangeable with American ones.

Premier has cut costs by minor design and manufacturing changes in recent years; most of these have been slightly detrimental, such as the change to a stamped wing nut in 1976 and to a flat, weak reflector brace about 1980. There have been many complaints about Premier bottoms cracking around the lower edge but reputable dealers will replace parts found to be defective.

Premiers made between 1978 and 1981 have a technical problem. The water valve tube ends about half an inch too high in the carbide chamber, so that special care is needed to see that the carbide charge is large enough to touch the end of the water feed. If it does not, the water will fall as separate drops on the carbide, causing the flame to flare and die rhythmically until the carbide swells enough to contact the feed end. In 1981 Premier redesigned the lamp to correct this.

Premier is the only carbide cap lamp currently in production. During a financial crisis in 1984, the original company sold its lamp operations to Metec Leeds, Ltd which, in turn, sold in 1986 to Caving Supplies, a caver-run enterprise. The lamps seem to be in good supply in 1990, with somewhat better quality control than in the problem years.

Justrite. Until late 1971, Justrite cap lamps were made of brass. In the 1950s and 1960s their best model for caving was number 2-844 shown in Figure 2. In general this lamp was acceptably rugged and reliable, and it became the standard U.S. caving light after the demise of competing makes in 1960. In later years, quality control was not of the best; leaks, cracks, and maladjusted valves gave occasional cause for complaint. The basic design is slightly deficient in having a flat front and back which reduces bend-resistance, and the reflector brace is flat and weak. A minor annoyance with late brass Justrites is the impossibility of removing the reflector without popping out the 9/32-inch burner tip as the wing nut is unscrewed, though this does make it possible to change tips without tools. Any usable parts of worn-out brass Justrites should be saved as they are obsolete and in demand.

Late in 1971, Justrite converted totally from the manufacture of metal lamps to new models made primarily of plastic. In the process, a completely different body design was adopted, with only the reflector and burner assemblies being interchangeable with the old brass styles. The plastic Justrite proved to be a regressive design in an inadequate material, difficult to use without clogging, and prone to break when dropped or to melt out the entire reflector assembly when pointed downward. The company gave up making them about 1984.

Figure 3—A Universal Auto-Lite lamp.

They may still appear in a few stores, but the wise caver will treat them as oddities, not as safe caving lamps.

Auto-Lite. The Auto-Lite lamp, made by Universal Lamp Company, Figure 3, was probably the most popular caving lamp when production was discontinued in 1960. Since then the lamps have come to be regarded as collector's items. They are in many respects the best of the standard brands and it is worthwhile to search antique and second-hand stores for them. In 1990 it was still possible to find good used Auto-Lites (usually of the round-hook style) in many areas at prices averaging $25 to $35.

The lamps are strongly built and have about 10% larger carbide capacity than Justrites. The Auto-Lite water valve usually seems more precise in its control than those of other brands. After 1930, Universal lamps were furnished with rubber "bumpergrip" bottom protectors. Original Universal tips, with a 15/64 inch end, are narrow enough that reflectors can be removed over them. Threaded Universal parts (bottoms, wing nuts, lighter spring caps, and hex nuts) are not freely interchangeable with Justrite lamps, though a rough fit can sometimes be managed.

The only serious defects in Auto-Lite design are in the hooks. After long use, especially if the bracket arrangement allows much flexing, the flat-hook tends to fatigue and break off at the narrow point just above the top rivet. The spring-clip on the round hook style often breaks or loses its attachment screw unless carefully handled.

Guy's Dropper. This brand was produced from about 1914 to the 1930s by the Shanklin Mfg. Company of Springfield, Illinois. In later years it was taken over by Universal, which manufactured it along with Auto-Lite until 1960. The "Dropper" is a good lamp and seems to have special prestige among cavers, perhaps because it is a little less common than Auto-Lite. However, it is doubtful whether it is quite as good as Auto-Lite on most points. Its most distinctive part is the patented, rotating sleeve water valve, which was intended to make cleaning easy, but whose more important effect is to predispose the valve to rapid wear and to make exact control of the water flow difficult. The Dropper's best points are the broad attachment of its flat-hook (even though not riveted, it is less liable to break than Auto-Lite's) and its particularly strong bottom shape. All removable parts except the reflector-brace (and the spring-clip on round-hook lamps) are interchangeable with Auto-Lites. In some areas Droppers are about as common in antique shops as Auto-Lites, while in others they seem unaccountably rare. Most late Droppers fortunately have flat-hooks.

Butterfly. The Butterfly lamp (also called Safesport Lamp on the box), imported from Hong Kong by Safesport Mfg. Company of Denver, Colorado, and by other importers in the eastern states, is essentially a poor copy of the Guy's Dropper, but without the rotating sleeve water valve. It was until recently available in many surplus and sporting goods stores, but went out of production a few years ago. It was made with both the round-hook and flat-hook attachment. Its only advantage is an unusually large carbide chamber. It is flimsily built and often leaky at vital joints. Butterfly bottoms and lighter parts will not interchange with other lamps. The thin reflector and its flat, weak brace are especially inferior. The gas tube is frequently soldered out of line with the hole in the bottom of the water chamber, allowing gas, water, and carbide to mix indiscriminately, rendering the lamp useless. Even when the solder joint is complete, the gas tube pulls out easily because it is cylindrical.

The Butterfly was never a dependable lamp and should be avoided. Safesport is now offering the superior Premier in its retail outlets, though mail-order caving suppliers may have lower prices.

Reflectors

Whatever lamp is used, proper choice of reflector is very important. Reflectors have been made in many sizes and forms. A common diameter is two and a half inches. The particular focus characteristics of these small reflectors vary depending on their shapes, but all of them tend to waste too much light to the side to be desirable. At the other extreme, the deep seven-inch type used on outdoorsmen's lamps for sharp focus is too cumbersome and fragile for general cave use. The four-inch parabolic, when available, will stand the hardest use and gives the best fuel economy since it focuses well at one half to one-inch flame levels. The standard Justrite or Premier four-inch chromed steel reflector is less expensive and more widely available; it works best for lighting large spaces but requires about a one and a half-inch flame for optimum focus.

Reflectors should be kept clean for maximum brightness. Dirty reflectors should never be scoured with abrasive cleansers; the surface will be scratched or the plating worn off. Toothpaste is the strongest abrasive that should be used, and that sparingly. Black coatings will rub off easily after soaking in vinegar for a few minutes. Unplated reflectors such as the Premier aluminum alloy or the stainless four-inch parabolic can be polished with a buffing wheel using jeweler's rouge.

Techniques and Efficiency

Basic operation of the lamp is very simple— merely load with carbide and water, turn the water valve on slowly, and wait until gas flows from the burner tip. Then light by cupping one hand briefly over the reflector to trap some gas and striking a spark by quickly sliding the hand over the lighter wheel.

However, getting the most out of the lamp is an art. Many users load the bottom only about half full of carbide, which ensures that the water will flow freely. Often this makes for short charge-life and lets the used carbide become soupy. With Justrite lamps, most cavers average about two and a half to four and a half hours between charges. This can be improved. First, use a charge which fills the bottom two-thirds full, but not more. When the flame begins to burn low, do not change carbide at once but check the water level and turn the water valve further on. If this has no effect, loosen the bottom half a turn, twist it a few times, tighten, and relight. This will open a water passage in the caked carbide and rejuvenate the flame within a few minutes. It may be repeated as necessary until the charge is completely used. Charge life of four and a half to six and a half hours is not uncommon with this technique. This is how I obtained the previously described seven and a half-hour average on one trip.

Troubleshooting

Before using a carbide lamp, take it apart and study it until you are thoroughly familiar with it and are sure it has no defects. If you understand your lamp, keep it clean, use it with reasonable care, and carry a tip cleaner and parts kit, you will rarely, if ever, have trouble that you cannot fix on the spot.

Nearly all malfunctions of carbide lamps can be attributed to one of the following causes:

1. A low flame that decreases on opening the water valve indicates that the lamp needs water.
2. A low flame that increases briefly on opening the water valve indicates that the carbide charge is used up.
3. A short and crooked flame is caused by a clogged tip; this is easily corrected with a tip cleaner.
4. A short flame may also indicate carbide caked around the water valve; correct by loosening the bottom and wiggling it. If these measures fail, check whether the water drips freely; if not, rinse the water tube to remove any dirt. In bad cases of clogging, apply suction to the water tank.
5. A "jumpy" flame indicates a wet filter, which usually results when an expiring charge has become flooded. Recharge the lamp and change the filter or dry it between layers of clothing. An emergency filter can be made from a piece of thick cloth.
6. Gas bubbling up through the water usually means either a clogged tip or water turned on too high. When associated with a wet filter, this may indicate a leak between the water and carbide chambers. If the leak can be located (it will usually be at the joint of the gas tube), temporary repair may be attempted with candle wax. A lamp thus repaired must be burned at a low level thereafter to avoid melting the seal.
7. Gas leaks around the gasket sometimes appear when a lamp is too loosely screwed together, has a bad gasket, is badly dented, or has threads heavily caked with deposits. If tightening or replacing the gasket does not stop the leak, try turning the gasket over or adding a second gasket. Threads may be cleaned by gouging with a knife, preferably with the leather punch blade.

The burner-tip orifice controls the mixture of acetylene with air, and its diameter is critical for brightness and economy. Tips that have been opened too wide by many reamings will produce a thick yellow flame and should be replaced. However, even if a tip is lost and no spare is on hand, the lamp will produce a dim and smoky fire adequate for emergency travel. (This should not be tried with the plastic lamps.) The reflector should be removed in such a case to avoid ruining its finish. Never light a tipless light until all air has been displaced from the inside; otherwise it could explode. This is not a hazard with the tip in, as an explosive wave in acetylene mixtures cannot pass through an orifice of less than 0.02 inch diameter (Lewes, 1900, p 563). This is more than half again the usual width of a tip orifice.

Old burners require more frequent cleaning than new ones, as the pores of the insert become impregnated with benzene and other polymers of acetylene which cannot be totally removed (Lewes, 1900). These residues catalyze further production of such contaminants, which then carbonize around the orifice. The sooting that may occur even on new tips when the flame is allowed to burn out slowly is more superficial. "Carboning" of the tip, in any case, is not as bad a problem as clogging from the inside.

Spare Parts and Accessories

A brush-type tip cleaner should always be carried in a convenient place, preferably tied or clipped to the lamp or lamp bracket, but not where it could jab the wearer. In addition, the cave pack should include a spare parts kit containing the following: at least one individual tip reamer (in case the brush-type is lost), tip, gasket, felt or filter, flint and (if possible) lighter spring, lighter spring cap, wing nut, and wind guard. Be sure each item will fit the particular kind of lamp used. All of these, except the brush-type cleaner, will fit into a 35-mm film can, with room to spare for a flashlight bulb and a few band aids. A short length of acid-core solder, with the ends heat-sealed, is a recommended addition to the parts kit. It is a good idea to keep a felt holder and felt plate at home, but these need not be taken into caves. A lamp will operate with the entire felt assembly missing, if gently handled so that spent carbide and water do not enter the gas tube.

Some possible improvements or substitutions are worth mentioning. For superior filtering, replace original felts with homemade copies of dense, open-cell, flexible foam, cut to fit around the side. These can be wrung dry when wet, and will not shrink like commercial felts. The material used must be acetylene-resistant. If standard gaskets for brass lamps are not available when needed, one and a half-inch O-rings can be substituted. These are not advised for general use because they do not support the lamp flange against dents. To keep a tip cleaner closed when not in use, unbend the eye enough to slip a ball-point pen coil-spring over the shaft and then rebend the eye to the original shape.

Matches are a vital part of any caver's gear. They are usually carried in "waterproof" cases which, all too often, prove not to be so when actually submerged. An excellent alternative is to tape a few matches to the inside of a container of fresh carbide. Carbide is a desiccant and the matches will remain dry as long as the carbide is good. Tape over the match heads to prevent friction against the carbide chunks. Another alternative is to carry a lighter in a waterproof container.

Hazards

The open acetylene flame is an obvious fire hazard. Carbide lamps should not be used near highly flammable surroundings (including dusty guano caves) or where the possibility of explosive gas or fumes is suspected (including the vicinity of auto gas tanks). When on climbing ropes, a low flame and constant alertness are advisable. With these exceptions, the worst that is apt to result from carelessness is a painful singe. Carbide lamps are very unlikely to explode from excess pressure, as both the water tube and the tip act as safety valves.

If a lamp leaks gas, the leaky spot may burst into flame. Such leaks are usually detectable by the disagreeable odor before they ignite. Leaks should be stopped at once (see Troubleshooting, above) to prevent such fires or small explosions and to avoid possible poisoning. For the same reasons, containers for extra carbide must be strong and waterproof.

The carbide flame itself is exceptionally clean burning (in single-jet tips) and is normally odorless. It gives off no carbon monoxide unless burning in oxygen-deficient air (Lewes, 1900). Its products are almost entirely CO_2 and steam. Carbide lamps are said to use several times less oxygen and to produce several times less CO_2 than candles or oil lamps (Parsons, 1906 and Morrison, 1908). Since a person at moderate work is apt, in breathing, to exchange O_2–CO_2 at about nine times the rate that a carbide lamp does (Paul, 1915), the flame should not be a serious threat to air quality even in small spaces.

Explosive gases, common in coal mines, are very rarely found in natural caves. Several deaths have occurred in caves artificially contaminated with hydrocarbon vapors in the vicinity of oil or gas fields or where waste petroleum had been dumped (Meador, 1965). Any scent of gas should be the signal to put out flames instantly and withdraw by electric light.

Since an injured person may have difficulty operating a carbide lamp, an accident victim awaiting rescue should not be left alone with a carbide lamp as his only source of light. In fact, for rescue work in general, electric light is preferable. The use of carbide requires time and attention that are needed for other purposes and rescue parties are likely to include persons unfamiliar with the use of carbide.

If carbide gets wet, it will quickly generate a cloud of explosive acetylene gas. All spent carbide that is not totally used up must be kept dry.

Lamps in Bad Air

If the carbide lamp flame begins to burn yellow and smoky, or goes out with no apparent cause — and particularly if all lamps in a party are affected — a dangerous displacement of air by carbon dioxide is indicated and quick retreat is in order. Such hazards are very uncommon in natural caves but may exist, especially where organic matter is decaying in stagnant air, as in debris-choked swallow-holes. **Carbide lamps are far from an infallible test for bad air, as they may continue to burn poorly** in still air at a CO_2 level as high as 25%, **well above the human danger point** (Smith, 1913). Labored breathing is experienced at CO_2 levels as low as three percent and is followed by headache, but cavers entering bad air may misjudge their symptoms and attribute them merely to fatigue, until they notice that their flames are extinguished.

Carrying Carbide and Water

Carry a personal reserve of carbide in a strong, airtight, **waterproof** container. Assigning all the carbide to one member of a party has a way of causing trouble. Most cavers prefer plastic baby bottles; the small (four-inch high) size will hold about eight ounces of carbide—enough for three or more charges, while the large (6½-inch high) size holds nearly a pound. Some cavers have used 35-mm film cans (1½ cans per charge). This has the virtue of allowing exact measurement of reserves, but handling many small containers is time consuming. The heavy-gauge plastic bottles of toner for duplicating machines are good carbide containers. A caver starting with a full lamp, one extra charge in a spare lamp bottom, and a small baby bottle full should have enough to last 15 to 30 hours in normal use. With lamp, extra bottom, and large baby bottle, about 24 to 48 hours of light are available.

For users of brass lamps, individually prepared charges in spare bottoms are a valuable adjunct to the main carbide supply, as they permit changing carbide merely by switching bottoms. The bulk and expense of such containers make it impractical to carry one's entire supply this way, but it is wise to have at least one extra bottom along. It will pay for itself when you need to change in a tight crawlway, on a rope, in the dark, in emergencies, or in any other situation where it is important not to delay the party. Premier bottoms now have a flanged screw cap and gasket for airtight sealing and may fit Justrites and (less often) Universal lamps, being intermediate in thread size. Also various commercial bottles (salad dressings, vitamins, etc.) have caps that will fit. In practical use, these work as well as original caps if the rim of the lamp bottom has not been damaged. The cardboard gaskets in such caps should be replaced by rubber ones for use in wet caves. A stout canteen or strong plastic bottle can be used to carry water. Allow about three ounces of water per two and a half-ounce charge of carbide, or one and a half to two fillings of water per charge. Lamp water is often not a major concern as it may be locally available in most caves. In emergencies, urine can be used. Its effect on flame quality is insignificant. But one should carry an adequate supply of water as many cave passages contain no water for long distances. Avoid muddy or sandy water. A separate water bottle for lamp water would allow refilling this supply without contaminating your drinking water.

Removing Used Carbide

Spent carbide, a paste of impure hydrated lime, is toxic and unsightly; good caving practice requires that it be removed from the cave and discarded out of reach of cattle or other animals—not dumped or buried in the cave. A tough plastic bag is the standard container. When the spare bottom system is used, the bottom can be emptied into the bag and refilled during rest stops. **Do not close spent carbide containers airtight** except briefly when they must be submerged in water—residual gas should be allowed to seep out. When emptying bottoms, do not pound them on rocks; brass dents easily. Sludge is best loosened by scraping with a blunt pocketknife blade, alternated with gentle tapping of the back of the knife flat across the bottom. Avoid getting carbide into the lamp threads.

A charge emptied while still generating gas freely may melt a plastic bag, as well as create a fire hazard. Cavers who habitually change before a charge is exhausted may find such bags unsatisfactory. The best solution is to use one's changes more efficiently; failing this, some heavier container will be needed.

Outdoor Use

Carbide lamps, where not prohibited due to high fire hazard, are excellent for night hiking and back-

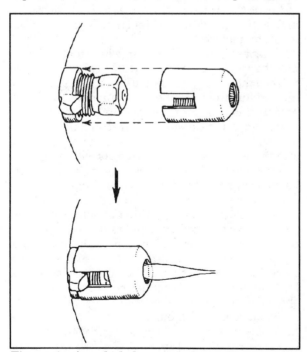

Figure 4—A carbide lamp windguard

packing. The diffuse light is ideal for walking, the lamp is a good hand warmer, the flame will light campfires in wet weather, and the problems of keeping batteries charged in the wilds are avoided. Lamps used outdoors (or underground in winds over 15 miles per hour) must be provided with a wind guard (or flame protector) as shown in Figure 4. A wind guard will also give the flame some protection from water spray near waterfalls. I believe that no maker now provides wind guards, but caving suppliers may still have stocks of old Justrite ones which can be adapted to other lamp brands by spreading the base. Homemade metal sleeves around the burners may also serve the purpose.

I have successfully tried carbide lamps as tent lights on winter mountaineering trips in sub-zero weather. Once in operation, the lamp generates enough heat to keep from freezing. However, the fire hazard becomes considerable when handling carbide lamps in such close confines. Water and damp, used carbide must not be allowed to freeze in the lamp after it is turned off. Even if the water has been poured out, the water valve usually freezes and must be rewarmed before the next use. Rubbing alcohol (70%) is said to be a safe and effective anti-freeze for carbide lamps, though it effectively shortens charge life in proportion to the amount mixed with the lamp water. The following table of freezing points is adapted from Whiting (1966):

Approximate alcohol percent by weight	Freezing point Degrees F.
20	14
25	5
33	-10
60	-34

Table 2 — Freezing points of alcohol and water mixtures. Liquor (100 proof = 50% alcohol) may be used in lieu of rubbing alcohol.

Obtaining Lamps

As of 1991, one should expect to pay $25 to $35 for a carbide lamp suitable for caving. New Premiers and parts are available from caving-club stores, from dealers advertising in caving journals, and from some surplus and sporting goods stores. Justrites, Auto-Lites, and Guy's Droppers in usable condition are still rather easy to find in antique stores, and sometimes second-hand stores and flea markets. Be sure the lamps are not cracked, corroded, or missing vital parts. In recent years at least one caver-dealer has offered reconditioned "classic" lamps at good prices (check classified ads in recent issues of *NSS News).*

Obtaining Carbide

Calcium carbide was formerly manufactured by several American companies including Union Carbide, Shawinigan, and National. In 1991 the only remaining U.S. producer was Elkem-American Carbide Co, PO Box 72, Marietta, Ohio, 45750.

Some sporting goods and surplus stores sell carbide in two-pound cans, but these are likely to cost more than $3.00 per pound. It is much more cost-effective for caving groups to order 100 to 300-pound drums direct from the producer or from caving-equipment suppliers who will ship. In such bulk orders, the cost may be as low as 50¢ per pound. For use in cap lamps, the "miner's lamp" (½-inch) size should be specified; for hand lamps or belt-generator lamps the larger "nut" size is preferred. Smaller ¼-inch and "rice" sizes are used in acetylene generators for welding; these will work in lamps but are less desirable. Calcium carbide is classified as a "dry flammable" hazardous material and is not allowed in the U.S. mail. UPS shipment requires special packaging, labeling, and surcharge. Large drums are best shipped by motor freight. Stored carbide will deteriorate slowly unless transferred to absolutely airtight containers. Do not store in cellars or damp places.

Cleaning and Storage of Lamps

One of the common causes of bad performance is the practice of letting lamps sit indefinitely without cleaning. Damp lime clogs parts, corrodes brass, and will eventually set like plaster. After each trip, the absolute minimum maintenance procedure is to scrape out the sludge as well as possible and let the carbide and water chambers stand open until completely dry.

Whenever time allows, or when malfunctions have happened, the lamp should be taken apart and washed thoroughly inside and out. Scrape and scrub all residue from the bottom (an old toothbrush helps). Remove the filter assembly and clean all parts. Scrub the threads and rinse and flush the tip and water valve. If hard deposits have developed, soaking for a few hours in vinegar will dissolve or soften them. Replace deteriorating gaskets or filters before they cause trouble. After rinsing, let all parts stand open to the air until entirely dry before reassembly. Lubricating the threads with petroleum jelly assures a smooth seal and reduces the chances of the bottom becoming "frozen" so hard that the lamp can't be readily disassembled. Store in a dry place — dryness is the most vital single aspect of lamp maintenance. When properly treated, lamps should work well for many years.

When removing a burner tip for cleaning, it is advisable to use a properly fitting wrench if possible. Never use vise-grip pliers for this; pressure is very likely to crack the insert.

Repairing and Restoring Lamps

Many lamps are thrown away for want of simple repairs. Missing parts can be replaced. Broken hooks can be duplicated with sheet metal; broken spring-clips can be replaced with coat hanger wire if originals are not available; cracks and punctures in metal lamps can be soldered.

When soldering, clean the metal well with vinegar or other acid followed by sandpaper, steel wool, or wire brush; use a small high-heat source of short duration. Beware of overheating the lamp; it is easy to make good joints leaky. To remove dents, take a stiff nail and round the head slightly; bend it suitably, clamp the point in locking pliers, insert the head into the lamp, and lever the dent up. If the dent cannot be reached in this manner, a small hole can be drilled in it, a bent wire inserted, and the dent pulled up. The hole should be closed with solder. A leaky water valve can often be readjusted by a simple procedure: Turn the lever two thirds toward full open, then direct a torch flame sideways against the top of the valve post while pressing down against the valve-ball until the solder softens, then remove the heat. If an old lamp is only soiled and tarnished, vinegar soaking followed by scouring and polishing often works wonders. (Vinegar attacks brass slowly, so should not be left in contact with the lamp longer than necessary. Several hours will do no harm.) Never use steel wool or abrasives on reflectors.

When buying a used lamp, turn the valve partly on and pull up and down on it to check for vertical play. If there is more than a trace of play, precision in water-flow control is lessened. Worn valve threads are usually impractical to repair, and if the valve is loose enough to rattle, the lamp may be considered worn out no matter how good it looks otherwise.

Summary of Recommendations

In situations calling for intermittent use, very bright, long-range light, highly efficient use of time, and/or ability to function underwater, electric lighting is recommended. For versatility, reliability, and ruggedness at low cost, carbide is superior. As the best carbide lamp system, I recommend a flathook Premier, Auto-Lite, Guy's Dropper, or brass Justrite cap lamp fitted with a four-inch, parabolic reflector or Justrite four-inch reflector. Include an extra bottom if available and a spare parts kit including a wind guard. Next choices, in order of descending quality, are round-hook lamps of the above brands and the Butterfly. All but the last one will generally give good service if not abused.

Recommended containers for the fuel supply: plastic baby bottle for carbide; spare lamp bottom with cap; heavy plastic bag for used carbide; and canteen or plastic bottle for water. Whatever system is used, learn how everything works, and keep components clean and well maintained.

References

Lewes, V. B. (1900). *Acetylene; A Handbook for the Student and Manufacturer*: MacMillan, New York, 977 pp.

Meador, T. (1965). "Why Not Dump It Here?": *Texas Caver* 10:212-213 and *Speleo Digest* 1965, Section 2:141-143.

Morrison, A.C. (1908). "Better Light and Air for Miners": *Mining World* 29:879.

Parsons, F. W. (1906). "Acetylene Lamps for Mines": *Eng & Mining Jour* 82:111.

Paul, J. W. (1915). "Notes on Miners' Carbide Lamps": U.S. Dept. of the Interior, Miners Circular 18, 10 pp.

Smith, E. E. (1913). "Acetylene as an Illuminant in Mines": *Mining & Engineering World* 39:1111-1113.

Whiting, D. (1966)-"Carbide Lamp Antifreeze": *Wisconsin Speleologist* 5:23-24 and *Speleo Digest* 1966, Section 3:36-38.

Chapter 3

ELECTRIC LIGHT SYSTEMS FOR CAVING

Tom Kaye
NSS 16356

Introduction

The main reasons for using an electric lamp are convenience and versatility. An electric lamp is reliable because its operation depends on only four simple parts: bulb, wire, switch, and battery, which means that little can go wrong. It is easy to carry spare bulbs and a small spare wire. Often these can be carried inside parts of the lamp.

Information is provided here about several electric light systems suitable for caving, most of which can be assembled by the user. Cavers without the necessary mechanical and electrical skills to assemble their own electric systems should consider buying one of the caving supplier's or commercial miner's lamps complete with a charger or choose a less expensive type such as a Justrite.

Because of the rapid changes that take place in the battery industry, no specific models of battery or charger are referred to in this article except for miner's lamps. The Wheat miner's lamp and the similar MSA (Mine Safety Appliance) miner's lamp have been around for many years and will probably continue into the future relatively unchanged.

Special Uses of Electric Lamps

Certain aspects of electric lamps make them especially advantageous for several kinds of caving and caving situations. One of the obvious advantages is the non-susceptibility of electric lamps to water, as opposed to the open flame of a carbide lamp. The normal operating voltages of caving batteries of four to six volts are low enough that total submersion will not result in any appreciable energy loss. Low water crawls and vertical pitches with spray and flying water droplets are typical situations where electric lamps are advantageous.

The focusable bright beam of the electric lamp makes it valuable in cave surveying. Checking for high leads and getting a good view of large passages are enhanced by the ability to concentrate the light output to a narrow beam. The focused beam is critically important in cave photography which often requires focusing the camera on distant cave features. A bright light cast on the subject is necessary for precise focusing of the lens. Even more important is the ability to illuminate distant features from the camera's viewpoint for compositional planning.

Choosing a Battery

Once you have decided to get an electric system, there are several decisions to be made. The number of possible electric systems that can be constructed, adapted, or purchased ready-made is large. The most significant difference between these systems is the type of battery used. Batteries fall into two categories: rechargeable and non-rechargeable. Rechargeable batteries can be re-charged 200 to 2,000 times, depending on the type, while non-rechargeable batteries are thrown away after they are discharged. For caving purposes, rechargeable batteries are preferable. Using almost any cost analysis scheme, even the more expensive rechargeable batteries come out cheaper than the cheapest non-rechargeable batteries. Only if you plan to use an electric system once or twice a year or less would it be advisable to avoid purchasing a rechargeable battery. Even though rechargeable batteries are the most cost-effective, cavers often start caving with an electric system based on non-rechargeable batteries.

The next most important consideration in choosing a battery is the capacity requirement. You will need to review your past caving trips and determine the number of hours that you will require your light source to operate per caving trip. For instance, if most of your caving trips are 8 to 10 hours long, you may want a battery that will provide 12 to 15 hours of light. On the other hand, you may at first be satisfied with a smaller capacity battery for your short trips or for use in vertical pitches with waterfalls.

Types of Rechargeable Batteries

Rechargeable batteries that are suitable for caving can be classified in five basic types: (1) lead-acid wet cell, (2) sealed lead-acid, (3) nickel-cadmium wet cell, (4) nickel-cadmium D-cell, and (5) rechargeable manganese. Each of these types has a particular set of characteristics. The following paragraphs provide a brief discussion on the most important aspects of the different types of batteries as related to caving use.

Wet-Cell Batteries. Lead-acid and nickel-cadmium wet cells both require vents of some type for use during the charging phase of the cycle. This is because these batteries will produce water vapor, hydrogen, and oxygen gases while they are being charged, especially when they near the state of full charge. To prevent these batteries from exploding during charging, they are designed with open air vents to relieve the pressure. Loss of water vapor through open vents requires that distilled water be added from time to time to replace that lost by vaporization and electrolysis. The usual type of vent is a screw cap which must be slightly loosened during charging. The vent caps of wet cell batteries must be protected from damage and accidental unscrewing in the cave, and yet you must be able to open them each time you charge the battery. This situation can be considered a disadvantage of wet cells since it requires that you build a battery case to adapt them to caving use.

Miner's lamps use wet cell batteries, but they are already suitable for caving purposes. Their vents are small holes designed so that even though they are permanently open, the liquid electrolyte cannot be poured out in any position. These batteries can be used in any orientation (such as in crawlways or walking passage) without worry that the electrolyte will spill. Miner's batteries are susceptible, however, to dust entering the vent holes, so these should be covered with electrical tape while caving. A pinhole in the tape for each cell window allows you to omit removing the tape each time the battery is charged. Underwater exposure of these batteries usually requires a little better hole-sealing technique. Such techniques will be discussed in the miner's lamp modification section.

All vented wet cell batteries require extra care in their storage, transport, charging, and use because of the chemical harshness of the electrolyte and the possibility of some of it getting out of the battery. The electrolyte of nickel-cadmium batteries is caustic potassium hydroxide solution and is chemically very similar to lye and drain cleaner. Even worse is the sulfuric acid electrolyte of lead-acid cells. Both chemicals can corrode rope and clothing among other things, and special care should be taken to avoid proximity problems in the storage and transportation of these batteries. Miner's batteries with their permanently open vent holes should never be transported or charged while upside down or even face down.

Even though you can't pour the electrolyte out, vibration and jiggling in a vehicle over a period of time could cause a minute amount to escape the vents if the battery is not upright or lying face up. The best way to transport these batteries is lying down and face up. The battery is then stable and the vents are straight up, away from the acid. Miner's batteries should not be stored for long periods in a completely enclosed space with rope because the air outside the battery is exposed to the electrolyte and could absorb a minute quantity of acid. Keeping rope and batteries in the same room or clothes closet would be techni-

cally safe, but keeping them in the same duffel bag or a car's trunk for several weeks would be inadvisable. The best practice is to keep batteries and caving gear, especially ropes, in separate places at all times, at home and in the vehicle. It is a good practice to always store and transport the battery in the same location so that any spilt acid doesn't get onto other caving gear.

Sealed Batteries: In addition to the wet cell batteries, there are the dry cell and the sealed cell batteries. These can absorb the gases produced during charging so they don't require vents. This is a major advantage for caving use. As opposed to vented wet cells, these batteries do not have the problems of susceptibility to water and dust or the possibility of the electrolyte leaking. They still require at least a carrying case since they do not have provisions for wearing them as do miner's batteries. The Justrite case for D-cells or an army ammunition belt pouch for a sealed lead-acid battery are examples of possible carrying cases for sealed batteries.

Circuit Breaker

All types of rechargeable batteries can put out a large amount of current if shorted. Because of the rigors of the cave environment, a circuit breaker in the system is a good safeguard against a hot lamp cord or damaged equipment. Small circuit breakers, $1\frac{1}{2}$ x $1\frac{1}{4}$ inch, are available from electronics supply dealers such as Poly Paks, Inc., South Lynnfield, MA 01940. Fuses and fuseholders are more commonly available, but they do not reset and you need to carry a supply of replacement fuses.

Charging and Discharging Differences

The different types of batteries vary widely in terms of recharge cycle life. A rechargeable battery will, after a number of discharge-charge cycles, gradually deliver fewer and fewer hours of service per charge. A wet cell nickel-cadmium battery has the greatest cycle life, with over 2,000 useful cycles. A nickel-cadmium D-cell has about 1,000 cycles of useful life. Lead-acid wet cells have a lifespan of about 500 cycles and sealed lead-acid cells have about 200 cycles. Rechargeable manganese batteries can only deliver about 40 cycles.

Batteries also differ in their discharge curve characteristics. The discharge curve of a battery shows the output voltage of the battery as it gradually decreases with time to the point at which the battery is considered dead. (Usually defined as a battery delivering only 80% of its rated voltage.)

The discharge curve of the nickel-cadmium battery is almost linear and remains constant throughout the discharge cycle. This type of battery produces a constant voltage and hence a light source of constant intensity. Although this is a desirable characteristic, there is a drawback. When a nickel-cadmium battery reaches its "dead" point, the voltage falls to near zero quite rapidly. This can be quite disconcerting if it happens in a cave. If a nickel-cadmium battery is discharged to this point, it is best to turn the light system off to avoid reverse charging damage to the discharged cells.

Lead-acid batteries have a discharge curve which is rather flat, but is not as horizontal as that of a nickel-cadmium battery. The lead-acid light system will produce a light which decreases gradually and at about the same rate throughout its discharge cycle.

Alkaline (manganese) and other dry cells used for caving have discharge curves which are curved downward, meaning that the light output will decrease more and more rapidly as the battery discharges. The discharge curve of lithium batteries is extremely flat, even more so than that of the nickel-cadmium. The lithium battery also differs in that each cell is three volts instead of the usual 1.5 volts and is very expensive for a non-rechargeable.

Miner's Lamp Modifications

Miner's lamps are increasing in popularity among cavers. They are well built and rugged for mining use and require little or no modification for caving use as opposed to most other electric systems. There are, however, modifications and additions that can be made which will improve their safety and versatility for caving use. The following discussions primarily apply to Koehler Wheat brand miner's lamps. Other miner's lamps are also useful for caving and the modifications can be applied to them as well.

The Wheat Lamp is designed to prevent tampering with while in the mine. This is primarily done to prevent explosions caused by the mine atmosphere coming into contact with electrical contacts. If you buy a miner's lamp, you will want to permanently remove the small cap screw that prevents the lens from being removed. You don't want to be prevented from changing a burned-out bulb while in a cave.

In a few cases, the metal posts that come up through the tops of the cells in a miners' lamp battery have become unglued. This condition allows small amounts of electrolyte to seep out. You may want to occasionally check for this condition and add epoxy or other adhesive if necessary.

Bulb Locking: The lamp bulb of the Wheat Lamp does not lock into its socket like conventional bayonet-base construction but is held in place by the glass lens in front of the headpiece. Although it is not easy to break the lens, the possibility does exist and represents a weak point in the Wheat Lamp. If the glass lens breaks, the bulb cannot be kept in place against the electrical contacts. To prevent the possibility of this happening, the glass lens should be discarded and

replaced with a transparent plastic lens. (Also, see step 2 of the bulb socket adapter section.)

Vent Hole Protection: Wheat Lamps are often used in underwater exploration as well as in expeditions that cause the battery to be submerged part of the time. The battery design includes vent holes which are necessary during charging. The holes connect to special vent chambers inside each cell which are designed to keep the electrolyte from dripping out when the battery is in a horizontal or upside-down position. The design, however, does not prevent water from entering the vents when the battery is submerged. Both plastic tape and self-tapping Number 8 sheet metal screws made of stainless steel have been used to temporarily seal the vent holes during battery-submerging cave trips. The tape method has not proven entirely satisfactory and the screws may not effect a sufficiently tight seal. Probably the best solution is to use screws in conjunction with rubber washers of the type used for faucet repair. Caution must be exercised, however, to always remove the obstructions from the vent holes when the battery is to be charged. Charging a battery with its vent holes plugged will cause the battery case to crack or even explode.

Short Circuit Protection: A circuit breaker (see section on circuit breakers) is a possible addition to a miner's lamp to protect it and you from short circuit problems. To install one, use a hacksaw to cut the lead band connecting the two cells of the battery under the cap. Solder the circuit breaker leads to the separated parts of the connector band. Completely cover the circuit breaker and all parts of the leads with PC-7 or other epoxy. With a small hacksaw cut, the connection can easily be remade by pressing a rock on it if the circuit breaker fails.

Spare Wire: Another modification of the Wheat Lamp is a fail-safe measure for wire and switch problems in the cave. A length of small gauge speaker wire can be coiled and stored under the metal top of the battery. If the switch or cord should fail for some reason, you can find places in the headpiece where you can attach the leads of the speaker wire to make the bulb operate. You may even want to attach a solder lug to one of the conducting metal parts inside the headpiece to facilitate an emergency connection. If you do step 1 of the following socket adaptation procedure, you can lead the emergency wire into the interior of the headpiece through the pry notch in the reflector if you enlarge it slightly. Otherwise, you can drill a small hole in the back of the headpiece and refill it with a removable amount of black silicone glue.

Bulb Socket Adapter: Wheat Lamps have a uniquely designed bulb socket which accepts the General Electric bulbs (BM30, BM30A, BM3232, and BM40l0) made for use in Wheat Lamps. The lowest amperage bulb available is the BM30A, rated at one amp. The light output of the BM30A is considerably brighter than that of a carbide lamp. There are bulbs, however, that will provide an amount of light near to that of a carbide lamp. The advantage of these bulbs is that when used with a Wheat battery, the light system will provide a steady light for much longer than the normal fifteen hours possible with a BM30A bulb. A Number 41 bulb when used with a Wheat battery will, for example, provide about 24 hours of light that is as bright as that of a carbide lamp. The catch is that the low amperage bulbs have miniature screw bases and require an adapter for use in a Wheat Lamp headpiece. Such an adapter can be built using the following steps:

1. Buy a Number 1157 automobile bulb. The Number 1157 bulb has a double contact index bayonet base like the Wheat Lamp bulbs.
2. Disassemble the lamp headpiece (you'll need a small Allen wrench) sufficiently to remove the sleeve that holds the bulb. On each side of this sleeve is a slit that accepts the guideposts on the sides of the bulb base. Using a needle file, you can lengthen these slits to allow the bulb to be rotated slightly and relax upwards as in a normal bayonet bulb and socket. The bulb can now be locked in place in the Wheat Lamp headpiece without requiring the lens to hold it in.
3. Wrap the bulb in a rag or piece of paper towel and pulverize the glass with a pair of pliers as much as possible, being careful to avoid damaging the brass sleeve excessively. If you are very careful, you can save the piece of opaque glass forming the base of the bulb. If not, salvage the two hemispherical contacts with their one-inch lengths of wire.
4. Buy a miniature screw socket from an electronics supply dealer.
5. Wheat Lamp bulbs have three contacts; two are the contacts on the base of the bulb and the third is the entire brass sleeve. The adapter should be wired so that the bulb works with either switch position of the Wheat Lamp headpiece. First, you must locate the contact on the old Number 1157 bulb that corresponds to the common contact of a Wheat Lamp bulb. Double contact index bulbs like a Number 1157 or a Wheat Lamp bulb have two small brass indexing studs on the sides of the bulb base; one is higher than the other. To make sure the bulb is used in the right position, as you hold the Number 1157 bulb sleeve with the upper indexing stud on your right and the lower on your left, the contact that is to be wired common is the base contact nearest you. Wire the base contact of the miniature screw socket to the one-inch wire connected to the common contact. Wire the threads contact of the miniature screw base socket to both the brass sleeve and the remaining one-inch wire of the Number 1157 bulb.

6. Push the miniature screw socket into the brass sleeve of the Number 1157 bulb, making sure that the contact wires remain visible and not excessively tangled. You could use an ohmmeter or a simple connectivity tester to make sure only the correct contacts have been made.
7. Screw in a Number 41 bulb into the miniature screw base and arrange the distance between the filament in the bulb and the two contacts at the base of the adapter so that it is equal to the corresponding distance in a Wheat Lamp bulb.
8. Slip pieces of cardboard or other insulating material into appropriate places between the miniature screw base, the brass sleeve, and contact wires to prevent shorting occurring during the rest of the adapter construction process.
9. Check the bulb filament to base contacts distance again and carefully unscrew the Number 41 bulb.
10. Fill the space between the miniature screw base and the brass sleeve with PC-7 or other epoxy cement. A toothpick can be used to force the epoxy into the spaces. Be careful not to get epoxy into the miniature screw socket.

Note: If you don't do step 2, then replace the word "filament" with the word "top" in steps 7 and 9.

A Number 13 bulb can also be used in a Wheat Lamp using the adapter. This bulb is lower in current than the Number 41 and it will give up to 50 hours of (dimmer) light per charging of the Wheat battery. If this amount of service per cave trip is preferable to the 24 hours of the Number 41 bulb, you may want to favor the filament to base distance of the Number 13 bulb in the construction of the adapter.

Replacing Miner's Lamp Electrolyte

If you made the mistake of going into a wet cave without plugging the vent holes of a miner's lamp and water enters the cells, or if the electrolyte becomes extremely dirty from dust entering the vents, you need to remove the liquid and replace it with fresh electrolyte using the following procedure. First, the battery should be charged as completely as possible, leaving the charger connected to the battery for an extra long time. This charging step gets as much lead as possible out of the discharge compounds and electrolyte, and back on the plates as pure lead. The charging should be done before attempting to remove any liquid from the battery. Be careful of liquid leaking out of the vent holes of an over-filled battery during charging.

After recharging as much as possible, all the liquid should be removed and discarded. This can be done using the plastic hose that fits into the vent holes. The battery should then be partially refilled (80%) with fresh sulfuric acid electrolyte (available at automotive supply dealers). After charging the battery again as much as possible, fill the cells to the fill line with more electrolyte.

Modifications to Other Electric Lights

Justrite electric lights and other similar types are about 20% of the initial cost of a Wheat Lamp with charger. However, they need several modifications before going underground. The elastic helmet strap should be replaced with a lamp bracket for helmet mounting. One model of the Justrite lamp comes with a caving bracket installed, instead of an elastic strap. A bracket can either be homemade or a bracket from a carbide lamp can be used.

The electric cord that is supplied with some of these lamps is flimsy and should be replaced with a stronger wire and attached in such a manner that any stress on the wire is not transmitted to the conductors or the connections. While making this new wire also make a spare.

In some of the lamps, the off-on switch is not cave worthy, and should be replaced with a sturdier one.

Battery Carrying Methods

There are several different methods of carrying a battery for an electric cave light. The most general consideration is where you want to wear your battery.

Usually, it is worn on a belt on your side. This placement conserves your narrowest dimension-front to back. To avoid the tendency of the battery to rotate around to your stomach while in a crawlway, you can run your belt through one of the battery's belt loops, then through one or two of the belt loops on your pants and finally through the other belt loop of the battery. The use of the special miner's lamp belt also helps to prevent sliding around. This kind of belt can be loosened to change battery position and retighten without too much worry about the battery rotating by itself. Europeans seem to prefer to wear their battery on the back on a waist belt. This method is probably less restrictive to leg motion and provides an even balance. You may want to try both methods.

Another point of contention is whether to wear the battery inside or outside your coveralls. The main advantages of wearing the battery inside the coveralls are that the battery is less likely to catch on things and the wire connecting the battery and the helmet can be run inside the coveralls, preventing any catching on rock projections. The main advantage of wearing your battery outside of your clothing is that it can easily be removed for extremely tight places. A compromise encompassing the advantages of removability and streamlining with clothes is to sew a large flap above the battery that can be fastened below.

Miner's batteries already have built-on belt loops so they can be worn on the body. The Justrite battery case for D-cells has a large clip for belt or pocket carrying. Other batteries are not specifically designed for wearing and require you to use a carrying method of your own design. The simplest method is to make belt loops out of heavy wire, such as coat hanger wire, and tape them to the battery with about three feet of fiber-reinforced tape. Surprisingly, the tape can last for five to ten caving trips. A much better method is to use the 6 × 3 × 2-inch army surplus belt pouch. Some sealed lead-acid batteries or nickel-cadmium wet cells fit in these packs. For better balance, you may want to remove the belt-connecting strap on the pouch and re-sew it in a higher position. Another method especially useful for nickel-cadmium wet cells, which are usually not as solidly constructed as sealed lead-acid batteries, is to build a case out of metal or other strong material and use a potting compound (silicone glue or thick epoxy) to secure the battery inside.

An occasionally seen rig consists of four nickel-cadmium D-cells mounted on the back of the cave helmet using battery-holding clips. Although this system has some obvious advantages, it is limited by the ultimate capacity of the D-cells which is 4-amp-hours per cell. In terms of light output, four 4-amp-hour D-cells will provide about eight hours of light slightly brighter than a carbide lamp. Of course, four extra D-cells can be carried in a cave pack to provide 16 hours of light potential. However, eight 4-amp-hour nickel-cadmium D-cells are not cheap. If you need more than about eight hours of light, you should not use D-cells. If you do want to use rechargeable D cells, make sure you get the 4-amp-hour kind, not the very common 1.2-amp-hour ones usually sold in retail stores.

Battery and Bulb Matching

The output of caving batteries ranges from three to six volts, and each kind has its own type of discharge curve. Each variety of battery will work best with only certain bulbs. Especially if you design your own electric system, you will need to know how to determine which are the most efficient bulbs for use with your battery.

Many electric systems use the Justrite headlamp which has a miniature screw base fixture. Considering all the small bulbs available, the miniature screw configuration provides the widest possible choice. There are many different miniature screw base and PR flange bulbs available for ten volts or less. From these, you will want to choose a main bulb to produce about two candlepower of light [equivalent to a carbide lamp with a flame approximately 1¾ inch long (Varnedoe, 1970)] and one or two efficient low-power bulbs. These low-power bulbs are useful as precautionary equipment in case an extra long caving trip is expected or if the time of a caving trip is unexpectedly increased.

Useful Bulbs for Electric Systems

Bulb Number	Design Volts	Design Amps	Design Brightness	Design Life (hrs)	Base Design
13	3.7	0.3	0.98	15	Min. Screw
27	4.9	0.3	1.4	30	Min. Screw
40	6.3	0.52	0.15	3,000	Min. Screw
41	2.5	0.5	0.5	3,000	Min. Screw
42	3.2	0.5	0.35	3,000	Min. Screw
157	5.8	1.1	8.1	50	Min. Screw
365	3.69	0.5	1.6	15	Min. Screw
403	4.0	0.3	0.98	30	Min. Screw
425	5.0	0.5	2.3	15	Min. Screw
502	5.1	0.15	0.6	100	Min. Screw
605	6.15	0.5	3.4	15	Min. Screw
1432	3.2	0.16	0.2	3,000	Min. Screw
1438	3.8	0.43	1.6	15	Min. Screw
1482	6.0	0.45	2.2	100	Min. Screw
1483	6.0	0.04	0.1	500	Min. Screw
BM30	4.0	1.2	4.9	250 x 2	D.C. Index
BM30A	4.0	1.0	3.9	250 x 2	D.C. Index
BM32*	4.0	1.2	4.9	250 x 2	D.C. Index
BM32A*	4.0	1.0	3.9	250 x 2	D.C. Index
BM3232	4.0	1.2/2.5	4.5/12	300/60	D.C. Index
BM4010	4.0	1.0/4.0	3.9/?	250/60	D.C. Index
HPR36	5.5	1.0	7.95	40	Flange
HPR50	4.42	1.17	6.76	25	Flange
HPR51	6.5	0.7	7.16	25	Flange
HPR53	4.0	0.85	4.77	25	Flange
KPR113	4.8	0.75	4.06	20	Flange
KPR118	7.2	0.55	5.23	15	Flange
PR12	5.95	0.5	3.1	15	Flange
PR13	4.75	0.5	2.2	15	Flange
PR15	4.82	0.5	2.0	30	Flange
PR18	7.2	0.55	4.8	3	Flange
PR30	3.75	0.86	2.25	40	Flange
PR32	4.8	0.7	3.2	30	Flange

All D.C. Index bulbs have two filaments.
* For Mine Safety lamp

Table 1 — Standard specifications of useful lamp bulbs for electric systems

The relative efficiency of different bulb and battery combinations can be evaluated by determining their brightness and expected hours of service per charge. To determine these things, one needs to know the design voltage (DV), design brightness (DB), design life (DL), and design current (DC) of the bulb being used, and the rated voltage and amp-hour capacity (AH) of the battery. Since batteries lose voltage as they are discharged, the calculations should be made using the average voltage (AV) of the battery. The average voltage is the voltage of the battery during the period between the beginning of discharge (use) and the point when the battery's rated amp-hour capacity has been spent.

Since each type of battery has its own characteristic discharge curve, the average voltage as a percentage of the battery's rated voltage can be used in designing a system. For the batteries most often used in cave lights, these percentages are:

wet cell lead-acid, 90
sealed lead-acid, 105
wet cell nickel-cadmium, 100
D-cell nickel-cadmium, 99
manganese rechargeable, 80
common alkaline non-rechargeable, 80

common carbon zinc batteries, 80

An electric system's average brightness (AB) (measured in mean spherical candlepower), bulb life (L), and the expected number of hours of service per charge (H) are calculated using the following formulas (Catalog of Miniature Lamps, undated):

$$AB = \left(\frac{AV}{DV}\right)^{3.5} DB \qquad L = \left(\frac{DV}{AV}\right)^{12} DL$$

Battery-Bulb Matchings

System	Bulb Number	Hours Service per Charge	Average Brightness	Bulb Life	Bulb Amps	CPH
A	13	49	0.9	21	0.30	44
	365	29	1.5	20	0.49	44
	41	24	1.8	38	0.61	43
	PR30	17	2.0	65	0.84	34
	BM30A	15	2.7	550	1.0	41
	PR50	14	3.3	300	1.0	45
	HPR53	18	3.3	88	0.8	59
	BM30	13	3.4	400	1.2	44
	BM3232	13/6	3.4/8.3	300/60	1.2/2.5	44/50
	BM4010	15/3.7	27/?	250/50	1.0/4.0	41/?
B	1483	196	0.1	338	0.4	19.6
	502	48	1.2	10	0.17	58
	1482	17	2.5	68	0.46	43
	605	16	3.5	14	0.50	56
	KPR118	16	4.9	17	0.51	78
	PR18	16	4.9	17	0.51	78
	HPR51	12	6.4	25	0.7	74
	157	7	10.2	22	1.14	71
C	502	29	0.5	150	0.15	15
	1432	21	0.9	17	0.20	19
	27	14	1.4	29	0.30	20
	PR12	8	1.8	146	0.45	16
	PR15	9	2.1	24	0.5	17
	425	8	2.2	18	0.50	18
	42	9	2.3	17	0.44	21
	157	4	4.6	360	1.0	18
	HPR36	4	5.4	45	0.94	23
D	502	85	1.1	14	0.16	94
	31	47	1.8	290	0.30	85
	605	28	3.1	20	0.49	87
	KPR118	28	2.8	133	0.5	79
	HPR51	21	5.4	65	0.7	113
	157	12	9.1	33	1.10	109

Battery-Bulb Matchings

System	Bulb Number	Hours Service per Charge	Average Brightness	Bulb Life	Bulb Amps	CPH
E	1432	70	0.83	23	0.20	58
	27	47	1.3	38	0.30	61
	425	29	2.0	24	0.49	58
	42	32	2.1	23	0.44	67
	PR15	28	2.0	30	0.5	56
	PR32	20	3.2	30	0.7	64
	KPR113	19	4.1	20	0.75	76
	HPR36	15	4.9	203	0.93	74
	157	14	4.2	480	0.99	59

System A: Koehler Wheat Lamp rated at 4 volts, 15 amp-hours (14.4 amp-hours). Average voltage is 3.6 volts.

System B: Sealed lead-acid battery rated at 6 volts, 8 amp-hours. Average voltage is 6.3 volts.

System C: Four nickel-cadmium D-cells rated together at 5 volts, 4 amp-hours. Average voltage is 4.92 volts.

System D: Five nickel-cadmium wet cells rated together at 6 volts, 14 amp-hours. Average voltage is 6 volts.

Table 2 — Characteristics of some battery-bulb matchings for five common batteries.

$$H = AH/\text{current} = AH/\left[\left[\left(\frac{AV}{DV}\right)^{0.55}\right](DC)\right]$$

Typical criteria for a good electric system are: a minimum of eight hours of service per charge at a minimum of 1.8 candlepower average light output, a minimum of ten hours for the bulb life, and a maximum battery thickness of 2½ inches. The best comparison of different bulb possibilities with the same battery is on the basis of candlepower-hours (CPH = (AB)(H)). This is the bulb's brightness at the average voltage multiplied by the number of hours per charge. Usually there are two or three efficient bulbs with almost the same CPH (although their brightness may differ) while the rest have only half this CPH or less.

Table 1 lists the bulbs most suited for caving along with their industry standard specification. The information in the table can be used to match batteries and bulbs using the bulb equations and characteristic average battery voltages. Table 2 shows such a matching completed for five common types of caving batteries. Both good and poor battery-bulb matches are included with the discriminating CPH ratings. Each battery has one good primary bulb of around two candlepower and a couple of secondary bulbs for long trips or emergency use.

Sources of Batteries and Bulbs

There are several sources of batteries and other equipment. The most obvious are the familiar caving gear suppliers (see Appendix D). In addition to complete electric systems and chargers, they have the Justrite headpiece and many of the varieties of bulbs. Another source is military and industrial surplus mail-order houses. These are especially good for liquid cell and sealed 4-amp-hour D-cell nickel-cadmium batteries and chargers. Miner's supply stores offer miner's lamps and chargers at good prices. Some of the miniature screw bulbs are difficult to obtain. One supplier, D. H. E. Electric, 1135 Okie St. N.E., Washington, D.C. 20002, seems to have all varieties (in boxes of ten only).

References

Chicago Miniature Lamp Works (undated) Catalog no. 7000: Miniature lamps, 33pp.

Varnedoe Jr, W. W.(1970) "Some Engineering Characteristics of Small Portable Electric Lights for Caving": *NSS Bulletin* 70:71-87.

Chapter 4

CAVE LAMP BATTERY CHARGING

Ray Cole
NSS 12460

Battery Chargers

Caving battery chargers range from those you buy ready-made to ones that are made from circuit diagrams. The factory-built ones are usually expensive, especially the ones sold by battery manufacturers for their batteries. If you don't think you have a working knowledge of the electrical aspects of caving lights and batteries then you better get a friend to help or purchase a commercial product that meets your needs. Battery chargers are only intended for use with rechargeable batteries. Under no circumstances should you attempt to charge batteries that were not specifically designed to be re-charged.

The least expensive ready-made charger you can buy is the small plug-in cube-type charger like the ones used with calculators and transistor radios. The problem is matching these up with your batteries. Since the power cubes are readily available used or new at electronic parts stores such as Radio Shack they should not be overlooked. Many caving batteries have terminal voltages around six volts. For these cells the power cubes rated for 6.0 volts DC at around 500 milliamperes are often suitable.

A relatively new and widely available variation of the power-cube is the charger for radio controlled race cars. Most of these chargers are made to use with either 7.2- or 9.6-volt nickel-cadmium (NiCd) batteries. They may not be suitable for use with other type of batteries such as lead-acid. Care should be used in using the "rapid-chargers" that are capable of charging nickel-cadmium cells in 30 minutes or less. These are best used with especially designed nickel-cadmium batteries and could result in a reduced number of charge/discharge cycles when used with standard cells.

Another inexpensive commercially made battery charger is the motorcycle battery charger available at motorcycle supply stores. These can be used to charge six-volt lead-acid batteries. Automobile battery chargers that have a six-volt switch position can also be used. Three silicon rectifiers in series can be used to bring these chargers down to an appropriate voltage for four-volt lead-acid batteries. The rectifiers are better than a resistor in this application since their voltage drop remains about the same over a wide range of charging currents.

Battery chargers can also be constructed from power supplies available from electronic parts suppliers as well as on the electronic surplus market. Adjustable power supplies that are regulated make ideal constant voltage chargers for lead-acid batteries. A fixed voltage charger such as a regulated power supply or an automobile charger will result in the charging current tapering off as the battery approaches full charge.

Of special interest to cavers is the "mobile charger" for using your car electrical system to charge your caving battery. One of these can be made by using a simple variable power resistor of approximately 20 ohms. The kind you want to look for is about ¾ inch in diameter and about 4 inches long (50 watt rating) that has a resistance of 20 ohms or less and a slide contact for varying the resistance. To drop from twelve to six volts at one ampere you need to set the resistor at about six ohms. Check the current with a meter as you begin to charge a completely discharged battery while the car motor is off. Set the resistor to give a current equal to one-tenth the ampere-hour rating of your caving battery. After you do this once or twice with a meter, you can put a mark on the resistor where the slide contact will be in the best position. The resistor should be mounted in a metal box or some other container to prevent the potentially hot resistor from coming into direct contact with anything in your car. The only other things you need are alligator clips to connect to the caving battery's terminals and a cigarette lighter plug to get 12 volts input. If you don't take advantage of your car's cigarette lighter fuse and want to connect directly to your car battery, be sure to include a fuse, both at your car's battery and in your mobile charger. An accidentally shorted car battery can quickly vaporize the wiring if the circuit is not fused.

Battery Charging Time

The length of time you should charge a battery depends on several factors: (1) the type of battery you have, (2) the current rating of your battery, (3) the current output from your charger, (4) the length of time the battery was discharged in the cave, (5) the current rating of the bulb used on the cave trip, and (6) how long since the battery was last charged. The calculations using these variables are not complicated at all, nor are caving batteries extremely sensitive to overcharging. It will help, however, to see exactly how they relate to get a feeling for how much you should be charging your battery.

The sixth factor is the only one that is difficult to compute. Essentially all batteries self discharge with time. The rate depends on the type of cell and its condition. Older cells will often discharge at a more rapid rate. Lead-acid batteries hold their charge better than nickel-cadmium batteries. A nickel-cadmium can loose 20% of its energy in the first month after charging. This is not a big problem for caving since batteries should be fully charged just prior to use.

The type of battery makes a difference in the amount of time needed for charging because some types are more efficient at converting the electrical charge into stored energy than others. For the two most common types used for caving, a lead-acid battery needs to be charged with about 110% of the energy (ampere-hours) discharged and a nickel-cadmium battery needs to be charged with about 140% of the energy discharged.

The ampere-hour rating of your battery determines the maximum rate at which you should charge your battery as well as the amount of energy that it actually stores. A good rule of thumb is the 10-hour rate. This is the rate at which a battery would be completely charged in a 10-hour period if it were 100% efficient. In other words, if your battery is rated at six volts and eight ampere-hours, you should charge it at a little over six volts and $1/10 \times 8 = 0.8$ amperes. If it was a lead-acid battery, this should take 11 hours and for a nickel-cadmium battery, it would take about 14 hours. Some care should be taken not to overcharge lead-acid batteries at the 10-hour rate. Nickel-cadmium batteries are more tolerant of this method of constant current charging.

If you are using a cube charger or other small charger that has a current rating that is less than a tenth of the ampere-hour rating of your battery, you have to charge for extra time to replace the energy. For example, if your battery is rated at eight ampere-hours and your charger is rated at 0.5 amperes you have to charge for $8.0/0.5$ or 16 hours to recharge a completely discharged battery (assuming 100% efficiency).

The amount you have to charge depends on the amount of energy actually discharged. The energy in ampere-hours that is discharged is simply the ampere rating of the bulb(s) used in the cave multiplied by the number of hours of use. For example, if you go on a 12-hour cave trip using a 0.5 ampere bulb for eight hours and a 0.15-ampere bulb for the rest of the time, you use $\left(8 \times 0.5\right) + \left(4 \times 0.15\right) = 4+0.6 = 4.6$ ampere-hours. If you charge at a rate of 0.6 amps and the battery is a lead-acid type, you need to charge for a minimum of $4.6/0.6 \times 1.1 = 8.4$ hours. Most batteries will not be damaged by limited over charging. Nickel-cadmium batteries can be charged at many times their 10 hour rate using constant current but

more care should be taken with lead-acid if constant current charging is used.

Charging Nickel-Cadmium Batteries

The following information applies only to nickel-cadmium batteries—do not attempt to charge any other type of battery with this circuit.

Nickel-cadmium batteries can be charged in numerous ways, but the basic problem is determining when they are fully charged. The technique described here avoids this problem by charging the nickel-cadmium batteries at $1/10$ their ampere-hour capacity. At this rate most makes can be charged for extended periods with no damage to the cells. By charging at this rate for 16 hours the cells will always be fully charged. Note that it is necessary to replace the energy used with 40 to 60% extra since the cells are not perfect storage devices.

The nickel-cadmium battery charger described here consists of a constant current device that delivers the same amount of current with a wide range of DC supply voltages for charging any number of cells in series.

The circuit is shown in Figure 1. This simple circuit is made possible by IC_1 which is a voltage-regulating integrated circuit with a low reference voltage of 1.25 volts. LED D_1, R_2, and R_3 are included to indicate that the battery is charging and that all connections are made. This feature can be omitted leaving just R_1 and IC_1. R_3 will have to be chosen experimentally due to variation in component tolerances. Select R_3 so that the LED D_1 is just clearly visible.

The charger will fit into an aluminum minibox measuring $2\,3/4 \times 2\,1/8 \times 1\,5/8$ inches. IC_1 must be attached to a heat sink or the metal case since it will have to dissipate many watts and will get hot. Use a conductive paste and insulating washer in mounting IC_1. The component placement is not critical. Test the charger by connecting an ammeter across the output terminals. It should read 0.38 to 0.42 amps. If the current is too high, it may be necessary to replace R_1 with a higher value such as 3.15 ohms.

To use the charger, connect it to a DC power source such as your car's electrical system, 12-volt power supply for your CB radio or ham rig, or a 12-volt battery charger. Any number of cells can be charged in series and as long as the charge-indicating LED is at full brightness you should be okay. Alternatively, you could insert a series ammeter. To calculate the supply voltage required, use the following equation where V_s is the minimum DC supply voltage and N is the number of cells connected in series:

$$V_s = 4.0 + 1.6N$$

For example: four cells require 10.4 volts while ten cells require 20 volts. You should be able to charge up to six cells in series using your car's electrical system while the car is running, but the charge current will decrease when you stop the engine since the car battery voltage will drop from 13.8 to 12 volts.

The DC voltage applied must be less than 30 volts more than the terminal voltage of the batteries being charged. If a large DC voltage is applied while charging a few cells, the charger will get very hot to the touch—it could become dangerously hot. This should not harm the charger since the integrated circuit will cut itself off if it gets too hot, then back on when it cools. Take care that no one, and especially children, comes into contact with a hot charger. It could cause burns. If you find the charger is too hot, it can be built into a larger case or a heat sink can be added to help dissipate the heat.

If you are fortunate to have a local electronic supply store all of the components should be available there. Many parts, including the LM317T ICs, are available at Radio Shack. An option is to use an LM350T instead of the LM317T. This IC will current limit at 3.0 amperes which is useful in charging multiple lamps in parallel or reducing the charging time. The following mail order supplier sells many of the parts including rechargeable batteries:

> Digi-Key
> 701 Brooks Ave S
> PO Box 677
> Thief River Falls, MN 56701-0677
> phone: 800-344-4539

To achieve maximum capacity from your battery, it should be charged just prior to use. Nickel-cadmium batteries lose energy quickly compared to non-rechargeable batteries. Avoid only partially charging the batteries, otherwise they might temporarily lose their maximum capacity.

Nickel-cadmium batteries can be damaged if a reverse charge is applied. This can happen if one of the series cells runs down to zero before the others while using your light system. To avoid possible damage to any of the cells, turn the light off as soon as possible after it starts to dim.

Miner's Lamp Charger

The miner's style of electric lamps have become popular with cavers due to their ruggedness, light output, large battery capacity, availability, and cost. Unfortunately the same cannot be said about the commercially-made chargers. The chargers described here will deliver a constant voltage charge to the battery either from 110 volts AC or DC from an automotive electrical system.

Always charge lead-acid batteries soon after use and leave them in a charged condition when stored. Remember to add distilled water to a battery only after it has been fully charged.

The preferred method of charging a lead-acid battery is to apply a constant voltage at the battery terminals until it is fully charged. The voltage

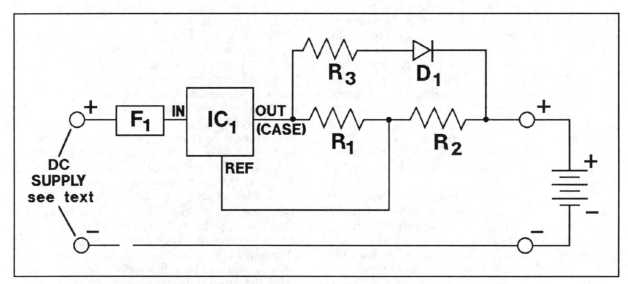

IC_1	National LM317T (1.5 amperes) or LM350T (3.0 amperes) Integrated Circuit
D_1	Red LED 1.6 volt at 10 milliamps
R_1	3 ohm, 5 watt resistor, 10% tolerance
R_2	1 ohm, 1 watt resistor 10% tolerance
R_3	0 to 20 ohm, ½ watt resistor (see text)
F_1	In-line 1 or 2 ampere fuse between DC supply and IN

Figure 1 — Constant current charger and parts list for 4-ampere-hour nickel-cadmium batteries.

applied will determine the time required for the battery to reach a full charge.

With the 14.4 ampere-hour capacity lead-acid battery used by Koehler, a voltage of 5.2 volts will produce a full charge condition in about ten hours or less if the battery was not completely discharged. Continuous charging at this voltage will not harm the battery but will require distilled water to be added to each cell periodically. The gassing and resulting water usage caused by the overcharging can be reduced by lowering the charge voltage after the battery is fully charged. A low voltage that will keep the battery charged is called the float voltage and for the Koehler lamps appears to be around 4.6 volts. If the lamp will not be needed for some time it can be fully charged at this voltage but that may take several days.

The circuit diagram for the miner's lamp charger is shown in Figure 2 along with the components. The DC voltage required can be supplied from a 12-volt car electrical system through a cigarette lighter adapter or other connection, or from 110 volts AC. The 110 volts AC must be converted to DC before it can be used. This is done by T_1 which reduces the AC voltage to around 14 volts which is rectified by D_1 and D_2 Electrolytic capacitor C_1 produces a smooth DC voltage. Be sure to observe the polarity on C_1. Since the 12 volts DC is connected through a diode, an OR arrangement results which will automatically select the greater of the two power sources. The resulting DC voltage is then applied to a combination voltage regulator/current limiter consisting primarily of IC_1. The output voltage from IC_1 is determined by the following equation (Catalog of Miniature Lamps, undated):

With Sl closed for charge

$$V_{out} = \frac{1.2\left(R_2+R_3+R_4\right)}{R_2+\text{part of } R_3)}$$

With Sl open for float

$$V_{out} = \frac{1.2\left(R_1+R_2+R_3+R_4\right)}{R_1+R_2+\text{part of } R_3}$$

The part of R_3 referred to in the above equations is the portion from the center contact to R_2.

With S_1 on, R_1 is adjusted for 5.2 volts for fast charge and with S_1 off, R_2 is adjusted for 4.6 volts for the float voltage.

The components will fit in a $5 \times 10 \times 3$-inch aluminum chassis. Component placement is not critical. Since the case of IC_1 is at the output potential, it must be insulated from the case and heat sink with a mica washer using heat conductive paste.

The type of connectors used to attach the electric lamps depend on the model of miner's lamp used.

More than one lamp can be charged at once but the total charging time may be increased. See

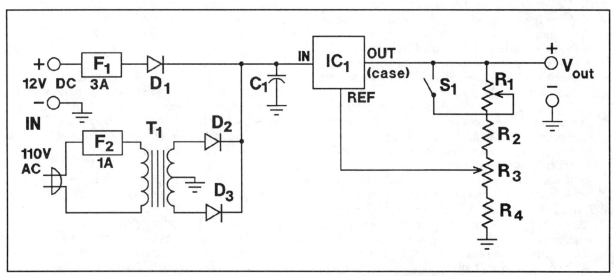

D_1–D_3	3 ampere silicon diodes	C_1	10 μfd 25 volt Capacitor
IC_1	LM317K (1.5 amperes) or LM350K (3.0 amperes)	T_1	Transformer 20 to 30 volt centertapped
R_1&R_3	100 ohm potentiometer		Heat Sink for TO-3 transistor case
R_2	180 ohm, ½ watt resistor		Conductive Paste
R_4	680 ohm, ½ watt resistor		Mica Washer Mounting Kit for TO-3 case
S_1	SPST switch	M_1	0 to 2 ampere meter (optional)

Figure 2—Miner's lamp charging circuit and parts list

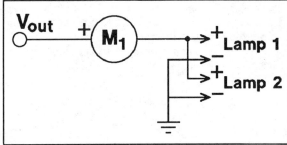

Figure 3—Connecting multiple lamps and the ammeter

Figure 3 for connecting an optional ammeter and connectors for additional lamps. The initial charge current will be about 1.5 to 2.0 amperes on charge and as the battery reaches full charge this current will drop to below 100 milliamperes, depending on the battery condition.

Again most of the parts can be purchased at a local Radio Shack store. An option is to use an LM350K instead of the LM317K. This IC will current limit at 3.0 amperes which is useful in charging multiple lamps in parallel or reducing the charging time.

Hints For Safer Caving With Electric Lights

The following suggestions may help keep you from ending up in the dark:
1. Check your equipment before each trip.
   a. All wiring should be solid with no broken strands.
   b. Clean and reconnect any doubtful connections.
   c. Replace any connectors, switches, sockets, or cords that are intermittent. Don't wait until they fail completely.
   d. Try using silicone grease on the electrical contacts. This material is available in automotive and electrical supply stores and helps reduce corrosion at the electrical contacts by keeping out the moisture.
   e. Rechargeable batteries should be fully charged as soon as practical before use.
2. Don't test electric lighting equipment in a cave. Check out your equipment in the safety and comfort of your home. You should know how much time to expect from each battery pack with your choice of bulbs.
3. Take at least three spare bulbs with you. You may run into a string of bad luck. Most bulbs are good for at least 10 hours—but that is only an average and a new bulb that is rated for a 30 hours could fail after a few minutes.

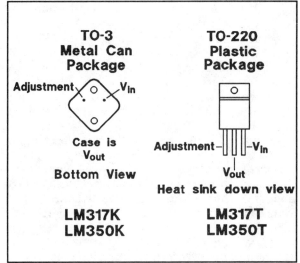

Figure 4—Pin connections for the LM317 and LM350 ICs.

4. Keep your equipment clean. This will help you in determining its condition and it will last longer. Clean water or a damp cloth is a good way to clean lamps and batteries that have been dragged through cave mud. Avoid submerging batteries that are not completely sealed. You should dry everything with a cloth and/or hair-dryer before it rusts.
5. You wouldn't go into a cave without spare parts for a carbide light. Electric Cavers should take the following with them in their cave pack:
   a. All the tools they need to disassemble their headlamps and battery packs. The list might include screwdriver, small pliers, and allen wrenches.
   b. Small knife.
   c. One foot length of insulated hookup wire for making emergency repairs.
   d. A backup headlamp cord (optional).
   e. Extra bulbs including low current replacements for emergencies.
   f. Spare batteries.
6. Finally and very important is the issue of how much reserve lighting time you should allow for. A good rule of thumb which applies both to carbide and electric is to have a reserve of 100%. Also for electric cavers you should take along lower current bulbs that will greatly extend your remaining battery life. The reduced light output might not be adequate for checking leads in the ceiling but can provide a useable level of light for extended periods of time.

Remember: **Three sources of light!**

Chapter 5

ADDITIONAL LIGHT SOURCES

Jim Pisarowicz
NSS 16872

Introduction

When it comes to light sources, the magic number is three. This usually works out to be a carbide or electric headlamp for general caving applications plus two additional sources of light for backup use in case the primary light source fails. Until recently, the two additional light sources carried by many cavers were a standard flashlight plus a candle and matches. With some recent advances in technology, the caver now has the option of several other sources of light which can supplement the primary light source.

Whatever backup lights are carried, remember that these will furnish the light that a caver must use when the primary light fails. **A caver must be able to safely exit a cave using backup lights!**

Before considering the many available secondary sources of light, consider why the standard carbide or electric headlamp, flashlight, and candle combination has worked so well over the years for so many cavers. This combination of light sources has proven itself over time because each source of light is relatively independent of the others. Consider the caver who chooses to carry three carbide lamps along on a caving trip and ends up losing his carbide container far into a cave. This single loss adversely affects not only his primary lighting source, but his backup sources as well.

There is a growing trend toward taking four light sources as caving trips become longer and more difficult. One of the "extra" three could be a duplication and totally independent of the primary light.

Flashlights

The most common secondary light carried by cavers is the standard flashlight. Most cavers prefer the smaller types, those using two C-cells or two or four AA-cells. Since this light is to be used primarily as a backup to a carbide or electric headlamp, the smaller capacity of C-cells or AA-cells when compared to the standard D-cell seems negligible. By using alkaline batteries and carrying extra dry cells and bulbs, a more than sufficient margin of safety can be achieved.

Several strong points can be made for both C- and AA-cell flashlights. First, both are small and light, an important consideration to every caver. In fact, all the AA-cell flashlights in general, and the Mallory brand in particular, are so small that they may be easily carried in the mouth in an emergency, thereby freeing both hands for climbing. Another important feature of these lights is that they are inexpensive. In fact, the Radio Shack version of the AA flashlight is often given away free or for a nominal charge at special promotions. Finally, both these flashlights, along with their components (bulbs and dry cells), can generally be found almost anywhere in the United States (and in other parts of the world as well).

Although many cavers merely purchase one of these flashlights, supply it with dry cells, and toss it into their caving pack, several suggestions can be made regarding caving and its relation to backup flashlights. One suggestion is that before you toss your emergency light into your pack or pocket, you reverse one of the cells so that if the switch is accidentally turned on, the battery does not drain. Another method, but not as foolproof, is to tape the switch in the off position. There is probably nothing so disheartening as to run into that situation where you actually do need your backup light, only to find that the battery is dead. In this regard it is generally a good idea to check the cells occasionally with a meter, or to replace them, even if they have not been used, to make sure that they are fresh. Carrying along extra sets of dry cells and spare light bulbs is also a good idea. The bulbs can be kept with your extra parts for your carbide or electric headlamp or in your first aid kit. If you are a photographer, remember that most electronic flash units use AA-cells, so if you need them, do not forget about these "extras."

Waterproof flashlights are occasionally handy but they are expensive. However, a relatively inexpensive waterproof flashlight is Eveready's Jr Skipper. This light uses two C-cells and even has room inside the case to carry an extra light bulb. There is also a D-cell size Skipper. Mallory AA-cell flashlights can be made waterproof by packing them with petroleum jelly. Although this procedure is messy, it creates a relatively good, inexpensive waterproof flashlight.

If a very waterproof compact flashlight is needed, consult your local scuba diving shop. One good, reliable waterproof mini-flashlight is called the Tekna-Lite and comes in various sizes. However recent models of the AA-cell Tekna-Lite have a flat brass spring contact in the base of the flashlight instead of a coil spring. This flat spring has been known to become smashed flat by the banging of the dry cells during rigorous caving, rendering the flashlight useless.

All of the Mag-Lite aluminum flashlights are waterproof and virtually indestructible. They come in almost any size imaginable and one should be just right for your cave pack. There are several different competing brands of aluminum flashlights on the market which are similar to the Mag-Lite. Some are just as good and some are not. Make sure that the dry cells do not directly contact the base connection of the bulb. They should be isolated by a spacer contact which takes the pressure off the bulb. If the bulb directly touches the top contact of the dry cells, the banging and jarring of caving will smash the base of the bulb, destroying it.

Another suggestion regarding caving flashlights is to attach a wrist or neck lanyard or retaining line to them. When a neck lanyard is used, be sure that its breaking strength is low enough to break before strangling you if the cord catches a projection while you are rappelling or if you fall. This cord can prevent the loss of your flashlight and provides a convenient way of finding the flashlight in the dark in a fully loaded pack. Merely attach the lanyard to your pack's strap and when you need the flashlight find the cord and pull.

The recent development of disposable flashlights needs to be mentioned. For the most part these look like the Mallory type flashlights except that when the battery is dead, you throw the entire flashlight away. (Outside of the cave, in the proper place!) Although these lights are inexpensive, there are several drawbacks to their use in caving. First, it is difficult to tell the state of their batteries when you purchase them. Shoppers occasionally "play" with them in the store by turning them on and off. This, of course, wears down the battery. Secondly, a cell cannot be reversed to prevent accidental discharge in your pack or pocket. Finally, many cavers have found that these lights have a tendency to corrode internally because of their exposure to damp cave environments. This is particularly serious with these lights since you cannot open them to examine their interiors as you can with standard flashlights.

Candles

Until recently, the most common third source of light carried by most cavers was a candle. The common plumbers or household candles were used and these can generally be found in many stores and most supermarkets. The plumbers candle is made of a special long-burning wax and is superior to decorative household candles. The wicks of these candles should be trimmed so that they can be easily lit. One drawback of standard candles is that they tend to drip wax in the cave which seems to be at odds with the National Speleological Society's

conservation message: "leave nothing but footprints." A simple solution to this problem is to bring along a piece of aluminum foil to catch drips. Remember that if you are using a candle as an emergency light source, you must be sure to take along matches or a lighter. Do not rely on your carbide lamp to light your candle for then these two light sources are not independent. An open candle flame is not a useful source of light while climbing and crawling through a cave. Its use is best reserved for those times you intend to remain in one location for a while.

Matches and Lighters

Matches carried during caving should be stored in a waterproof container and kept with the candles. Matches will also stay dry if carried in a carbide container but will be lost if the carbide container is lost. To maintain complete independence of light sources, one should use a container separate from that used to fuel the carbide lamp. In addition to the matches in a waterproof container, some sort of rough surface to use for striking the matches is generally handy. Occasionally cavers are confronted with the situation in which they have dry matches, but no dry place on which to strike them. A small piece of sandpaper or emery cloth kept in the waterproof container with the matches works well.

With the advent of the disposable lighter, many cavers have opted for carrying them in lieu of matches. To be sure, this modern day convenience makes lighting lamps and candles a simple matter of a "flick" but there are certain disadvantages inherent with lighters. For one thing, most disposable lighters burn butane which is turned on by pressing a lever and ignited by a spark from a piece of flint. Unfortunately for cavers, this lever may be accidentally turned on so that all the butane escapes. Not only does this render the lighter useless but it fills your pack with highly explosive butane which will be ignited by the next handy carbide flame. This problem with disposable lighters may be circumvented by wrapping an elastic band around the lighter under its lever or by using a nondisposable lighter which burns lighter fluid.

A second potential disadvantage of most standard lighters is that the ignition is from a spark created from a flint. When the flint gets wet, occasionally it does not spark. This problem may be avoided by using a piezoelectric lighter which utilizes a piezoelectric crystal to provide the initial spark for ignition. These crystals seem to work even when wet from being submerged all day long. Unfortunately, these lighters have recently become very expensive.

A third danger of some disposable models is that they may melt or explode if burned continuously for an extended period of time or if the case is ruptured by being hit or dropped. Still, lighters tend to be easier to use than matches and have the added advantage of being able to be used as a candle-type device for a short period of time. Both of these features make them an attractive alternative to matches.

Chemical lights

The most recent innovation in lighting technology to reach the caving community has been the advent of chemical lights, generally known as Cyalumes® or lightsticks. These chemical lights consist of a plastic tube, six inches in length, containing a glass ampule of activating chemical floating in a green luminescent liquid. When the plastic tube is bent sufficiently to break the inner glass tube, the two solutions mix, and instantly produce a bright, yellow-green light when the lightstick is shaken.

The light output of a chemical lightstick during its first hour of operation is equivalent to an AA-cell flashlight but the light is diffused in all directions. By carrying a piece of aluminum foil, a reflector may be constructed to direct and concentrate the light. By drilling two pairs of holes in your carbide lamp reflector and using twist-ties or ty-wrap cable ties, a chemical lightstick may even use the standard carbide lamp reflector.

There are several advantages and disadvantages to using chemical lightsticks as a backup light source. One advantage is that although the intensity of the light gradually diminishes over a period of several hours, the human eye is particularly sensitive to its yellow-green color. Also, whereas a candle or flashlight of similar size will no longer be useful after about three hours, the chemical light will continue to glow for 24 hours or more. This can be an important source of morale for a caver lost in a cave. Lightsticks also work even when submerged and, unlike open-flame light sources, do not burn oxygen, an important consideration if caught in a bad air section of a cave or when involved in tight crawling or digging situations. Finally, unlike most light sources which may be

damaged by dropping or being bashed around, if a lightstick is "damaged" all it will do is start working!

This final advantage of lightsticks is also a disadvantage in that the stick may be accidentally "turned on." This may be prevented by storing the light in a cigar tube or a piece of lightweight pipe (aluminum, copper, or PVC) — Some cavers have gone so far as to place the lightstick in a piece of pipe and then sewing the pipe right into their coveralls. Thus this light source will always be with them.

Another disadvantage of these lights is that they are sensitive to storage in air, moisture, light, and heat. Because of this, they should always be left in their foil wrapper until ready for use. Unfortunately, this means that you cannot tell whether or not the stick has been damaged until you are about to use it. Lightsticks should not be subjected to heat as this tends to reduce their efficiency (i.e. do not store them in the trunk of your car). These sticks also deteriorate with time. They have a "shelf life" of about two years under normal temperatures and are best stored in a refrigerator. Finally, note that each lightstick may only be used once.

Mantle Lanterns

The Coleman Lantern, or other mantle-type lantern, produces a good bright light, but is of limited use in caves. These lanterns use Coleman fuel, kerosene, or special tanks of butane for fuel. They are carried by a wire handle at one's side.

In large walking passages, one of these lanterns will be enough for several people and the entire passage will be lit except for a shadow directly above the lantern. But there are many disadvantages. A hand is required to carry the lantern, making easy climbs difficult, and they must be carried upright which becomes a problem in crawlways. The glass globe and mantle are easily broken. Extra mantles can be carried and replaced. However, it would be difficult to carry extra globes. The glass can be taken out for cave use where there is no wind. Lanterns are seldom used by cavers but at special times one can be handy.

Chapter 6

YOUR CAVING HELMET

Jim Pisarowicz
NSS 16872

Have you ever wondered about your caving helmet? Sure, you know that it protects your head when you stand up and the room isn't as tall as you are and it provides a good platform to mount your lamp—but would it actually save your life in a fall? And what would happen if a falling rock hit you on the head? Maybe you should think some more about your caving helmet because, after all, you entrust the safekeeping of your most vital body system to your helmet.

Unfortunately, there isn't any single federal specification that is complete enough for caving helmets. This is not surprising for Robert Berger of the American Society of Testing Materials, National Bureau of Standards in Washington, D.C. has noted: ". . . few standards exist for any type of helmet." Should we as cavers then expect some sort of safety standard for our helmets? Of course, we should; but those that exist are inadequate at best. In this regard, the federal Z-89 standard covers the cushioning of your head from top impact (i.e. falling rock), but does not mention side impact (such as a tumbling fall down breakdown or swinging fall as when on belay). On the other hand, the federal Z-90 standard covers the cushioning of side impact, but does not mention top impact. Just to get things straight, let's look at these two standards.

American National Standards Institute ANSI Z-89.1

In order to meet this standard, a helmet must have a suspension or lining in the top that reduces the transmitted force of a steel ball weighing eight pounds dropping five feet onto the top of the helmet to not over 850 pounds.

American National Standards Institute ANSI Z-90.1

The chin strap must have a strength of at least 300 pounds. When a headform "wearing" a helmet is dropped six feet onto a solid floor, striking on the side of the helmet, the maximum deceleration of the headform should not exceed 400 gs. If the head weighs 11 pounds, that amounts to 4,400 pounds of force.

You may wonder why the maximum allowable force is 4,400 pounds sideways and only 850 pounds from the top. This is because during side blows the brain is encapsulated in the skull and hence protected against deformation. But in top

blows, the hazard is fracture of the neck vertebrae, a different problem. At intermediate angles, the problem is complex and is not addressed in either standard.

To complicate things even more, there are figures available which seem to indicate that if you could remove your head, hold it out at arm's length and drop it on the ground, there would be no helmet on the market that could protect it adequately. This does not mean that helmets are worthless when it comes to protecting your head from rock fall or just plain falling down in a cave, but it does mean that no matter what you wear on your head, you'd better use its contents as much as possible to keep from getting into trouble in the first place. This philosophy is well summarized in the following statement from the Snell Foundation (a helmet testing organization established by race car drivers): "The protection given by any protective headgear is necessarily less than complete. The best helmet is but one link in a long chain of safety including safety education."

Granted that the preceding statement is true, what sorts of things should you look for in a good caving helmet? John Armitage (1966) noted some characteristics of good climbing helmets. Although cavers and climbers are often worlds apart in the equipment they use and how it is used, Armitage's comments on helmets seem reasonable:

1. The helmet must be on your head when you need it. The chin strap must be designed to hold the helmet on your head, both in a tumbling fall and in normal climbing (i.e. caving).
2. The helmet should not be heavy or bulky or restrictive of hearing.
3. The shell must be rigid enough to spread the load of an impacting object to protect against skull fractures.
4. The shell must resist penetration by pointed objects.
5. The helmet must have an energy-absorbing lining around the head band area to cushion side impact in a tumbling fall.
6. The cost should not be too high.

To Armitage's points, the Mountain Safety Research Group added:

7. The helmet must have an energy-absorbing suspension to reduce the peak force of a top impact (falling rock).

8. The side-to-side rigidity must be reasonably good.

Okay, granted these points, what about helmets commonly seen being worn by cavers?

Helmets

Most cavers wear some sort of modified construction type helmet. The reason for this is simple — these helmets are cheap and do provide some protection (i.e. when banging your head on the ceiling). Unfortunately, most cavers will rig these helmets with inadequate elastic chin straps. If one starts to fall down a slope, the helmet is likely to be lost immediately. The head can take a terrific beating as the caver rolls and bounces down the slope. Also, these helmets often only meet the Z-89.1 standard and so it is questionable whether the helmet would protect the caver even if it stayed on the head during a fall as described above.

Pick up one of these helmets and squeeze the sides together. It is possible to move the sides inward at least an inch or so without all that much effort. This is also true for other "caving" helmets that are sold. Try the above procedure on one of the Speleoshoppe's "Deluxe Caving Helmets" (circa 1979 or before). Remember that just because it's sold as a "caving helmet," does not mean that it is safe for all kinds of caving. The Speleoshoppe's helmets do have adequate suspension systems which should keep the helmet on in a tumbling fall.

On the positive side, it can be said that most of these helmets are reasonably cheap, lightweight, fairly cool, and do protect the head from falling objects, bumping your head, etc. But, if you intend to do vertical caving, or are planning to do lots of caving, perhaps a better helmet should be in your future.

Just because you go out and spend $40, $50, or more for a caving helmet does not mean that you should not shop carefully. If you are going to spend this much money, you will probably be looking at so-called "climbing helmets" (Bell, Joe Brown, MSR, Ultimate, Petzl, etc.), and for the most part these will provide your head with much more protection than the modified construction type helmets.

First, these helmets tend to be expensive. There is a definite difference between $15 and $45. If we were all required to purchase these expensive helmets for caving, many of us probably would not have started to cave.

Second, many of these climbing helmets are hot to wear, almost unpleasantly so even in alpine caving areas. Some cavers have tried to remedy this problem by drilling holes in their Ultimates, Bells, or Joe Browns to provide ventilation for their heads. The MSR helmets come

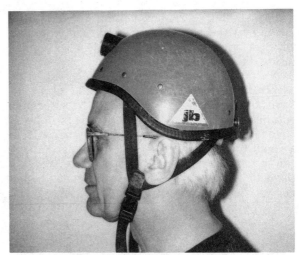

Figure 1 — A Joe Brown climbing helmet equiped with an L-1 lamp bracket. This helmet has an adequate strap with a rigid two-point attachment. The strap has been modified with a Fastex® fastener for easier removal in tight places. (photo Ladonna Rea)

with holes already designed into the helmet. In the case of the former three mentioned above, it should be noted that by drilling holes you may compromise the added protection provided by these helmets. They were not designed to have holes drilled in them and no one knows how these holes affect their primary function of protecting your head. Also, holes in the helmet shell (and this goes for the MSR helmet as well) provide a place for a falling rock to "catch" thus transmitting its falling force onto a small portion of the helmet. Without these holes, a rock would probably merely glance off the helmet with its force being dissipated accordingly.

Thirdly, you should carefully inspect any climbing helmet for other desirable caving and/or climbing qualities. For instance, although most climbing helmets have excellent strap systems for holding the helmet on your head, it is sometimes difficult to get these helmets off when confined in tight or awkward places. Also, since most of these helmets were not designed with caving in mind, adding a lamp to the front of them often causes them to tip forward, especially with the weight of a carbide lamp. This, of course, means that even though you may have spent a considerable amount of money on your helmet, modifications may still be required to its suspension system.

The "slip through" fastener on the chin strap of one of these helmets can be carefully replaced by a Fastex® quick release buckle. Filing a little slope into the gripping edge of the male part of the Fastex® buckle will make it easier to release under tension.

None of these helmets come with lamp brackets, so one must be added. Remember to be careful when installing your bracket so that you do not end up with screws, bolts, or any other rigid projection which is longer than half the thickness of the foam inside the shell of your helmet.

A useful helmet accessory, especially for carbide cavers, is a stout rubber band, such as can be cut from an old inner tube. When pulled across the bottom of one's lamp, it helps keep it from being jarred off at bad moments. Other objects, such as a small flashlight, lighter, notebook, pencil, etc., can be temporarily carried on the head by slipping them under the band. This is especially useful when negotiating deep water.

To be sure, climbing helmets will protect your head better than the construction type helmet. Their manufacturers are more con-cerned about their products. Bell and MSR tell their customers that should they have a bad fall, the helmet should be returned. These manufacturers will test the helmet and replace it if it is found to be defective.

The helmet question is still up to the individual caver. Hopefully, you can assess the amount and kind of caving you do and how that relates to this information about caving helmets. So when looking for a helmet, be informed and be observant, for after all, it's your head.

Reference

Armitage, J. (1966): "A Report on Helmets for Climbing": *Summit* 12(3)(17-22).

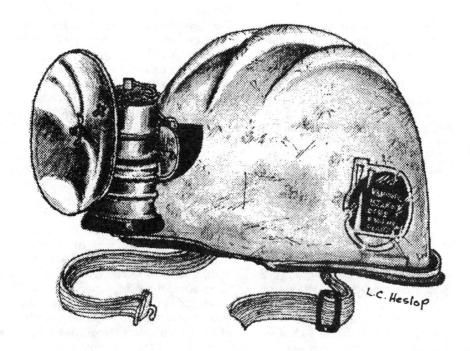

Chapter 7

CAVE PACKS

Alan Williams
NSS 9700

Selecting A Cave Pack

Any caver, before entering a cave, must be carrying a certain minimum amount of gear to ensure his safety: three sources of light, hard hat, spare parts, water, food, etc. (See Chapter 10, General Equipment.) In addition, the equipment list can quickly expand to include vertical gear, survey equipment, camera gear, and many other items depending upon the nature of the cave being visited and the interests of the individual caver.

Most cavers solve their transport problems by stuffing all the gear they can't wear into a cave pack. Cave packs are found in an almost endless variety of shapes, sizes, weights, and modes of attachment to the human body. However, a few grand generalizations can be made about their desirable characteristics. A cave pack should:
1. Be of rugged construction.
2. Be as compact as possible.
3. Allow for comfortable carrying.
4. Have a trouble-free method for opening and closing.

Some specific descriptions of the kinds of cave packs in general use by cavers follow:

Military Surplus Packs. A majority of cavers have found the answer to their cave pack needs in the large variety of "Army" side packs, field packs, and bags available in surplus stores throughout the country. The selection is not quite as varied as it once was, and certain desirable styles are becoming scarce, but a caver can find a suitable pack if he looks hard enough.

Army packs are inevitably made of durable heavy canvas, have secure closure devices, and usually come with their own array of carrying straps. The most common type in current use is the "gas mask bag" in all its many varieties. These packs are usually not larger than a foot in any dimension. They are designed to be slung over the shoulder by a single strap (the mode generally preferred by cavers). A typical gas mask bag is capable of holding the gear for most caving trips, providing you don't bring along all kinds of camera,

Figure 1—A variety of cave packs: 1–Field Phone bag. 2–German gas mask bag (note button closure). 3–Small waterproof pouch. 4, 5, & 6–various styles of gas mask bags. 7–Polyethylene pig. 8–Field pack (photo Alan Williams).

surveying, and vertical equipment. A selection of gas mask bags and other packs is shown in Figure 1.

Another surplus pack in general use is the so-called "field pack." Originally designed to be carried on the shoulders like a knapsack or suspended on the hips by a webbing belt, these packs have approximately twice the capacity of an average gas mask bag, yet are still relatively compact. They are usually fitted with an assortment of small straps and buckles intended for fastening oversize items to the outside of the pack. Field packs have only short, "knapsack" type, straps for carrying and must be fitted with a longer shoulder strap if this is desired. The larger capacity of these packs is useful when camera gear, etc. is being carried, eliminating the necessity of carrying two gas mask packs.

A surplus pack or any type of cave pack that is larger than a field pack verges on the impractical (immovable when you stuff it full of gear). Oversize packs, up to duffel bag or backpack size, occasionally are required for an elaborate expedition but generally the smaller the better for convenience

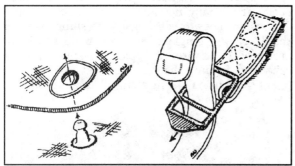

Figure 2 — Eyelet-snap and buckle-and-strap closures.

and ease of carrying.

There are two common types of closures on surplus packs: the "buckle-and-strap" and the "eyelet-snap," illustrated in Figure 2. Both closures are acceptable, but the eyelet-snap type is subject to fouling by mud and grit. Vaseline® packed into the snap before a trip will reduce this clogging. Almost any cave pack with snaps, after a few cave trips, will have one or more of these snaps rendered unworkable. Diligent post-trip cleaning can help alleviate this problem. When the eyelet-snap no longer functions, a piece of string or shock cord can be fastened in the eyelet and hooked to another part of the bag to close it. The buckle-and-strap closure is virtually foolproof, although it requires more manipulation to open and close than a functional snap type.

Zippers are occasionally found on surplus packs. They are even more subject to fouling than snaps and should be avoided. Less common are button closures (usually on foreign-made packs). Buttons

are simple and trouble free as long as the button holes are tight and the buttons don't tear off.

Ammunition Boxes. Many cavers use these military surplus metal boxes as protective containers for their camera gear. Two sizes are readily available: .30 caliber and .50 caliber, the .30 caliber box being the smaller of the two. The use of ammo boxes as cave packs is a questionable practice with regard to the well-being of both the caver and the cave. The metal box is hard and unyielding, with eight sharp corners to chip any flowstone they might touch. The box is heavy and ungainly to carry. Unless somehow tightly fastened to the body, it will be continually hitting shins, knees, and hips. An ammo box in good condition is watertight and thus may be useful for caving trips involving lots of crawling in stream passages.

Both advantages of ammo boxes — protection and water-tightness — can be achieved using soft cave packs and appropriate methods of wrapping and cushioning vulnerable items. For the well-being of both you and the cave, avoid ammo boxes if at all possible.

Miscellaneous Surplus. Many other surplus items are available which have application in cave packing. These include:
1. Belt pouches of various sizes.
2. Waterproof bags.
3. Sheaths.
4. Leather pouches.

If every surplus pack disappeared tomorrow, a caver's life would be more difficult and much more expensive. However, alternative packs do exist and are some good ones are growing in popularity.

Polyethylene Pigs. This ingenious and inexpensive pack is made from two identical one-gallon polyethylene jugs, usually bleach or anti-freeze bottles. The bottom one quarter of each jug is cut away, allowing the two to be pushed together, one inside the other, as shown in Figures 1 and 3. A carrying strap is attached at both jug handles. Often a second short strap or shock cord is attached

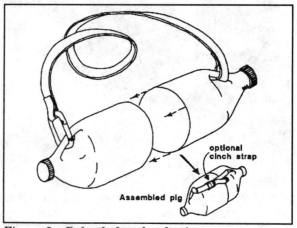

Figure 3 — Polyethylene bottle pig.

which can be cinched tight to further ensure the pig won't fall open.

Your Own Body. Some cavers find they can dispense with a separate cave pack altogether. They do this by adapting their clothing, usually coveralls, into a cave pack. By sewing additional pockets in strategic places, along the inside of the legs and arms, for example, most gear can be stowed in an out-of-the-way place. This method of packing is effective on "routine" trips, where the caver knows exactly what will be needed to safely visit the cave and no extraneous gear will be required. Of course, one should never skimp on the recommended essential gear in order to avoid carrying a separate pack!

Day Packs. Manufactured for hiking outdoors, these packs are vastly inferior to surplus packs for caving. Usually they are a bit too big and bulky, made of too-light material, too difficult to open and close securely, and too expensive. However, they are acceptable for a few trips until something better can be obtained.

Hip Packs. These packs are made for skiers and bicyclists. They are put on like a belt with the pack fitting snugly across the back at hip level. These packs are compact, but suffer from the disadvantage of any pack which is tightly attached to the body: there are inevitably situations where the pack must be removed to negotiate tight or awkward places.

Custom-designed Packs. While the possibility of dreaming up a completely original pack style is slim, there are many individual touches one can apply to improve an existing pack or to assemble a new one. These touches range from simply tying on a length of webbing as a shoulder strap to reinforcing pack corners with epoxy or leather patches to experimenting with Velcro® closures. An interesting home-made pack consists of an inner-tube-like circle of canvas three feet in diameter. Items are placed into compartments in the tube. The pack is carried like a bandolier in most situations, but can be unslung quickly and dragged if necessary.

Specially Manufactured Caving Packs. There are several sources of packs which are designed and manufactured specifically for cavers. This category is exemplified by the Lost Creek pack. Lost Creek packs were designed by an Indiana caver who became tired of constantly replacing his military surplus pack after wearing it out on just a few trips. These packs are made of ballistic nylon with a urethane coating for water resistance. Ballistic nylon is the material from which bulletproof vests and flack jackets are made.

These packs, while expensive, are probably more economical for the serious caver because they are virtually indestructable and have been proven to last for from five to ten years of hard caving. Lost Creek packs are available in many sizes and configurations. The carrying straps are arranged so the pack can either be worn as a backpack or carried on the side, under the arm. Special packs are available to fit Wheat or Justrite electric light batteries along with some spare parts and a small flashlight.

Packing the Cave Pack

Once the desired cave pack is obtained, there are a number of hints on how to efficiently fit all that essential gear inside. One of the most useful and widely used pack items is the plastic baby bottle, either without the rubber nipple or with the nipple trimmed to form a gasket. Baby bottles come in four and eight ounce sizes. They are light, compact, watertight, and extremely rugged. An eight ounce bottle will hold six to eight charges of carbide, i.e. up to 16 hours of light. Cave foods such as gorp, Granola, or M&Ms fit conveniently inside. Spare parts, flashbulbs, water—all can be carried in baby bottles. A baby bottle is made more cave-worthy by cementing together the two pieces of the screw cap. Mark the bottle used for carbide so you won't have an unexpected mouthful of carbide for lunch.

Plastic food storage bags have also found their way into universal usage. Obviously, they are not as rugged as baby bottles, but doubled bags can securely wrap just about everything that goes into a cave pack. Carefully wrapped items will be waterproof inside plastic bags; but for long periods of immersion in water passages, baby bottles are more reliable protection. The one-gallon size bags are the most versatile and many cavers prefer the "ziploc" style of closure. However, do not get mud in the ziploc threads if the bag is to be reclosed.

Other containers for packing include snap-lid film canisters for spare parts, pieces of foam rubber for wrapping cameras, rubberized bags for camera or surveying gear, and any sort of handy box or bag a resourceful caver can come across.

Carrying the Cave Pack

No arrangement for carrying a cave pack will be trouble-free in every situation. However, here are some recommendations to minimize the struggle. By far the most favored method of carrying a pack is to sling it at hip level by means of a single strap passing over the shoulder. This loose attachment to the body allows for immediate removal when necessary to negotiate tight spots. Little or no hesitation in "caving rhythm" occurs since this pack can be swung easily out of the way or removed entirely without interrupting forward motion. The pack is most conveniently slung at hip level. Slung lower, the pack continually beats against the thighs; slung higher, the shoulder strap becomes too short to pass easily over a helmeted head. Many cavers like a

Figure 4—A Lost Creek pack being carried with a combination of a shoulder strap and a waist strap. (photo Scott Fee)

waist strap on their pack in addition to the shoulder strap. A waist strap will hold the pack next to the body preventing it from swinging loose. A pack held in place with both a shoulder and waist strap will not have to be removed as often as those packs with only a shoulder strap. Also a pack that does not swing around can be more efficient to carry.

Cave packs carried like a knapsack on the shoulders present frequent inconvenience in caving. While this pack is more comfortable to carry when walking upright, it is necessary to stop to remove it or put it on—a situation that will occur before and after every crawlway.

A good indication of the practicality of a given cave pack is to note the amount of time it is carried in the hand. A pack which must be constantly taken off, or which is difficult to put on, will most often be carried by hand. This is an undesirable situation, since both hands should be free. A convenient pack will have to be removed only for the tightest crawls and will seldom be hand carried.

Another good rule to follow is: take your pack with you wherever you go in the cave. The quote, "I'll leave my pack here while I check this lead for a few minutes," is a familiar one. The result, 50% of the time, is that 20 minutes into the "little lead," the caver must madly dash back to his pack to change carbide. Either that or he yells back for his friends to "Come on through, and bring my pack with you!" Pulling this trick too often results in disgruntled companions.

Finally, a point of caving etiquette regarding cave packs is to resist the temptation to pass your pack across every obstacle to someone on the other side. Occasionally, it is more efficient to hand all the packs through at one time; but many cavers overuse this technique—making their fellow cavers pause and help them continually. It is good for a caver's soul to wrestle his own gear through the cave with minimum help.

Chapter 8

CAVER'S CLOTHING
AND INSULATION

Thomas E. Miller
NSS 10183

Essentially, cavers wear clothing for only two reasons: protection from the sharp, abrasive cave surface and as thermal insulation from air, water, and rock. Among cavers, modesty is not always considered sufficient cause.

To address these two concerns, clothes worn in active caving must be durable and warm; they must also fit well enough to allow safe and comfortable caving for extended periods of time. Caving encompasses crawling, rock climbing, and rope and ladder work—the perfect caving garments will not only allow contortions in belly-crawls or squeezes (both forward and backward) without coming off or apart, but also will not restrict movement during delicate climbing maneuvers on rock, rope, or ladder.

The safety aspect of proper clothing should not be ignored. Under most circumstances it is more important than a knowledge of proper rope techniques or owning the latest, most advanced equipment. Minor wounds or low-level hypothermia brought on by inadequate clothing greatly increase the risk of injury due to impairment of physical reflexes and common-sense judgement. And of course, much of the enjoyment of a caving trip can be lost due to physical discomfort or worry.

Dress Appropriately For Each Cave

No two caves are identical, and each varies in the amount of crawling, wetness, or climbing involved. There are often radical variations in routes within the same cave and significant variations in temperature and moisture between caves in different regions of the continent.

The three primary factors (price aside) determining dress for a caving trip are moisture, temperature, and degree of activity. Water, cold, and waiting all increase insulation requirements. The combination requiring minimal insulation would be that of a dry, warm (55° Fahrenheit or warmer) cave with a small party in frequent motion. Accompanying a large photographic party in a northeastern stream cave with vertical work is one of the more stressful situations (some might call it a nightmare).

Determining the clothing to be worn on a trip can be made easier, with safer and more enjoyable results, if each caver is aware of the conditions under which the trip will be taken. Comprehending the route and purpose of the trip is as important for the novice as it is for the experienced caver following unfamiliar companions, or entering an unfamiliar cave. Discuss what you will be doing in the cave with the trip leader or your companions to determine the length of time to be spent and the amount of crawling, walking, climbing, etc. How wet is any mud to be encountered, is there water, and is it to be crawled in or waded through? Make sure the trip purpose is understood, as well as the numbers of people involved—these will indicate the extent of activity, or how much sitting and waiting will occur. Trips where there are large numbers of people, where route-finding will be a problem, where vertical caving is involved, or where slow-moving photography or surveying is planned, are all situations where more or warmer clothing is required to offset the increased waiting time.

Lastly, be skeptical. Cavers' memories being what they are, the difficult aspects of most caves are usually under-rated, and a little over-preparation can help.

Clothing

Outer Protection: The primary function of the outer layer is to be durable enough to protect any insulating layers beneath. Depending on the severity of the trip, it may function as both protection and insulation. It should be large enough to allow insulating garments to be worn comfortably underneath. If your caving trips occur too frequently to allow proper maintenance and cleaning between trips, or there is wide variability in the severity and conditions of trips, more than one set of outer wear may be needed.

There are three ways to address this need:
1. Old clothing, such as a jacket, sweatshirt, or shirt and jeans, may be purchased cheaply at used clothing stores, but have the disadvantage of wearing out quickly and separating when backing out of tight crawls. Loose shirt tails may pose a hazard if they tangle in the rope or descent gear. Cotton clothing also provides little warmth if damp or wet.
2. Cotton or cotton blend coveralls or overalls are readily available in most department stores.

Figure 1—Three choices in outer clothing. The caver on the right is wearing cotton coveralls over old street clothes. The caver in the center is wearing a flannel shirt and blue jeans. The caver on the left is wearing a nylon caving suit. (photo Scott Fee)

Those with synthetic blends (e.g. polyester) are more durable than pure cotton.

The outer pockets of these garments tend to catch on rock projections, formations, or the like so many people sew or glue them shut; it may be useful to open them to the inside of the overall, or even transfer them. Although one or two inner pockets may be useful, filled pockets can become an uncomfortable or bulky discomfort in tight crawls.

Males might also enjoy the advantages of a two-way zipper that can be undone from the bottom as well. Zippers often jam in muddy conditions, so cleaning after each trip might include light oil on a metal zipper or silicone lubricant on plastic.

Cotton coveralls wear out rapidly at the points of greatest contact—the knees and seat. They can either be resewn or reinforced, or new material can be quickly and easily glued (to clean material) using "Canvas Grip," available from most cave equipment distributors.

3. If you can't sew your own coveralls, numerous sources are available that sell "Designer" cave-coveralls designed specifically for caving. Nearly all of these use synthetic fibers such as Kevlar or PVC. Most are extremely tough garments that lack outside pockets and usually have one or more interior pockets. The best choices will also feature a hood (possibly detachable, and useful for retaining body heat and for protection from waterfall spray), and a zipper/velcro or zipper/snap closure combination—zippers often fail under

muddy cave conditions and the alternative closure method can be very useful.

It is well to remember to test an oversuit for proper fit before deciding to purchase it for cave use—this may involve a lot of stretching, crawling about, and embarrassment on the floor of the store where you purchase it.

Insulation: Cotton, wool, and synthetic materials (e.g. polypropylene) are the choices for the insulating undergarments worn beneath the protective outer suit. The primary advantage of cotton is its cheapness. But under any damp conditions—mud, water, perspiration—it loses much of its insulation ability. Both wool and the synthetics retain their insulating capacities when wet. Synthetics have one advantage over wool in that they drain more easily than wool and do not become as heavy. Some of the synthetics, such as polypropylene, are capable of wicking moisture away from the skin to an outer garment.

Recently, reasonably-priced undersuits designed for caving have become available. They are usually made of synthetic pile-fleece, and are of full body length.

Footwear: Boots must be capable of providing both ankle support and traction. Unfortunately, top-quality leather boots with Vibram-like soles can cost twice as much as cave-coveralls, but will have a life-span considerably shortened by abrasion and constant soaking. Some outdoor stores sell used boots or "seconds" at very low prices. Lastly, leather tends to be high-maintenance, requiring cleaning, oiling, or greasing for maximum life.

Other alternatives are "combat boots" found in surplus stores, and some of the inexpensive hiking boots sold in some of the larger department stores (K-Mart, Wal-Mart, etc). They may be slightly cost-effective, but they are generally of inferior construction, wear out very quickly, and provide poor traction and ankle support.

Any type of leather boot can be dramatically bolstered in life span through the early application of a coat of epoxy, "Shoegoo II," or a similar product, to the toes, stitches, and the sides opposite the instep.

One of the best solutions to the problem of footwear is often simply a pair of rubber boots of the type used in farm work or pouring concrete. They are inexpensive, rotproof, easily patched if holed, and sufficiently high (just below the knee) to be waterproof in a surprising number of situations. It is useful to make sure the particular boot purchased has a good tread design (some are relatively smooth, which provides poor footing and should be avoided). Some of the softer rubber boots give better adhesion on mud and rock than does Vibram. The boot should fit snugly with whatever is worn inside; lined boots make it easier to insert your feet.

Although they are fine in many stream situations, if the water overtops the boot they have the disadvantage of filling and becoming quite heavy. This is obviously remedied easily by lifting the leg back at the knee and letting them drain, but can become annoying in some situations. They can also accumulate sand and mud inside which may need occasional emptying. This can be largely remedied by wearing the coverall legs outside the boots. These boots (or "wellies" as they are called in England) are popular among English and French cavers, which should be sufficient recommendation to most of us.

Rubber boots are probably the most cost-effective solution to foot gear at present, but for circumstances requiring much "technical" climbing, they do not match the capabilities of a good leather hiking or climbing boot.

"Tennis" shoes, running shoes, or the like should be avoided, if at all possible. They provide little in the way of traction or ankle support, and are often contributing factors to problems encountered during cave trips.

The actual distance covered on most cave trips is so short that blisters are rarely a problem, except if the same boots are worn enroute to the cave and the trail is long.

Socks, etc: Wool, or some of the "pile-type" synthetics, are preferable to cotton for keeping feet warm. If the caves visited require wading, and are cold (55° Fahrenheit or below), the purchase of a pair of wetsuit socks provides agreeable warmth. The wetsuit socks should not be confused with wetsuit booties — these have a hard outer sole suitable for walking, but are difficult to fit into most boots. The hard bottom sole can often be *carefully* cut away. Wetsuit socks can be made at home with sufficient neoprene and glue for much less than their commercial selling price.

Gloves: Not everyone wears gloves, even in colder, sharper caves. Cotton, leather, and coated (rubber, nylon, etc.) gloves are the main options.

Cotton is cheapest, but wears very poorly (sometimes not even lasting a full trip) and gives little warmth when wet.

Leather is more expensive, and eventually deteriorates after repeated wetting and drying.

The coated gloves generally offer the best value: unless immersed completely they remain dry inside giving insulation superior to cotton or leather, they do not rot, and they wear very well. They are easily cleaned and holes can sometimes be simply repaired with a sealant such as silicone. They may scar on rope descents if the descent rate is very rapid, but they are more than adequate for a safe, gentle descent.

It is often useful to wear something beneath the outer glove. Some people wear thin rubber "dish washing" gloves on surveying or photography trips where instrument cleanliness is an issue. These are reported to keep the hands warmer as well.

"Fingerless," or "Millar" mitts of wool or polypropylene worn inside the glove also provide excellent hand warmth even when wet.

Knee and Elbow Pads: Crawling is a common feature of caves, and most people have pain thresholds low enough to require some knee padding. The best protection is probably provided by a hard, thick outer layer over foam rubber, such as represented by Rockmaster. These types of kneepads, however, tend to be bulky and heavy, with straps that can become painful if the cave also contains substantial sections of walking.

For caves with a mixture of passage sizes, or with unfamiliar passage, basketball kneepads offer an excellent compromise of protection and flexibility. They can often be worn beneath coveralls, their chief disadvantage being the difficulty of removal. Basketball kneepads also wear out faster than the hard rubber kind if worn on the outside of clothing. The life of the pad can be extended by gluing canvas or other cloth to the outside and replacing as necessary.

Elbow pads can sometimes be of advantage in tight, lengthy crawls.

Headgear: The essential component of headgear is a helmet, a GOOD helmet. Although a rock climber's helmet may seem extravagant (perhaps twice the cost of a construction helmet), the basic question should be, "What do you think your brain is worth?" (See Chapter 6.)

A helmet serves the function both of freeing the hands for climbing by holding the light source, and of protecting the head from falling rocks or from slamming into the ceiling during travel or falls. As such, it should be firmly attached to the head, preferably with a quick release strap. An elastic strap can permit the helmet to fall off during unusual maneuvers or falls, taking with it not only the protection for the most valuable part of the body, but also the primary light source.

Helmets also can serve a valuable insulation function: below 50° Fahrenheit, 40% or more of the body's heat loss occurs from the head. In higher latitudes or elevations, this insulation may be insufficient, particularly during extended rests, or on survey and photography trips. In such cases, a "balaclava," ski-mask, or other hat of wool or polypropelene can be an asset, carried perhaps in a ziploc bag until needed.

Inside the helmet itself, an emergency vapor barrier for the entire body can easily be carried. This could be as simple as a large, unused garbage bag in a ziploc baggie (to prevent tearing the garbage bag), or one of the light "one-use" space blankets. Either is small enough to be duct-taped to the inside helmet top, and might be invaluable during any long wait.

Other Items

Maintenance: Cleaning and upkeep prior to a caving trip (and preferably as soon as possible following) can be as important as having the proper equipment. If your equipment is torn, broken, or too muddy to function properly before entering a cave, it will likely suffer shorter than normal life expectancy, or fail when needed. Holes in clothing are certain to get larger. Gear and lights that are failed and wet can simply be dead, unnecessary, wet weight to carry through the cave. Everything in your pack should have a potential function, and gear that is not working increases the risk of an unpleasant experience.

Gear Transport to the Cave: Two plastic bags are useful for a cave trip: one for the wet, muddy clothes and gear that result from the trip and the other for clean clothes into which to change following the trip.

Handkerchief: One or more of these may be useful for cleaning or drying survey gear, cameras, etc., tieing hair during a rope descent, or as head insulation.

Intermediate Level Caving

Many (most?) cavers find the simple clothing combinations described above to be adequate throughout their caving careers, particularly in the southern half of the United States where caves are usually warm, if not always dry.

But with a desire for enlarged caving horizons comes a need for more complicated (and usually more expensive) garments, often as an attempt to counter colder and wetter conditions that prevail in the mountains and higher latitudes. Such gear is beyond the scope of this book: it may include an entire or partial wetsuit (with booties, hood, and gloves), or the use of a latex farmer john undergarment such as those sold in Europe

by Gomex (see *NSS News* July 1985, p.243). Scuba rental stores are often bargain places to purchase slightly used wetsuits, particularly in the fall and winter.

Purchasing Gear

A variety of enterprises offer equipment for caving (see Appendix D), often with free catalogues or shipping service. Many of these advertise in the *NSS News*, or can be found at the various national and local conventions of cavers.

PRICING COMPARISONS (approximate 1991 prices)			
MODERATE		INEXPENSIVE	
cave coveralls	$ 70	Jeans, sweatshirt cotton coveralls	$ 0-50 $35
pile-fleece undersuit polypro underwear	$40 30-50	Cotton longjohns	$10-20
rubber boots climbing boots	$15 $150	rubber boots leather boots	$15 $35
coated gloves	$5	cotton gloves	$2
2 pr wool socks wetsuit socks	$15 $25	cotton socks	$2/pr

[The above prices are for new items—it is often possible to purchase used equipment from caving clubs or members, garage sales, newspaper ads, etc. Some clubs rent gear for low fees. This is one of the advantages of being involved with a local club.]

Cavers on this continent should also be aware of the tremendous diversity of specialized caving equipment offered by foreign dealers (particularly in Britain and France). It is usually of excellent quality, and depending on the monetary exchange rate, is often cheaper than purchasing U.S. equipment, even with shipping. These catalogue dealers are listed in caver magazines such as *Descent* and *Caves and Caving* (Britain), or *Spelunca* (France).

Summary

So, find out about your trips in advance and prepare for the expected conditions. Maintain and clean your gear and spend as much to purchase it as you think you would be willing to pay in the cave to have the item you were too cheap to buy beforehand.

Chapter 9

THE SELECTION, USE, AND CARE OF ROPES FOR VERTICAL CAVING

Kyle Isenhart
NSS 12327

Most cavers are eventually faced with the need for a piece of rope. They may need 5 feet or 1,500 feet. They may need a handline or a main rappel and prusik line. They may be in free space or against a wall, dry or wet, clean or muddy. They may even be doing technical rock climbing underground. All these factors can affect the selection of the proper rope to use.

In many parts of the United States there are very few vertical caves and an active caver may spend many years underground and not need a handline, much less a rappel and prusik rope. However, in most caving areas at least a few caves with significant vertical development are found. This discussion is directed to novice cavers and the more experienced horizontal cavers who wish to enter these vertical caves.

In most cases, an individual's introduction to vertical caving is under the leadership and direction of an experienced vertical caver. That individual or his club will usually provide the necessary ropes and equipment for the introductory vertical trips. During these trips the new caver can see what types of ropes and equipment his trip leaders are using.

After these first trips, the new caver may decide to purchase his own rope. While there are people who own very few ropes and mechanical ascenders, in the realm of vertical caving this condition is the exception rather than the rule. People who only occasionally do vertical caving often own several hundred dollars worth of equipment.

The most important item in all vertical caving is the rope. Whether it be a handline, belay line for a ladder climb, or rappel and prusik line, *it must not fail.* The selection of a high quality rope suited to the applications is a necessity. But acquiring a good rope is only the beginning. It must be maintained properly and properly used or it will deteriorate and become unsafe.

The selection of a rope, as mentioned earlier, depends upon many things. One thing it should not depend upon is price. Even the most expensive ropes are cheap when compared to medical bills, disability, or even death. Every person's life on a trip may well depend on the rope. At such times a few dollars are meaningless. Fortunately, the finest ropes available today are relatively inexpensive. Except for the specialized dynamic rock climbing ropes, top-quality ropes sell in the United States

for around $50 per 100 feet. While there are hundreds of ropes on the market today, they vary in only two things: material of construction and type of construction. This discussion will address only three basic types of rope construction.

The oldest and most common type of construction is twisted, usually called laid (Figure 1A). The second and less common type, usually restricted to rope of ½-inch or less in diameter, is the solid braid. The third type is usually called kernmantle (Figure 1B). This type consists of two basic layers. The core or kern, and the outer, braided sheath called the mantle. The inner core can be braided, highly twisted, or have nearly parallel strands. In some cases combinations of two or even all three core methods are used in a single rope. This discussion will be limited to the laid and kernmantle ropes of nearly parallel core construction as they are the most common caving ropes. Both types have advantages, but due to the low stretch and non-twisting characteristics of the kernmantle ropes, they are more popular for main rappel and prusik lines.

There are more laid ropes available than kernmantle on the general market, but fewer laid ropes suitable for caving, so we will examine them first. Their main advantages are as follows:

1. Low cost and ease of manufacture, hence a lower potential selling price.
2. They are easily inspected for damage. However, under high loads, failure usually occurs first in those filaments closest to the center of the rope, thus it must be untwisted slightly to inspect for this type of damage.

Their main disadvantages are:

1. They twist or spin in free space when a weight is suspended from them.
2. They have high stretch which is not easily controlled.
3. Their outer surface is rough due to the three or four strands used to make up the final rope.
4. Since all filaments in the rope make up the main load-bearing unit, loss of strength from abrasion can be rapid.

The first two disadvantages have been the major reasons for laid ropes losing their position of leadership in caving use compared to the kernmantle ropes.

The other type of construction we will examine is the kernmantle. Its main advantages are as follows:

1. Very little or no tendency to spin in free space when a weight is suspended from it.

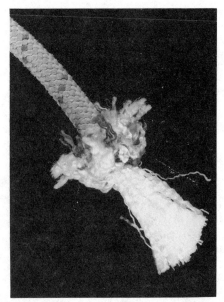

Figure 1—A laid Goldline rope on the left and a kernmantle Blue Water rope on the right with the outer sheath pulled back.

2. Controlled stretch, usually quite low.
3. High abrasion resistance. Almost all the load on a kernmantle rope is carried by the core. Therefore abrasion of the sheath has very little effect on the total strength of the rope.
4. The outer surface of the rope is smooth.

The main disadvantages of kernmantle ropes are:

1. A tendency to have tensile load failures in the core strands before any visible failure occurs in the sheath.
2. Due to the tightly braided sheath, it is not possible to visually examine the core strands for damage without ruining the rope.

These two disadvantages are still major problems for manufacturers and users of kernmantle ropes and are mainly responsible for their failure to totally displace the laid ropes in this country as rappel and prusik lines.

Within the laid and kernmantle categories, there are also individual differences. The laid ropes' main differences are the rate of twist in the strands, the direction of the twist (left or right), and the tension under which the twisting was done. For caving purposes a rope of hard-lay construction is preferable to a rope of standard ("marine") lay. A hard-lay rope is much stiffer than a standard-lay rope. It usually has less stretch and improved abrasion resistance. This hard-lay characteristic is achieved by increasing the rate of twist and tension during the manufacture of the rope.

There is a large number of variables in the manufacture of kernmantle-type ropes. This chapter will deal only with a very few which, in the author's opinion, relate directly to the rope's utility in most caving activities.

For caving, a kernmantle rope should have high abrasion resistance. One method of accomplishing this is by adjusting the tension, braiding pattern, strand size, and/or denier so more yarn can be put into the sheath, making it thicker and hence more abrasion resistant. Some people feel it may also be accomplished by using a large denier yarn of high quality and twisting it at a high rate before braiding the sheath. The problem that happens with a too heavy sheath is that an imbalance between the sheath and core can occur causing all sorts of stretch and load-absorbing problems. The sheath can also carry too much of the tension loads and premature tensile failures of the sheath can occur.

Another desirable characteristic in a caving rope is high strength. All good quality kernmantle ropes have very high strength. But again, the balance between the load-absorbing characteristics of the sheath and core must be maintained for optimum strength.

Another important characteristic of rappel and prusik ropes in particular is moderately low stretch. When compared to laid ropes at loads between 200 and 600 pounds, kernmantle ropes have much less stretch. However, when subjected to shock loading, such as when someone falls several feet and then the rope comes suddenly tight, very low stretch can be a major disadvantage. Since this type of shock loading can occur during caving activities, the rope should have enough stretch to have some shock absorbing ability. For rock-climbing activities there are special ropes with low stretch under low loads and extremely high stretch when high loads are required. Low stretch ropes made for caving are not suitable for belaying where the climber may fall several feet before being caught by the rope.

The next area of importance in ropes is the material of construction. Because of their tendency to lose strength rapidly and to rot, natural fiber ropes should not be used for caving activities. Ropes made of cotton, manila, sisal, or other natural fibers are no longer used for caving.

Synthetic fibers that are commonly used for ropes include nylon, polyester, polypropylene, and various types of polyethylene. There are many types of each of these synthetic fibers. In general, ropes made of nylon, polyester, and polypropylene have all found some acceptance in caving circles. The polyethylene ropes are usually too weak and stretchy and melt at too low a temperature to be used. There are many polymer manufacturers world-wide. These polymers are made into synthetic yarns by numerous yarn manufacturers. These yarns are then made into rope by the various rope manufacturers. So, getting a rope made of the right type of the right polymer from the right size of yarn into the right type of rope construction for your use can be a complex problem. Fortunately, the rope manufacturers usually sort through all the various materials available and select the ones they feel are best for a particular type of rope. As a consumer, you must trust the rope manufacturer to make the right decisions. In different parts of the world different synthetic yarns are available to the rope manufacturers. Because of this, the type of rope in use in various areas may be different. The machines used to manufacture the ropes themselves are also different in the various countries.

In the United States, the preferred material for caving rope construction has been type 6-6 nylon. Within the broad class of this type of nylon, there are many different grades for various uses. In the United States polyester ropes are not popular for caving, but they are used quite a bit in Europe. In many caving areas inexpensive polypropylene ropes are used for handlines and, in some cases, for short rappel and prusik lines. Small diameter polypropylene ropes are popular for prusik knot construction. The nylon ropes generally have a better balance of strength, elongation, and abrasion resistance than those made, of other materials. These improved properties are more than enough to offset their greater cost.

When deciding what rope to choose for a handline, consider how often one certain length will be needed and if it is worthwhile to buy a special rope for that purpose. If a rope will be used exclusively as a handline, it should be large enough to get a good grip on and usually of laid construction. The laid rope is rough on the surface and facilitates gripping by hand. The author uses 1/2-inch polypropylene laid rope for handlines. It is sufficiently strong, easy to grip, and inexpensive. A handline is usually short, 15 to 50 feet long. If you only need a 25-foot handline, it isn't very practical to carry a 150-foot main prusik line instead. Active vertical cavers often have to cut their long main prusik lines because of worn spots from ledges, etc. In this way, many cavers acquire a number of short ropes of handline length.

The selection of a main rappel and prusik line is a little more complicated. Kernmantle ropes are currently in vogue for this purpose; few people still prefer hard-laid ropes. Kernmantle ropes are generally preferred because of their lack of spin and low stretch, making them much better on long, free drops. On wet drops the laid ropes tend to splash more water on the rappeller than kernmantle, but when coated with a sheath of ice, the increased stretch and spin characteristics of the laid ropes help them to de-ice and be easier to ascend. At the present time in the United States, over 90% of the main rappel and prusik lines in use by cavers are of kernmantle construction. Worldwide there has been a tendency toward using smaller diameter ropes. While 7/16-inch (11-millimeter) has generally been the standard in the United States, 3/8-inch (10-millimeter) is in fairly common use. Occasionally, smaller ropes (8- and 9-millimeter) are used in specialized and advanced rigging. Beginners are advised to gain experience with thicker ropes first.

The most important thing to remember when using a rope is that it must be protected from damage. Ropes should not be overloaded. They should be protected by sturdy pads wherever they contact rough surfaces. Whenever possible, extremely tight bends and knots in the loaded portion of a rope should be avoided. Ropes should never be walked on or dragged along the ground. They should be kept clean. A dirty rope is not a status symbol. Mud and dirt on a rope not only destroy the rope, but damage expensive descending and ascending equipment.

Ropes should be washed regularly. Use either one of the special rope washers available or wash the rope in a large front-opening washer. Use a good detergent, warm or hot water, and a fabric softener, which is helpful to re-lubricate the yarn filaments that make up the rope. The importance of taking care of a rope cannot be over-emphasized. After being cleaned, the rope should be inspected inch by inch following each trip and before storage. Store the rope in a cool, dry place out of direct sunlight. Protect the rope from exposure to acids and alkalines. Remember that a rope you trust your life to is for that purpose only. A rope used to tow a car is a tow rope, not a rappel and prusik line or a handline.

Where to purchase a rope for caving is the final question. If you are looking for a handline, you might find one at a local hardware or marine supply store. If you want a rappel and prusik line or a special dynamic rock-climbing rope, you will have to go to an outdoor sporting goods store or a mail-order catalog. In recent years some people affiliated with caving in the United States have set up small "travelling stores" from which they sell all sorts of supplies for caving, including ropes. Their addresses are given in Appendix D. When you buy a rope, try to make sure it is of high quality. Companies such as West, Sampson, and Wall have been making good ropes for many years. For those people desiring a hard-laid nylon rope, Goldline has always been the standard. Originally manufactured by Plymouth, later by the Cordage Group, it

was eventually dropped as a product. It has been recently reintroduced as Goldline II. Kernmantle type ropes especially designed for caving use such as Blue Water, PMI, and Edelrid Superstatic are excellent ropes. PMI and Bluewater manufacture dynamic kernmantle ropes in the United States for rock climbing. A number of European sources exist including Mammut, Edelrid, and Maxim.

Always buy the best rope available, use it only for its intended purpose, protect it from damage, keep it clean, and inspect it regularly. Get proper training in rope work and don't take chances.

Remember: **It's your life that's on that line.**

Chapter 10

GENERAL EQUIPMENT FOR EACH CAVER

or
What to Bring on a Cave Trip

Ed LaRock
NSS 14362

This chapter is designed to bring together other parts of the manual into one checklist or guide to what items to bring on a cave trip. As a result some items, such as lamps or cave packs, which have been detailed elsewhere, will need no explanation when mentioned here. Items to bring on a cave trip can be broken down into the "basic necessities" that **each caver should carry on every cave trip** and "optional items" that depend largely on the type of cave trip planned, some of which may be distributed among the cave party.

The basic necessities should be taken on even the "easiest two-hour" cave trip since unexpected events may lengthen your trip underground. The basics should be carried in a handy, easily reached place as they may be in frequent use.

The Basics

Primary Light Source and Helmet—the light should be helmet-mounted to leave your hands free and to always illuminate your line of vision. The helmet should have a good chin strap.
A. Carbide Lamp

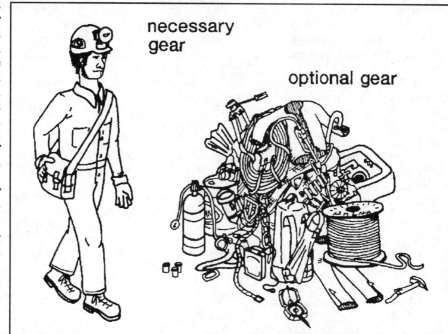

necessary gear

optional gear

1. Spare carbide and water for the lamp—at least twice the amount you plan to use.
2. A container for your spent carbide—never dump spent carbide in the cave.
3. Spare parts such as an extra lamp bottom, tip, felt, gasket, wing nut, flints, and a tip cleaner.
B. Electric Headlamp
  1. Spare batteries—again twice the amount you think you'll need.
  2. Spare bulbs and any other replaceable electrical parts.
Extra Light Sources—at least two independent sources that can be used to exit the cave.
  A. Most commonly carried are a flashlight, perhaps with a wrist strap, and a candle with waterproof matches. Often some chemical lightsticks with aluminum foil to make a reflector are substituted for the candle and matches. Many cavers carry a spare carbide lamp charged and ready to go in addition to a flashlight and chemical lightsticks or a flashlight and a candle with waterproof matches.
  B. Waterproof matches or a cigarette lighter are also useful to carry. Be wary of butane lighters. If the butane leaks or is spilled, a tremendous explosion can occur.

C. Candles are useful during rest stops or while repairing items. They are a poor light source for traveling.

General Items that Everyone Should Have – Remember, things break or get lost. Your trip will be more comfortable, safe, and enjoyable if you are not inconvenienced.

A. Small pair of pliers needed for lamp repairs, tightening rappel racks, etc.
B. Pocket knife to sharpen pencils, cut webbing, make repairs on lamps, open cans, and so on.
C. Some electrician's tape or duct tape for all kinds of repairs.
D. Short lengths of string and wire can be very useful.

Food and Emergency Gear

A. Food and drinking water.
  1. Requirements will depend upon the length of the trip and the individual.
  2. Each person should at least carry some small emergency food item on any trip, i.e. a candy bar or food sticks.
B. A space blanket (which may deteriorate with time if wet) or a large, heavy duty plastic bag – these are excellent emergency insulators or body wraps that have prevented many cases of discomfort, or even hypothermia, and should always be carried.
C. A small pocket-sized first aid kit.
D. A short length of cord or webbing for use for pack strap repair, emergency lamp mounting, arm sling, handline, or rigging point.
E. A small whistle for signalling.
F. A pencil and paper for leaving or taking notes.
G. A list of rescue phone numbers (which could be left at the vehicle or the entrance) and some coins for emergency phone calls.

Optional Gear

Optional caving gear will often depend upon the type and length of the cave trip you are planning such as a mapping trip or a vertical cave trip.

General – useful items for someone on the trip to be carrying.

A. Some removable flagging tape for marking the way in a new or complex cave and for survey stations when mapping. It can also be used to mark off trails and areas of delicate speleothems.
B. A map of the cave (if one is available) in a plastic bag.
C. A compass.
D. A watch.

Survey or Mapping Gear – should be packed in a separate sack or baggie in a cave pack.

A. Compass and inclinometer.

B. Waterproof notebook – this is also useful for leaving notes for other parties, that is if you also have pencils.
C. Measuring tape, 25- to 100-foot length.

Photography Gear – packed in a waterproof case such an a surplus ammo can or a specialized camera case such as the Pelican case.

Vertical Gear – each person on a vertical cave trip should have his own complete set of vertical gear, possibly in a separate sack or pack for convenience.

A. Ascending/climbing gear.
B. Descending/rappelling gear, including gloves.
C. Seat and chest harness(es).
D. Rope – carrying shared by the members of the caving party.

An Extra Long Trip or Expedition – this belongs in a separate category beyond basic caving. However, extra food, lighting supplies, wet suits or exposure suits for wet caves, sleeping gear, and larger and specially designed packs should all be considered for long, strenuous trips underground.

Finally, items brought on a cave trip will have to be transported in some way, but more importantly they should be individually dirt resistant, waterproof, and durable. Several hints on containers and "cave proofing" are summarized below:

All contents of the cave pack(s) can be placed and sealed inside a plastic trash bag for transport through wet caves or near sumps. This will also cause the pack to be buoyant.

Plastic containers, baby bottles, film canisters, and double ziplock baggies are rugged and usually waterproof for carrying almost anything.

Condoms have been used successfully to carry small clothing items such as socks and underwear through sumps and bathtubs.

Water containers with "flip tops" are handy for filling carbide lamps.

Drinking water should be carried in a separate container since a caver may want to refill his lamp water bottle with water from the cave.

It is wise to use a piece of plastic bag or wrap as a container. Seal to prevent leakage or contamination.

Collapsible plastic containers take up less space as the contents are used up. They can be compressed and stowed away until needed or after they are empty.

In conclusion, the chance of a mishap or inconvenience while in a cave can be greatly reduced if every caver in the party is carrying his or her own basic cave necessities. Provisions for optional gear should be worked out with the trip leader before the trip.

Hope Uhl explores a clean washed canyon in Carma Cave, Costa Rica, during the 1989 Costa Rica Expedition. (photo Scott Fee)

Chapter 11

CAVING SAFETY

Ray Cole
NSS 12460

Introduction

Your chances of serious injury or even death while caving can be reduced by being aware of the dangers involved, by having adequate knowledge of equipment and techniques, and by cultivating good caving sense. Unfortunately for many, the needed knowledge comes only after years of caving experience and association with other cavers.

Statistically, caving accidents are mostly attributed to poor judgement, little or no caving experience, or falls. Important reading for all cavers should be the annual report, *American Caving Accidents*, published by the National Speleological Society. Since the same types of accidents keep repeating themselves, needless deaths and injuries might be prevented if every caver read just one of these yearly reports.

Dangers in Caving

The most common causes of caving accidents include drowning, falling, being struck by falling objects, and hypothermia.

Drowning: Unfortunately, accidents related to flooding caves often result in fatalities. Many of the deaths could be avoided because they are the result of inexperienced cavers ignoring the signs of rising water and entering caves that are known to flood. Some caves flood so quickly that they are safe to enter only in the coldest winter weather when surface water is frozen. However, caves often flood due to rapid melting of snow when a sudden weather change occurs. This is especially true when rain falls on frozen and/or snow-covered ground and natural water absorption is prevented. As a result, large quantities of run-off can flow directly into low-lying cave entrances. The experienced caver looks for the telltale signs of a cave that floods. The most important of these are low-lying caves that drain large surface areas with either dry or active streams present and organic material lodged in crevices in the walls and ceiling of the cave. If you are ever trapped in a flooding cave, head for the highest section possible. Several cavers have drowned while trying to leave a flooding cave instead of retreating to safety.

Flooding is not the only cause of drownings in caves. Cavers have always been challenged by sumps (where the ceiling dips below the water level) and the alluring quest for what lies beyond.

Whether using scuba equipment or free diving, going through a sump is risky business. The dangers associated with this include bad air when resurfacing, disorientation, no visibility due to disturbed sediment, and underwater mazes. If you need to go through a sump, we recommend that you contact members of the Cave Diving Section of the National Speleological Society for proper advice and training.

Falling: To reduce the risk of falling, one should avoid jumping and uncontrolled sliding down slopes, wear proper footwear, check and discard any faulty or worn vertical equipment, obtain proper training in the use of vertical equipment, use a proper belay when exposure dictates, always use a belay on a cable ladder, and use common sense.

Falling Objects: Accidents caused by falling objects are best avoided by always wearing a helmet, staying clear of the base of drops and climbs, and securing all items of equipment so that they will not drop on cavers below.

Hypothermia: The temperature of the body core is about 98° Fahrenheit. If this temperature drops more than a few degrees, the body can no longer function properly. Even if placed in a warmer environment, the body core temperature may continue to drop, resulting in certain death unless the condition can be reversed. This condition, called hypothermia, or exposure as it has often been referred to in the past, can kill the unprepared. A factor in many caves that accelerates the loss of body heat is the presence of water. A person immersed in 54° Fahrenheit water has about 2½ hours to live but loses the ability and will to function normally much sooner. The most common situation where hypothermia occurs is climbing in waterfalls, where, because of fatigue or equipment failure, the caver is no longer able to climb or descend. Without assistance from his caving companions, death is the usual result. The situation is best avoided by rigging drops out of waterfalls when possible and by using wet or dry suits when lengthy exposure to water is required or anticipated.

Other Hazards: Not all caving problems involve injuries. A few people do get lost in caves, become stuck, or are unable to climb up a ledge or rope to get out of the cave. Exhaustion and a lack of light (or light failure) may cause someone to become lost who might otherwise have found his own way out of the cave.

Serious cavers seldom become lost in caves since they keep careful track of their whereabouts and are careful to note important landmarks in the cave. A caver with enough experience is not bewildered by the cave environment and feels as comfortable as a woodsman walking in a forest. An easy place to get confused is at the intersection of two passages, one smaller than the other. It can be harder than one might think to find the smaller passage. By leaving a highly visible arrow made from reflective tape, the location is easily found again. The reflective marker can be picked up on the way out and reused.

Everybody gets stuck occasionally when caving and it doesn't take a new caver long to learn to remain calm and in control when it happens. In some cases, extra clothing can be removed so that a little extra clearance can be obtained on the second try.

Potential hazards in the cave, other than the cave itself, may involve the equipment carried by cavers. The flame of a carbide lamp, the most common piece of caving equipment, can cause serious burns. Another common situation occurs when the base of the carbide lamp has not been screwed on tightly or a poor gasket is used. Gas escaping around the bottom suddenly bursts into flames. A burned hand may result when the startled caver reaches for the lamp without first extinguishing the flame.

Electric lamps are not without their problems. A shorted headpiece with a high current capacity battery could produce a dangerously hot cord. All such cords should have an in-line fuse. Acid electrolyte leaking from a lead-acid battery can dangerously weaken nylon ropes and slings.

Caving Emergencies

What do you do when something goes wrong during your caving trip? Most situations of an injured or disabled person are dealt with by members of the group involved. If the group is not able to handle the situation, it will be necessary to quickly get outside help. Suddenly, you realize just how alien the cave environment can be. Caves are often located in remote areas away from roads, population centers, and the local rescue squads that the modern city dweller too often takes for granted. To further complicate matters, help could be needed in an area that is many hours into the cave, beyond crawls and down drops, making the removal of an injured person a difficult technical problem.

When needing assistance, you can either wait until someone comes looking for you, or you can send two people for help. If you send for help, you must have one person stay with the injured person. The two cavers going for help should leave any extra supplies, including clothing. For this reason

a caving party of four should be considered as a minimum group and, of course, you should never cave alone.

The primary objective is not to rush the victim out of the cave, but to keep him alive (to stabilize the victim). First aid should be administered. All cavers should have first aid training. Extra clothes should be placed under the injured person to prevent heat loss due to conduction to the cold, damp cave floor. Keeping an injured person warm is vital since he will probably be in shock. Large plastic trash bags make nice bivouac shelters, especially with the warm glow of a carbide lamp inside. Don't burn yourself or the victim and leave a vent hole for a little air circulation. A "people sandwich" is a good way to keep warm. To achieve this effect, place a person on either side of the injured party.

When members of the party seeking help reach the surface, they usually will rely on the telephone to communicate their need. Many parts of the country have special telephone numbers for the purpose of coordinating cave rescues. If the number is not known, first try 911, then call the local sheriff. Whoever is called must be told that you have a caving emergency and you must state the nature of the problem. Make sure the person you are talking to has the telephone number of the telephone you are calling from. Then have someone available at that phone until the rescue has been completed. In addition to local rescue personnel, the law enforcement authorities in caving areas may have information on area cavers as well as the regional cave rescue coordination number to call for additional assistance.

If you are using a pay phone and have limited change, tell the operator that it is an emergency and he or she will stay on the line with you, allowing as many calls as necessary. It is vital that the persons calling for assistance remain where they can be found by the rescuers and that they be available to lead teams and equipment to the victim. With any luck the people with the necessary skills and equipment will soon be on the scene to successfully complete the rescue operation.

An opportune time to rally your fellow cavers and/or grotto members to do the things that should have been done to prevent an accident is soon after an accident has occurred. The first of these is a training program for new cavers. Such a program is a good chance for the old timers to brush up on the basics as well as to assist the new cavers. This manual a makes good basis for such a course. Don't forget, caver training must include training trips to caves.

You should find out where first aid training is available in your area and encourage members of your group to enroll and learn essential life-saving skills. First aid courses are available through the American Red Cross and Emergency Medical Technician programs.

Learn the telephone numbers for cave rescue coordination in the areas in which you go caving. Publish these numbers in your newsletter frequently. Print them on small cards that can be carried easily and distribute them to local cavers. Groups wishing to participate in cave rescue should contact the National Cave Rescue Commission of the National Speleological Society.

Preparation

The best way to promote safety is to start before the caving trip. Consider these points: get yourself in shape; caving is a strenuous activity. Learn all you can about the cave you will visit and pick caving companions carefully. When selecting your caving companions, consider what the others would do if something happened to you. A minimum of four cavers in a party is best. Now consider the basic items of equipment used for caving.

Equipment

What to take along on a trip depends on the nature of the cave, expected length of trip, special personal requirements, and experience. Experienced cavers just take along what they will need plus adequate equipment for emergencies. Today, the trend in caving is to pack light so you can go fast and far. Thus, it becomes even more important to consider each item of equipment for safety.

The helmet should have a lamp bracket, cord loop on the rear for electric lights, and a quick release chin strap.

Cavers should have boots with good support that come at least up to the ankle. While lug soles are good for walking on rock with small scree, they will pick up large quantities of sticky cave mud. They should not have metal hooks for the laces. These will catch on cable ladders. Tennis shoes do not give adequate support or provide much protection.

For the primary light source, carbide or electric lamps are most commonly used. It is essential that this light source fit on the helmet to allow two hands free for caving. At least two backup sources of light such as an extra carbide lamp, flashlights, or chemical light sticks should always be carried. If a flashlight is used as one backup, you should have spare dry cells and bulbs. Ordinary carbon-zinc dry cells should not be used for caving since they have a short shelf life and may have very limited capacity when used. The alkaline variety hold their charge much longer and provide added capacity for an extra margin of safety. Chemical light sticks quickly loose their effectiveness when exposed to the air. Examine the foil wrapper and discard your light stick, or let the kids play with it, if the foil is damaged.

Include fuel and parts for all light sources. For carbide cavers this means an adequate supply of carbide in a strong, waterproof container, water, a container for spent carbide, and extra tips and felts. A spare base containing carbide is useful for a quick change. Tiny pliers are helpful to replace tips and a tip cleaner or reamer is necessary. Electric cavers need extra bulbs, a small knife, a screwdriver, and any special items required to service their equipment.

It is a good idea to include with your first aid equipment items that are necessary for survival in the cave if unexpected events lengthen your stay. Survival items include: large plastic bags or a space blanket, high energy food, waterproof matches, candles, and a whistle. Another use of first aid supplies is to treat those minor ailments and injuries that, while not life threatening, often occur and detract from the enjoyment of the trip. While not essential, these include: aspirin, band-aids, and an elastic bandage for sprains. Another category of first-aid equipment is necessary for dealing with life threatening bodily injury. Here the contents depend somewhat on the expertise of the caver, but every kit should contain these minimum items: change for at least two telephone calls, sterile dressings, razor blades and/or scissors, adhesive tape, and butterfly closures.

While being far from an adequate amount of medical supplies for treating injuries, this is about all the average caver is willing to pack with him. If much more is added and the kit isn't used often, it will soon be left out of the cave pack. The remaining essential items needed for treating serious injuries would have to be improvised. For example, bandages can be made by cutting strips out of clothing. Likewise, a makeshift splint can be improvised by rolling heavy items of clothing. Far more important than any supplies on hand is knowing the right thing to do.

Package the first-aid items in a waterproof container. Individually packaged items are more likely to survive the rigors of caving. After each trip replace items that have become damaged.

If you require special medication, be sure to have it with you and inform the other members of your group of this fact.

Food for a short caving trip need not provide all the nutrient and vitamin content found in your daily diet. The cave food should be high in carbohydrates and sugar to supply the large energy requirements the body needs while caving. An extra ration of high energy food is good to have just in case your stay in the cave is longer than expected.

The Trip

After having found out about the cave to be visited, you will probably put together your equipment in advance to make sure you'll have everything you need. You can make a checklist to be sure.

Explain your caving plans to another caver or your family. Make sure that these people know who to call if the need arises. In the unlikely event you do not return by the allotted time, they will make arrangements to get help to you. You must realize that they can only do this if plans have been explicit. As a caver you must be cautious about meeting your schedule if you are going to expect help when needed. Have at least one waterproof watch in the party. Realize that most caving trips take longer than you expect them to. Don't be too optimistic in setting your return time. Also consider the time required to get from the cave to a telephone if you are running late.

After all the training, planning, and packing, it is quite a relief to finally get into the cave. Once in the cave the most difficult decision most cavers face is when to start the trip out. Generally, if any member of the party indicates it's time to start out, then you should do so. Caving should not be made a do or die activity, dying is an actual possibility. Know your group's ability and learn not to push their physical endurance.

Chapter 12

DRIVING TO THE CAVE

Tom Rea
NSS 5683

Many caving trips involve several car loads of cavers driving to the cave caravan style. Sometimes only the lead vehicle knows the location of the cave. Many years of experience with this style of driving and many frustrating experiences have led the author to formulate the following set of guidelines or rules for safe, effective caravan driving.

1. Everyone should know that a caravan is planned and agree to participate.

This may seem obvious, but problems have occurred when participants did not know they were in a caravan and went their own way, leading other participants astray. One time the author was in the lead and turned onto a side road while the second car in line continued straight ahead, leading a caravan of seven or eight cars into limbo from which the trip never recovered.

2. Each driver should recognize and follow the car immediately in front of him.

The author has had the experience of having caravan members pass him on the highway and then complain at the destination that they were left behind, even though they arrived first!

3. The leader must be able to instantly recognize the last car in line.

It is important to keep the group together. If the group becomes separated, it is the leader's responsibility to get it back together. He can most easily know the group is together (assuming group members follow the rules) if he can readily identify the last car in his rear view mirror. If the last car is nondescript, rearrange the caravan or add a strategic bit of flagging tape.

4. The leader should obey all traffic laws and caution signs.

The author was once following another caver to an unknown destination through a town that was strange to him. The leader turned right at a red traffic light in spite of several signs prohibiting this maneuver and then took off at a speed at least ten miles per hour over the speed limit. Being reluctant to get a traffic ticket, we became hopelessly lost.

It would be best to stay a few miles per hour under the speed limit. It is always easier to lead than it is to follow and your guests may feel rushed and confused if you push the limit.

5. Participants should not allow a gap to develop or follow too closely. Maintain a two-second interval.

Traffic safety experts agree that a two-second interval between vehicles is a safe interval at any legal speed.

"Foreign" cars that inevitably get between caravan members can be handled by increasing the interval and slowing to about five miles per hour below the speed limit. The interloper will pass at the first opportunity and be gone.

6. The leader should be aware of a "stale" green light and slow down to allow it to change to red rather than hurry through.

If group members are trapped by a light and stop, as they should, the group will inevitably become separated. If they do not stop, they will be in danger of causing an accident or being arrested.

Most traffic signals at rural intersections are actuated by the traffic. If there is no car at the intersection, the light probably will not change. If a car approaches on the side road, the light surely will change.

7. If the group becomes separated by traffic, a navigation error, or traffic signals, the leader must pull over to the side at the first safe spot before making any turns and allow the group to reform.

He should not pull out until the last car has pulled in behind him. After such a stop, the last car should pull out as soon as he safely can after the leader and block the lane for the rest of the caravan members.

8. The group must agree on a procedure to follow if someone other than the leader has to stop.

A caravan member may have to stop unexpectedly for any number of reasons. If he just stops, the group will be split if the leader does not realize that a stop was necessary. One good way is for the driver who has to stop to turn on his headlights in the daytime or his four-way flashers at night. The other drivers should relay the signal forward to the leader who, of course, should stop at the first safe opportunity.

9. The leader must consider the capabilities of the least maneuverable vehicle in the caravan.

On a western trip the author was driving a Suburban loaded with five other cavers and their caving and camping gear. He was following two people in a mini-truck over mountain roads. After not having seen the leader for 45 minutes, having passed many likely looking side roads, and not being sure of the location of either the destination or the campground, tempers were rising. Finally the leader was sighted waiting at the side of the road. He said, "I wasn't going to turn off until you showed up." It would be better to be patient and keep your whole caravan in sight.

10. Changing lanes can be easily and safely done if it is planned well in advance.

The leader should slow down slightly and signal his intention to change lanes. The last car should immediately claim the lane, blocking further traffic from passing. The leader can then change lanes when the lane is clear behind him, followed by the rest of the caravan.

Needless to say, everyone in the caravan must know this procedure and the leader must plan his turns well in advance. This technique will not work on the spur of the moment.

11. Caravan members must not pass each other.

This should go without saying but considering most Americans' agressive driving habits, it could happen unconsciously. After stops and during lane change maneuvers, group members should not panic when the last car pulls out as if to pass.

12. If the leader misses a turn, he should continue on, stop as soon as it is safe, explain the situation, and turn around.

A quick maneuver will usually split the group and may cause an accident. The leader must swallow his pride, admit the mistake, and correct it as gracefully as possible.

13. On long drives, choose one or more easily found alternate meeting places.

It is likely that someone will get lost on a caravan drive of 100 miles or more. Pick an easily found and identifiable public place that is known to the leader and has room for the whole group to park together. Make sure each group member knows where the alternate location is. Pick a reasonable expected time to reach that spot and a reasonable waiting time for lost participants. If the group is separated when the alternate is reached, the leader must wait until the waiting time has expired.

14. On long drives, designate some stay-at-home as the communication link.

Every participant should know the name and telephone number of the communication link. If someone becomes hopelessly lost he should call the communication link before the agreed waiting time at the next alternate meeting place expires and explain the situation. If someone does not show up at an alternate meeting place by the end of the waiting time, the leader should call the communication link to see if the person has checked in or to leave instructions for him.

15. Participants should consider all maneuvers by the leader as strong suggestions, not orders.

Do not drive into an accident or traffic ticket because your leader did something stupid. Do not race to beat red lights or go on through a light that has turned red. Do not wildly change lanes in heavy traffic in an effort to keep up.

It is the leader's responsibility to keep the group together. If you get lost or behind, continue to drive safely, lead the people behind you, and look for the rest of the group waiting along the right side of the road or at the next alternate meeting place.

16. CB radios make caravan driving a lot easier.

The caravan should choose a channel of their own, not try to use 19. Cavers usually use channel 2. Every member of the caravan who has a radio must know the channel the group is using. The leader must know which cars in the caravan do not have a radio. If there are only a few radios, the best use can be gained if the leader and the last car have a radio.

Chapter 13

MOVING THROUGH A CAVE

Roger W. Brucker
NSS 1999

Introduction

Caving can be very strenuous, especially if you are not in good physical shape. Even those who run or swim, for example, may complain of sore muscles after a tough cave trip. Caving uses muscles you never knew you had; their pain will inform you of their presence! The best cure for sore caving muscles is to go caving again right away. After months and years of caving you will wonder how you could have hurt so much.

This chapter is not about pain, however. It is about how to obtain the most pleasure from caving. Happiness comes from learning how to move through a cave so that you enjoy it to the fullest, see everything, and waste the least amount of energy. We will look at the relationship between mental attitude and physical condition. We will see how to harness your eyes to the task of moving with the least effort. We will learn some tricks of experienced cavers. And we will talk about the relationship of movement skills to getting back out of the cave safely.

Mental and Physical Aspects

There are many good books about physical fitness. Their message boils down to the fact that you will feel better and be healthier if you are fit. You also will enjoy cave exploring more because you will have more endurance, you will be able to go places that require hard physical effort, and you will be putting your body and mind on the adventure line. Doing something "neat" out on the far edge of adventure can make life more satisfying. You may gain exciting new insights on the world around you and you may meet new friends with attractive qualities far beyond the everyday. For some, caving is indeed living.

The thought of going caving may produce fears. These are natural and healthy. In fact, the person who claims to be fearless in the presence of the unknown is either dishonest or insensitive. This fearfulness or apprehension is useful if it causes you to check your equipment one more time, to take a last look at the map before you enter the cave, or to check the rigging on a drop after the "expert" has told you the knots are okay. When you hear expert cavers tell morbid jokes before going into the cave, you will know they too are feeling the same excitement or fear that you are. Jim Dyer, one of the best cavers ever, used to unnerve new explorers in the Flint Ridge Cave System with the dry comment, "Now when we get to the Bottomless Pit, I want you to tie up the legs of your jeans. It's a very scary crossing on a slippery ledge, and we want to be considerate of anyone who happens to be below." Jim was as brave as any caver, but he knew fear also.

Your brain is the most important part of your body in moving through a cave. Your eyes are the second most important. Try to cultivate a habit of looking at the spaces you will move into and analyzing how your body will fit them. Imagine yourself and what you will be doing next. Will I have to duck to get under that low ledge? Can I keep my head a little higher if I go under where that notch is? If I lead with my left foot, where will my right foot hit? Such questions may seem forced and silly, but they soon become automatic. By themselves, questions are not very useful, except that they force you to make some future guesses about your body's fit and movement through inner space.

These guesses are then quickly proven right or wrong as you move. You are cultivating the habit of making predictions and obtaining instant feedback. Using this technique, you will rapidly learn how to move easily and naturally through the toughest cave. Your guesses will get better. As an example, when you whack your helmet on the ceiling, you may see that the headlamp on your hardhat fails to illuminate a blind area immediately above it. You adjust to this by checking out low ceiling ahead of your light's blind spot.

Some cavers who have tried this prediction and feedback method have reported astonishment at how rapidly they learned to move. A few have reported dreams of flying through a cave with ease, their bodies gliding through the smallest and most convoluted passages.

Physiologists might explain this mind-body mastery on the basis of kinesthetic theory. Natural athletes seem endowed with such awareness at an early age. But no matter how clumsy you are, you can improve your caving movements. Good cavers can become excellent—measured by endurance—by learning the method of imagining your own body moving ahead of where you really are.

The third mental aspect of good caving is to develop an attitude: "I will conserve energy at every opportunity." This sounds like a recipe for becoming lazy, but it is very practical advice for enjoying caving to the fullest. What this means is you should rest every muscle you can every chance you get. The practice will help you ward off fatigue and will keep you alert and happy long after others on the cave trip are bombed out. Don't rest too long, though, because you will become chilled and your muscles will stiffen.

You can conserve energy by not using more than you need, or by replacing it with food. Good cavers do both. Let's talk about food first, since that is the easiest, and most misunderstood, way to conserve energy. Energy is calories. Most cavers carry candy bars, whose sugar is a handy source of quick energy. In as little as 15 minutes after eating a candy bar, you may feel less tired and more alert. On the other hand, energy from candy bars seems short-lived, and many cavers report that they feel more tired than ever after the candy "lift" wears off. A few cavers report upset stomach from "candy over-load." What you eat and how it affects you is a highly individual matter, of course, and you should experiment with what you eat until you know your own needs.

One eating strategy that has worked for many years in the Mammoth Cave System, where cavers go for 20 hours or more, is to eat a variety of foods in the cave for longer lasting energy. A typical meal may consist of canned boned chicken or turkey or beef stew, canned fruit, and a candy bar. Such meals are eaten 45 minutes or so before the cavers grow hungry, so there is no lag while energy levels work back up from low levels. Eat a large meal containing fats before entering the cave. Fats are slowly metabolized and provide energy for a long period of time.

A mental attitude of conserving energy can be cultivated just as easily as the predictive-feedback method of learning how to move. You ask yourself, "How can I do this with less effort?" Then you try acting on your answer. If you are resting, for example, your answer may be that sitting up takes more energy than lying down, so try lying down. Elevate the legs above the level of the torso while lying down; to some, this seems to relax the leg muscles. Practice regularly, you will work out your own little tricks for reducing exertion and prolonging your strength. Also try asking other cavers for pet methods of being lazy in a cave.

Tricks of Moving Easily

Here are some tricks of moving easily through caves that have proven useful for over 25 years. No doubt the list could be expanded by any caver. The discovery of practical ideas like these can increase your sense of joy from caving.

Keep your head up. Keep your head as high as possible, whether you move through vast galleries or chest-compressor crawlways. It will improve your posture, and will make it easier to move along briskly. In a passage four feet high, for example, you may have a choice. You could crouch. You might even squirm on your belly. Choose the crouch, keeping your head as high and close to the ceiling as you possibly can. Will you hit your head? Sure! But that is why you sport that expensive hardhat. By clonking your hardhat on the ceiling a few times, you will improve your aim. That is, you will learn just how high you can carry your head without colliding too often with the ceiling. If you never collide, you are moving with your head

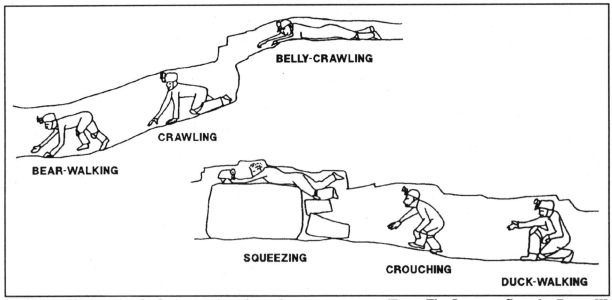

Figure 1—Various methods for moving through a cave passage. (From The Longest Cave *by Roger W. Brucker and Richard A. Watson, ©Cave Research Foundation, 1976. Used by permission.)*

too low. Also, with impressive scars and scuffs in your hardhat, people will believe you are an old-time hard-core caver rather than a greenhorn. However, when in low passages where speleothems line the ceiling, stay below them.

In many crawlways there will be a channel or groove in the ceiling. If you track along with your head up in that groove, you will spend less energy. In chest-compressors and belly crawls you may see experienced cavers remove their hardhats. The extra inch or so of headroom this provides may make a big difference in the ease of moving. Moving small, loose pebbles out of one's way in chest-compressors is easy to do, saves much wear and tear on the body, but is often neglected.

Stay level. When you walk along a trunk passage or come to a room in a cave, there may be many routes ahead. You could climb to the bottom, go to the top, and so on. The energy-saving trick is to eyeball a level line from you to the place you want to go. It may take you over breakdown blocks and swing you wide of a direct bee-line. But the level route will require less energy to traverse. Pick out intermediate landmarks to head for to keep you straight on your course. The same applies to walking in a passage. If you encounter a rock, either step over it or walk around it, but do not use it as a stepping stone. This requires elevating the body and is a needless loss of energy.

Balance yourself. There are many different tricks to trim and balance yourself while moving and resting; all will give you an extra measure of energy. For example, you are crouching along through a low passage with your arms moving naturally along your sides. Bent over, you are unbalanced. To trim yourself, swing your pack over your buttocks and hold the straps in your hands locked together behind you. The redistribution of weight to your hips unloads your trunk and shoulders, and you feel you can almost fly through the passage with much less effort than you have been expending.

A related trick is to fit your pack with a waist strap in addition to a shoulder strap. Two straps distribute the weight for better balance. Be sure, however, that you can still move your pack around as a handy counterweight when you need to. Run some experiments climbing a steep, slippery slope and you will soon see that the pack, when moved around or held out from the body, can help or hinder your progress. In general, don't take your pack off except in the tightest passages.

Some cavers add counterweights to the back of their hardhats to balance the overhung weight of the lamp on the front. A way to balance yourself at rest is to remove your pack. If you are carrying a load, such as coiled ropes, try to distribute the load evenly on your body, or carry a load in each hand. With just a little thought, balancing will become automatic to you in nearly every caving situation.

Climb easier with layback methods. An experienced rock climber seems to flow up a cliff in one continuous liquid movement. If you watch each move closely, you will see a number of moves in which one muscle is pitted in opposition to another. For example, the climber may jam a fist back into a smooth-walled crack in the face. He then pulls outward with his arm and lifts with his shoulder as he pushes against the face with his feet. He literally walks upward. He is held on the face by the opposition of forces — pulling with the arm and pushing with the legs. He uses muscle power to overcome gravity. To be sure, a climber would soon tire from such exertion. Layback climbing, which uses this method, is for getting past places where there seem to be no handholds, or where overhangs project to block more direct moves.

There are many places in caves, and not just on pitches, where layback methods will conserve energy and make otherwise difficult maneuvers rather easy. One such instance is ascending a standing line on knots or mechanical ascenders to the place where the line bends over the protected edge of a drop. Getting over that lip is the problem. You could use brute-force. But the easier way is to grasp the standing line above the lip, pull with your arms, and push out with your feet in opposition. Your body will neatly swing out and upward, passing the lip in a smooth movement. The others will thrash and dangle, rip clothing, lose equipment from pockets, sweat and swear — while you just smile.

Don't save layback methods just for spectacular moves. Their real utility comes in the dozens of ways you steady yourself here and brace yourself there — where there are no apparent handholds. Variations include crossing ledges by pressing the ceiling with your fingers in opposition to your leg muscles on the ledge. Chimneying uses muscles in opposition, pressing outward on two sides to maintain your headway or position in slippery canyons. While the chimney moves seem natural, the layback moves do not, even though they operate the same way. Practice will make them second nature.

Catalog comfort tricks. A variety of ideas will make movement in a cave easier, even though the ideas don't seem to relate to moving along. For example, try to stay dry, but if you must wade eventually, don't spend energy avoiding wading. If you are going to spend a long time moving in water, take a salt tablet. Caving dehydrates the body and caving in water will chill the body. Dehydration plus chill causes cramps in some cavers, perhaps caused by insufficient electrolytes in the body. If you swallow a salt tablet, chances of cramping are reduced, and you will be able to move with ease.

Another trick related to chilling and the slow-down of movement that occurs is the use of the Palmer Furnace, as perfected by Arthur N. Palmer.

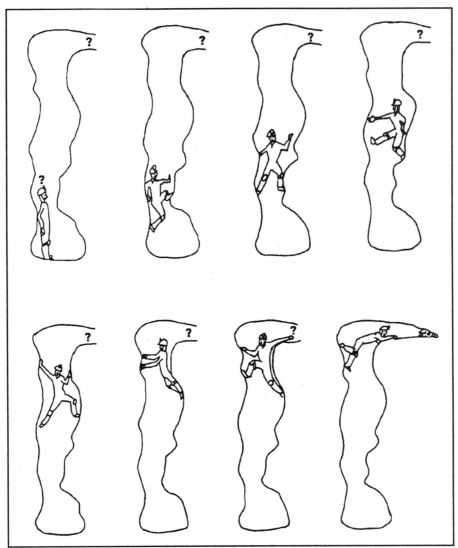

Figure 2—Chimneying. (From The Longest Cave *by Roger W. Brucker and Richard A. Watson, ©Cave Research Foundation, 1976. Used with permission.)*

When you are cold, you sit down. Remove your carbide lamp from your hardhat. Pull out your shirt from your body and hold the lamp at the bottom edge, so the heated air rises through the "chimney" created between your body and the stretched-out shirt. After a few minutes you will have a toasty, warm belly and a better attitude. (Caution: Jenny Anderson used the Palmer furnace one day on a wet trip. Unknown to her, the lamp heated the cave key that was dangling from a lanyard around her neck beneath her sweater. When she straightened up, the hot key made a searing brand on her chest. The pain did not improve *her* attitude!) Variations can involve crouching on all fours over the lamp, or having a friend hold the lamp under the back of your shirt. When you warm up, get moving again to restore energy.

Sit on your gloves when you pause to rest on a damp floor. That's another way to ward off chills,

which rob energy. If you take off your gloves in a dry cave, lay them on your legs to keep them warm. Good knee pads also save energy. Mix up the way you move through long, monotonous passages; crawl on one side, then the other, then crouch, then roll. Invited on a photo trip? Take an extra sweater. The slow pace will make molasses look fast, and you will freeze without extra clothing. After you have caved for a while, you will have your own catalog of tricks for staying comfortable.

Look Where You Go

As we have seen, movement through a cave depends on seeing the cave—really seeing it. Some cavers will tell you that they only see a cave when they are surveying a passageway. The slower pace gives them time to find and observe things that they would miss by going along at a brisk pace. You may be in a party with other people, and thus may not be able to set the pace you want. That should not prevent you from sharpening your powers of observation.

Watch the caver in front of you. His lamp illuminates the route a good distance ahead. If he has trouble, learn from his experience.

Turn around frequently and look behind you. Passages often look entirely different heading the other way. When you come to a change in the character of the passage, see if you can spot the reason. Has the bedrock changed? In Mammoth Cave one time, Will White and George Deike were struck by a passage that changed abruptly from an oval tube to a rectangular cross section. By leveling, they also discovered that the slope had changed, too. They concluded they had found the place where a vadose water passage above the water table had turned into a phreatic water passage below the old water table. You, too, can find and solve puzzling mysteries in caves if you keep your eyes open.

One place to be especially wary is where passages join. Examine all junctions from different viewpoints. One practical reason to do this is that junctions are confusing, and if you have to lead the party out, you will want to be clear about which way to go. Prominent landmarks deserve a second look for the same reason. Watch that you don't make the mistake of one caver. He loudly named a rock in the middle of the passage Dog Rock, because you had to lift your leg to crawl over it. He didn't realize that other rocks in that passage and many others resembled it. When it came his turn to lead out, he blithely led the group down a passage he had never been in. He knew he was on the right route when he shouted "There's DOG ROCK!" Only it wasn't, as he found out an hour later when he gave up in disgust at being lost. Make sure landmarks are unique before you name them.

All this emphasis on leading out and not getting lost is not just related to safety. Many cavers never really look at a cave until they experience the hopeless feeling of being lost. Then, by god, they pay attention! The Cave Research Foundation has found that good cavers are ready to become good party leaders only after they have experienced the "Uh-Oh! I am lost!" feeling. Then, and only then, do they observe the cave clearly enough to travel through it responsibly.

The Marked Route

In the bad old days of long ago, cavers used to smoke direction arrows on the walls of passages, with the head usually pointing back toward the entrance. Marking walls is a form of vandalism that detracts from the natural appearance of the cave. But directional markers are sometimes placed in new discoveries until the cavers learn the routes.

In the Mammoth Cave System about a mile of virgin cave is discovered every month. Often, four or five different survey teams will move into it to chart and explore it. They will mark confusing junctions by building small cairns, with an adjacent rock pointing the way back toward known cave. Or a sharp-pointed rock may be propped up for the same purpose. Directional notes are written on paper and left. At a few very confusing junctions, the notes were replaced with rectangles of cement board with permanent felt marker direction messages on them.

In some caves explorers leave route markers in the form of flags or bits of plastic survey marking tape. The general rule is to underdo it.

Getting Back Out

We have looked at ways of making movement in caves easy, and at ways of seeing the cave and remaining oriented. But what about those situations that can restrict or eliminate movement in caves? (Death is nature's way of telling you to slow down.)

Safety is discussed at length in Chapter 11. Yet, no consideration of moving through caves would be complete without commenting on dangerous situations.

Floyd Collins considered himself an expert caver. Yet, in 1925 he got himself trapped in a cave. He died there, despite earnest rescue efforts. Never mind that he violated every rule of caving, the point is he got into a situation where nobody could help him. There was no room to crawl past his body, which completely filled the solid rock tube in which he was encased. The rescuers found themselves in crawlways the size of wastebaskets—with no room to move. The moral, of course, is don't move into anything you can't get out of, and especially into places where nobody can rescue you.

If you come to a pit and you can see a passage leading off down at the bottom, don't plunge in. Ask yourself, "How will I get out?" and "What if we all get down and the rope breaks?" When you have figured out the worst that can happen, you may be ready to brave the unknown with common sense and a healthy respect for the risks.

If all this sounds like fear to you, you may recognize that we have nearly returned to our starting point. Some cavers psyche themselves up by studying maps, others by cleaning and packing their equipment. To paraphrase a famous explorer, "The caver who meets the unexpected is unprepared." If you try out these ideas about moving in caves, if you keep your eyes open, and if you think about what you are experiencing in a cave, you'll love to come back again and again.

Chapter 14

FITNESS AND NUTRITION

Louise Hose
NSS 13138

Fitness

The most important piece of equipment a caver can possess is a fit body. Fitness is the ability to accomplish a task with a reasonable degree of efficiency without undue fatigue. Adequate fitness often makes the difference between a pleasurable experience and a miserable time. Cavers' fitness should be sufficient not only for their usual caving activities, but also for emergency situations where someone's survival may depend on the fitness level of the others in the group.

Judging a person's fitness by their bulging muscles or ability to run a mile under six minutes is a popular misconception. Fitness is specific to the task to be performed. The term does not describe a general state of health. Top professional athletes, highly fit for their vocations, have been given general physical fitness tests and were judged to be unfit in their cardiovascular endurance or muscular strength that was not specifically required by their sport.

Knowing what fitness is makes it easy for the caver to improve his or her level of fitness for caving. There are two simple ways to change from unfit to fit without much time commitment or special training. The first way is to reduce the intensity of activity. If a person feels unfit to keep up on an eight-hour exploratory trip, perhaps beginner training trips or family-oriented trips would be more appropriate.

The second way to improve one's fitness without training is to improve one's efficiency. Moving through a cave or up a rope at a slow but steady pace is more efficient than moving quickly and taking frequent rest breaks. The human body works best when, like all machines, it operates at a constant rate. Cavers should pace their speed and not stop often. When rest stops are needed or desired, make them brief. After starting any strenuous physical activity, it takes a while for the circulorespiratory system to catch up to the demands of the body. If one stops for long, the heart slows down. This makes it more difficult to resume activity at the previous level. The same principles, of course, apply to the hike to the cave.

The state of one's fitness depends on a number of factors, including the suitability of the body structure for the work to be performed, the effectiveness of the organs and systems supporting the effort, and the view the person takes of the task.

The first of these, the shape and size of one's body, is termed anatomical fitness. It becomes obvious in caving that a 48-inch chest and tight crawlways are not compatible. Tall people often have an advantage on many climbs. Tight chimneys may favor short cavers. Because of the great variety of activities involved, it is impossible to describe the perfect body type as is often done in other sports.

Perhaps the one statement that can be made is that being overweight is rarely an advantage. Not only is it difficult to move the extra bulk through squeezes, it also means more weight for the legs to carry and the arms to lift.

Physiological fitness is far more complex, yet more alterable, than anatomical fitness. It refers to the ability of the respiratory, circulatory, homeokinetic, muscular, metabolic, and temperature-regulating systems to support performance.

It is often assumed that caving requires a high level of circulorespiratory fitness by placing considerable demand on the heart and lungs. However, in a set of preliminary tests conducted by the author on the heart beat rate (a test for detecting strain on the heart and lungs) of cavers as they negotiated various cave obstacles, this assumption was generally not supported, except during lengthy rope climbs. So, while circulorespiratory fitness may improve general fitness, it may not be essential to most activities in the cave. Outside of the cave, however, the considerations are different. Similar tests indicated that hiking to caves and ridge walking often placed considerable strain on the heart and lungs. It is suggested that cavers maintain a high level of circulorespiratory fitness to be prepared for difficult hikes to caves, long rope climbs, and those rare times in a cave when it may be helpful.

Any activity which raises the heart rate to 120-130 beats or more per minute for 15-20 minutes several times a week will improve one's circulorespiratory fitness. Jogging, swimming, and rope jumping are some of the best activities. Tennis, squash, and bicycling are good when done vigorously. Aerobics classes are popular and can provide a fun means of training. "Cross-training" (participating in a variety of physical activities) is the buzz-word of today's active people and it is an excellent way to prepare for caving trips.

Caving is primarily a body-lifting activity. Cavers typically lifts their bodies, not another object, from place to place. The amount of strength needed, therefore, is related to the caver's own weight. But caving is one place where it is advantageous to have more than enough. A great amount of strength is not overkill. A strong person needs fewer muscle fibers to perform a given act. When those fibers tire, others can be called upon. This gives the muscle greater endurance by allowing part of it to rest during activity.

To develop muscular endurance, exercise and weight training can be helpful. Push-ups, pull-ups, sit-ups, running, and other exercise can develop strength. Notice, also, weight training, not weight lifting, is suggested. The purpose of weight training is to develop strength, endurance, and flexibility. One should use relatively light weights and the individual activity should be repeated 8-15 times. Weight lifting is practiced only to increase the amount of weight one can lift.

Weight training can be extremely helpful to cavers. For example, leg presses can be beneficial in preparing for trips that will involve a lot of rope work. But, do not neglect the rest of the body. Caving places demands on the entire body. The back and abdomen are less obvious but important muscle groups for a caver. Most cavers planning to haul loads, such as camp duffels, through a cave will find weight training almost essential for optimal performance.

Remember to retain flexibility. Exercising one set of muscles without exercising the opposing muscles can result in a great loss of flexibility. For example, a person who does bench presses (exercising the extending muscles of the arms) should also include rowing lifts (using the flexing muscles in the arms) as a part of the weight training program.

In all activities that are extended over a period of several minutes or more, homeokinetic fitness becomes important. This form of fitness refers to the body's ability to establish and maintain a steady state at elevated levels of physical activity. Limiting factors include the maintenance of adequate blood sugar levels, the preservation of optimal pH, and the provision of an adequate oxygen supply. The proper function of the nervous system, in particular, depends upon preventing homeokinetic breakdown. In extreme cases, collapse and coma occur. Improving overall caving fitness seems to be the best means of improving homeokinetic fitness.

Metabolic fitness describes, among other things, the body's ability to produce energy. Caving, an endurance type of activity that requires considerable energy, demands a high level of metabolic fitness. Diet plays a major role in metabolic fitness. In fact, all of the systems that contribute to caving fitness can be affected by diet. Eating properly before and during a caving trip can make a difference.

The demands made by the cave's environment on the body's temperature regulating system are extreme. Although caves are generally cool, dehydration and heat exhaustion can occur. The body is cooled by the evaporation of sweat. The hotter the body becomes, the more it sweats. In high humidity environments, like caves, little evaporation takes place so the body tends to stay hot and sweat profusely. Consequently, there may be a great loss of water and electrolytes, leading to heat exhaustion if the caver does not drink adequate fluids. Intense thirst, headaches, weakness, dizziness, and muscle cramps are all indications of this problem.

The problem of over-heating is one burden on the temperature regulating system. The other is over-cooling. Getting wet, and especially staying wet, can rapidly cause hypothermia. Sitting still or moving too slowly to generate body heat at the same rate that it is lost can also bring it on. Hypothermia is a condition that is induced by lowering the body core temperature. Intense shivering, muscle tension, numbness, and stumbling are symptoms of its early stages. Lethargy and disorientation are symptoms of a more advanced stage; death can occur.

Improving fitness of the temperature regulating system is largely a matter of buffering your body against the cave environment. Efficient movement, adequate food and water intake, appropriate clothing, and good overall physical fitness offer the most effective buffers.

The high elevation of alpine caving makes activity more difficult and one's performance decreases due to the decreased density of air. It is best to remember this limitation and move more slowly. Athletes at the Olympic Training Center in Colorado are reminded that the body actually deteriorates during the first few days at high altitude. Remember that your performance is likely to be most affected by the stress about three to four days after arriving. After that time, the body will rapidly start to acclimate and function better.

Lastly, the most important factor in endurance is motivation. How willing a person is to endure discomfort and fatigue can seriously affect his or her performance. A lack of motivation may result from all night, pre-caving car rides, recent illness, colds, allergies, toothaches, hangovers, or just a lack of interest. Though not incapacitating, a "low" feeling should always be taken seriously as it reduces one's efficiency, endurance, and overall performance. For safety's sake, it is better to spend a day on the surface when motivation is minimal.

An adequate level of fitness for the type of caving a person plans is not difficult to achieve and is essential to the protection of the caver, the entire caving party, and to the cave itself. An overextended caver becomes careless. Carelessness can endanger all members of the caving party and increase the chances of damage to the cave. Adequate fitness can help prevent these problems.

Nutrition

One of the most important substances that the body needs during a caving trip is adequate water. Dehydration can be a serious problem, even in cool caves. Unfortunately, drinking just enough water to meet one's feelings of thirst is not always adequate. A caver needs to make a conscientious effort to assure that enough fluid is consumed during a cave trip.

Probably the best way to assure sufficient fluid intake is to drink fruit juices or commercial electrolyte drinks and water at regular, frequent intervals. While alcoholic beverages, like beer, may be temporarily thirst quenching, they actually tend to dehydrate the body and upset the body's fluid balance. By dilating the blood vessels, alcohol also increases the chance of suffering from hypothermia. Coffee is popular and provides fluids for the body. But, it is a stimulant to bowel action and thus is inadvisable prior to a trip into a cave.

What a caver should eat before a trip into a cave is probably as debatable as what an athlete should eat before competition. Basically, a balanced diet that provides all the necessary nutrients without an excess of calories is best.

Athletes and cavers today generally agree that a diet high in carbohydrates is best immediately before and during strenuous activity. Energy comes from a combination of glycogen and fat. Glycogen, stored in the muscles and liver, is a product of carbohydrate foods. While carbohydrates are not essential to sustain life and a large amount may be harmful in a sedentary diet, they are important to the active person.

For long, difficult trips, cavers may find it advantageous to increase the percentage of carbohydrates in their diet. Many serious athletes who participate in endurance events practice a technique called carbohydrate loading. This involves a dramatic increase in the percentage of carbohydrates in their diets prior to strenuous competition. This technique is of limited value to cavers but may be of some help to cavers who are preparing for a very long, strenuous trip. Most good, modern books on nutrition for athletes give a summary on the advantages, problems, and procedures for carbohydrate loading for those serious cavers who may be involved in expeditions where endurance demands are great.

More important than pre-trip meals are in-cave meals. Frequent light snacks are beneficial in providing energy to keep going and to maintain body temperature, thus preventing hypothermia. Foods high in carbohydrates are good for cave food. Suggestions might include dried or fresh fruit, honey, hard candy, granola bars, and other quick energy foods. For the more creative caver, backpacking magazines often have recipes for high energy trail mixes and bars that can be prepared at home. One of the best foods for the cave is fruit juice in eight or twelve ounce cans. Fruit juice cans tend to be a little bulky for a cave pack but they provide the simple sugars needed for quick energy and the liquid needed to prevent dehydration. Cans are sturdy and stand up well to being dragged through a cave. Glass containers should never be taken into a cave.

Foods that are chosen need to meet several requirements. Listed below are a few features to consider:

1. The food should be simple and relatively neat to eat. When a caver is covered with a layer of mud, "finger-lickin" chicken is not appetizing.
2. The food should not require refrigeration or cooking.
3. Foods should be packaged to withstand abuse. Use nothing breakable. Sandwiches, crackers, grapes, and chocolate bars are often smashed so badly during the caving trip that little is left of their original form by the time one is ready to eat. Foods should be packaged in a waterproof container or bag to help keep dirt and water away from the food. Air-tight, plastic containers (baby bottles, Nalgene, and Tupperware products for instance) work well.
4. If the trip is a long one, pack food that can be eaten as several snacks throughout the day.
5. Food taken into the cave should be palatable. No matter how nutritious it is, food helps only if it is eaten.
6. Quick energy foods are best. Choose foods high in carbohydrates.
7. If the food taken into a cave has waste left over, make provisions to carry this material out of the cave. Apple cores, orange peels, and oil from canned meats do not belong in the cave environment. If something is brought into the cave, it should also be removed by the caver.

It is always best to pack more food than one expects to need. Trips commonly last longer than expected. Also, should an accident occur or hypothermia become a problem, extra food could make a crucial difference.

Eating correctly both before and during a caving trip can add energy and increase the pleasure of a trip. On work trips or during difficult exploration, proper nutrition can help add to the amount of work accomplished. The results can be well worth the small amount of time needed to assure that proper food is eaten before and during a trip.

Chapter 15

FIRST AID

Eileen Carol
RNC, MN, MPH, PhD, FNP
NSS 12945

An extremely important, yet often overlooked, aspect of caving is first aid. The purpose of this chapter is to introduce the caver to the more common accidental threats and injuries prevalent in the cave environment. No step-by-step guide to treatment is intended here as entire books have been written for that purpose. However, an attempt will be made to offer some general guidelines for action. From that framework, it is intended that the caver will be motivated to obtain more specific knowledge and training in first aid. The responsibility for preparedness remains an individual and personal obligation.

Prevention

Prevention of accidents remains by far the most effective policy. This includes preparedness and knowledge in the areas of:
1. the caving environment to be encountered
2. the caving skills and techniques required for the specific cave (horizontal and vertical)
3. good physical condition
4. knowledge of your own ability and the ability of those members in the caving party
5. proper clothing and equipment (and maintenance of that gear)
6. adequate fuel for the body (food and water)
7. other associated stress factors such as minor illnesses and psychological elements
8. a minimum of three cavers on a trip.

Other considerations include:
1. prevention of overheating
2. prevention of hypothermia
3. abstinence from alcohol and drugs
4. sensory deprivation
5. knowledge of other cavers' physical and/or mental disorders.

Preparedness also includes the consideration for specific injuries that might be encountered within a given cave or caving locale. The importance of becoming knowledgeable about hazards before entering the cave cannot be stressed enough. The conditions of the hike to the cave must also be included. Forethought alone can often be enough to divert any possibility of accident or injury.

Local cavers are an excellent resource in any area. They can provide information relating to the cave hazards, as well as the available first aid and rescue personnel and routine. Local cavers should be contacted prior to a trip into an unknown area.

First aid knowledge and skills are included in preparedness. The American Red Cross provides both standard and advanced first aid courses at minimal cost. Short courses in Cardio-Pulmonary Resuscitation (CPR) are taught by either the Red Cross or the American Heart Association and are a necessity. Consult your local telephone directory. The National Speleological Society has the National Cave Rescue Commission (NCRC) for a resource. (See the current NSS Members Manual for the address of the National Coordinator of the NCRC.) Hopefully, cavers will pool their talents and resources to devise and offer caver-oriented first aid courses on a local level.

First Aid Kit

A basic first aid kit is an integral part of personal caving gear. This can be small and light enough to be unnoticeable—until it is needed. Contents should be placed in a waterproof or water-tight container (largemouthed plastic water bottle, plastic case, metal tin, etc.). Contents should include:
1. one large, heavy plastic garbage bag
2. a few large and small band aids
3. large paper clips, tongue blades, or pencils to be used as splints
4. 1-inch or 2-inch-wide rolls of adhesive tape
5. mixture of 1 teaspoon salt and ½ teaspoon baking soda wrapped in a plastic bag (used to make one quart of "shock" solution)
6. a few 3×3 or 4×4 gauze dressings
7. matches in waterproof container
8. a few aspirin (wrapped in plastic)
9. a clean handkerchief.

Optional items include:
10. a small elastic bandage
11. 1-inch-wide gauze roll or roll bandage
12. butterfly closures
13. a small bar of Dial soap
14. small container of Betadine antiseptic solution.

A more complete first aid kit should always be kept in the car for severe injuries. The location of the car key should be known by all trip members. The kit should include the following items:
1. more 4×4-inch gauze dressings and some large-sized ones

2. roll bandages of assorted size and lengths (can be made at home from prewashed cotton muslin)
3. triangular bandages
4. splints (pneumatic, wood, metal)
5. small camp stove and fuel
6. small pot and two cups
7. water
8. wool blankets
9. extra webbing, ropes, pulleys
10. spine board (for caving spine board plans, contact the National Cave Rescue Commission.)
11. heavy plastic sheeting.

Common Injuries

It is impossible to predict all the hazards and injuries that can occur in a caving situation. The locale of the trip will dictate specific possibilities. The arduous, arid hikes into the Sierra Madre Oriental of Mexico will offer different hazards compared to the cold, wet caves of the mountains and northwestern United States.

In general, the more common injuries to be encountered, in order of probability, include:
1. exhaustion
2. dehydration
3. wounds
   a) lacerations
   b) abrasions
   c) contusions (bruises)
   d) minor burns
the more serious:
4. hypothermia
5. sprains, dislocations (to be handled the same as a fracture)
6. fractures
   a) neck and spine
   b) femur and long bones
   c) pelvis
   d) other bones
7. shock
8. cessation of respiration
9. cessation of heart beat
non-trauma problems include:
10. insect and snake bites
11. infectious agents (rabies, histoplasmosis)
12. food poisoning from improperly prepared caving food and/or contaminated water.

Often, injuries occur in combination and can aggravate each other. Some degree of shock and hypothermia should always be anticipated. The more significant and life-threatening issues will be dealt with separately.

Open Wounds

Open wounds include abrasions, incised wounds, lacerations, and puncture wounds. Severe bleeding occurs with the most serious of these injuries. Management includes the control of bleeding, prevention of contamination, and immobilization of the part involved.

Minor wounds generally need only to be covered with a clean dressing (handkerchief, cloth strips) bandaged in place. Because these are not life threatening, treatment can be delayed.

Major deep wounds require immediate action to stop severe bleeding. Bleeding from the arteries, if left uncontrolled, will result in heavy blood loss, shock, and possibly death within minutes. To stop severe bleeding:
1. Apply direct pressure on the wound with a clean dressing. If one is not available, use your hand and apply firm pressure. Be sure you don't cut off the circulation.
2. Elevate the affected limb.
3. If bleeding persists, apply pressure on the pressure point nearest the wound but between the wound and the heart. See Figure 1 for the location of the pressure points.
4. When severe bleeding is controlled, apply a compression dressing and tie in place (scarf, sock, webbing, strips of cloth). If blood soaks through, don't remove the dressing, but apply an additional dressing on top.
5. Apply a tourniquet ONLY as a last resort. This may lead to amputation of the limb later on. It should only be used as a life-saving measure when a limb has been destroyed or amputated. The simplest tourniquet is a belt, webbing, or cloth wrapped about two inches above the wound and pulled just tight enough to stop the

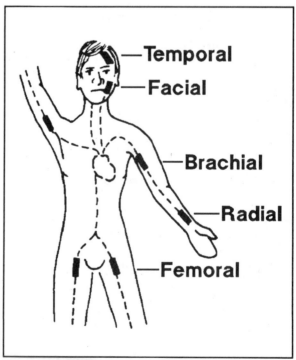

Figure 1 — Body pressure points

flow of blood. With a narrow belt, wire, or thin rope, you run the risk of cutting into the victim's skin. Do not cover the tourniquet as it could go unnoticed. Once a tourniquet is applied, never remove it for any reason. If it were loosened, clotted blood could enter the heart and lungs causing death.

6. Puncture wounds generally don't bleed freely. One of the most serious is to the chest wall, which may collapse the lung. Seal off a sucking wound as soon as possible. If clean dressings or bandages aren't available use air-tight material such as plastic wrap, a baggie, or aluminum foil — and bandage in place. If no dressing is handy, use your hand. If a spinal injury is not suspected, turn the person onto his injured side.
7. When an object has penetrated into a person, never make any attempt to remove it. You risk severe hemorrhaging if you do. It is important to immobilize the object so it won't cause any further damage. Pack folded clothing around the object to keep it steady and fasten in place with tape, elastic bandage, or strips of clothing.

Hypothermia

Hypothermia occurs when there is a fall in body temperature. When heat loss is greater than heat produced, the body defends itself in order to protect the vital organs. The first reaction is to shut down the circulation to the skin, the external muscles, and the limbs. This is done to maintain the "core" temperature of the blood flowing to the vital organs. However, as the core temperature decreases from 98.6° Fahrenheit, the progression from drowsiness to coma can be very rapid, with death occurring in less than one hour. Never assume a hypothermia victim to be dead until attempts to revive him in a hospital have failed.

The wet and cold environment of most caves provides prime conditions to foster hypothermia. Water — whether from rain, snow, or perspiration — conducts heat away from the body 200 to 250 times faster than air. Other aggravating factors include improper clothing, exhaustion, lack of food intake, drugs, and alcohol.

Hypothermia often gives little warning. Initial reaction to the cold is goose pimples and shivering. If the heat produced by shivering doesn't keep up with the heat being lost, the body's temperature will fall. With the slowing of the metabolic rate, mental and physical changes occur. As the victim drops out of conversation, he may appear discouraged or depressed. Uncoordinated, slow, and labored movements may occur. Simple tasks become difficult, judgement will fail, and sleepiness may occur.

Try to prevent hypothermia before it occurs. Preventive measures include:

1. Proper clothing of several light, loose layers that will trap air and provide ventilation
2. Wool and polyester fabrics (PolarGuard, Dacron, Hollofil II) retain some protective value when wet; whereas cotton and bird down do not.
3. High heat loss areas such as the head and neck should be protected at all times.
4. Good physical condition is important.
5. Adequate food and water intake are fuel for heat maintenance.
6. Neoprene wet suits are a must for extremely cold, wet caves.
7. Pace yourself and avoid fatigue.

Know the early signs of hypothermia and leave the cave environment immediately. Symptoms of hypothermia in yourself are:
1. intense shivering
2. fatigue
3. numbness
4. stumbling
5. poor speech
6. poor orientation
7. careless attitude

Look for signs of hypothermia in others:
1. poor coordination
2. slowing of pace
3. stumbling
4. forgetfullness
5. hallucinations
6. thickness of speech
7. dilation of pupils
8. decreased attention
9. careless attitude

The darkness of the cave and spacing of party members may hinder the recognition of hypothermia. Long waiting intervals at vertical drops and pitches can also aggravate hypothermia. If the condition is discovered early enough, leaving the cave won't present a problem. However, this decision must be made for each situation. Forcing someone to get out of the cave on his own may worsen hypothermia and add to the danger.

When being evacuated, the victim must be watched closely. He must be carefully protected from even minor hazards in the cave. Caution must be taken to belay even simple situations.

Removal may have to be delayed or stopped if the hypothermic condition worsens. If this happens, help should be sent for and other members must maintain the victim. Very wet top clothing must be wrung out and extra clothing from other party members put on — but not at their expense. Rubbing the limbs has no value. A garbage bag or space blanket is an asset, especially with the heat from a carbide lamp underneath aimed at the victim's chest. Insulate the victim from the cold, wet ground. Provide warmth from others huddled around him. Have him huddle, sitting in a thigh-to-chest position to maintain his body warmth. Feed him with any available nourishment, especially hot and sweet things. Offer encouragement and reassurance at all times. Give absolutely no alcohol or drugs, as this increases the heat loss.

Injuries or shock aggravate hypothermia. Under any circumstance the condition of the victim dictates whether he can safely evacuate himself. If his speech is impaired, or if his muscle function is impaired so he is unable to move along the cave passage in a coordinated manner, then he should not be forced to move on. Outside the cave, warming should be slow and gradual, and may require medical assistance.

Know the factors that can lead to hypothermia—cold, wind, wetness, and a likely victim. Prepare for the worst. Plan to refuel the body at regular intervals. Keep moving as much as possible.

Shock

Traumatic shock can occur from all types of injuries, even minor ones. If not treated, it can become life threatening. Once bleeding has been controlled, you must deal with assessing and treating shock. For assessing shock:
1. Early signs of shock are clamminess and bluish or pale skin color. Checking the skin color and temperature will be a problem in a cave.
2. Check the pulse. If the rate is over 100 beats per minute, the victim is probably in shock. The pulse may be too faint to be felt at the wrist, but can be felt better at the carotid artery at the side of the neck or in the groin.

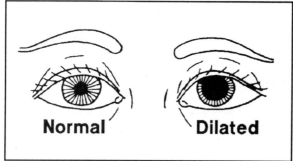

Figure 2—Eye condition.

3. Check the breathing. There may be rapid, shallow, irregular breathing.
4. A person in shock may also be restless, anxious, complain of thirst, and become nauseated.
5. Check the pupils of the eyes (also a problem in the cave). If they are widely dilated (see Figure 2), he may be in severe shock.
For treating shock:

1. Victims in shock should be kept lying flat, with clothing and blankets under and over the person. External heat applied at this time will draw blood away from the vital organs and to the skin and should be avoided. The lower limbs should be elevated slightly, about eight to twelve inches. The exceptions follow:
   a) If a person has severe facial wounds or is unconscious, place him on his side to prevent the possibility of fluids being drawn into the lungs.
   b) If he has difficulty breathing, the victim may be placed on his back with his head and shoulders propped up—only if he doesn't have a spinal injury.
   c) With a head injury, the victim may be kept flat or propped up. Do not elevate the rest of the body higher than the head.
2. Fluids should not be given if the person is half-conscious or unconscious, if help is immediate, or if the victim is nauseated. If rescue is more than an hour away, which is most likely in a cave accident, a "shock" solution of tepid temperature is recommended (1 teaspoon salt, ½ teaspoon baking soda to one quart of water, to be sipped, about ½ cup, at 15-minute intervals). If a person becomes nauseated, fluids must be stopped.

Closed Wounds

After bleeding and shock are under control, you can check for other injuries such as internal bleeding, fractures, and damage to the brain and spinal cord.
1. Gently feel the head for any depression or injury. If a hard hat is on, you have to remove it to do this. Always suspect neck injury in persons with head injuries. Avoid moving them unless you must do so in order to protect them from further harm.
2. Check the neck, feeling for lumps and bony protrusions. If the victim is conscious ask him to:
   a) wiggle his fingers and toes
   b) squeeze your hand hard with each of his hands
   c) Push against the palm of your hand with each foot.
A weak or absent response indicates probable spinal cord injury.
3. When you suspect spinal injury, do not attempt to move the victim, bend his back, or raise his head.
4. If you must move him for further protection and don't have a spine board, use as many individuals as are available for a six-man carry. Equal numbers of people should be on either side of the victim. Gently, the hands should be worked under the victim, to midline. Upon first command the victim should be lifted to waist level.

On second command they should rise to their feet. The same procedure should be used in reverse to lower the victim to a safe location. When lifting, the rescuers should use their legs, not their backs.

5. Examine the eyes, nose, ears, and mouth for blood or clear fluid.

6. Closed fractures and internal bleeding have the same signs as shock. In addition, the person may vomit blood and have a rigid abdomen. There is nothing you can do directly for internal bleeding in the field. You can insure a good airway, give nothing by mouth, and reassure the victim.

7. Gently check the ribs for fractures, asking if he has any pain or tenderness. Place in a comfortable position, generally on the side of the injury. If he has trouble breathing, raise his head and shoulders (or give artificial ventilation).

8. Feel the pelvic area for tenderness and deformity. With a pelvic fracture, the victim should be immobilized from his waist to his feet (rolled jackets, blankets). Then treat him like he had a spinal injury.

9. Check the limbs for deformity. Look for bones protruding through the skin. A clean dressing or handkerchief, moistened with clean water, can be placed over protruding bones to protect them. Do not attempt to straighten out any fracture. Keep the victim lying quietly.

10. Dislocated or broken fingers do not have to be splinted in the field. You can protect them by wrapping a clean cloth or handkerchief around the hand involved.

11. In the case of fractures, splint the involved limb in the exact position you found it. Use any available materials. You may have to wait for these to arrive from outside the cave. You can use strips of cloth or rolled clothing to immobilize the fracture.
    a) For fractures of the upper arm (humerus) splint to the side of the body.
    b) For fractures of the leg (femur, tibia, fibula) splint to the uninjured leg.
    c) Always immobilize the joint above and below the fracture. If no pulse is present, move the limb only enough for the pulse to return and then resplint in that position.

Though a good assessment of the victim is conducted with removal of the clothing, this is impractical and unwise in a caving accident. Leave all clothing and boots on the victim. Begin to treat for and protect him from hypothermia.

First Aid Guidelines

Common sense knowledge is the basis for action in administering first aid. Several broad guidelines will be presented. These will provide a logical course of action for thinking through and acting in a first aid situation. Table 1 can be used as a learning tool to assist you in becoming knowledgeable in assessing an injured individual. These are also important factors medical personnel will want to know.

The goal of first aid is to administer aid quickly, correctly, and with calm assurance. One must assess the injuries, know what to treat first, and know how to treat. The limitations of your own first aid ability must also be recognized. More harm can be inflicted if you are unsure of what you are doing.

Before a caving trip, it is important to determine what individuals will be in charge if there is an accident or injury. This will prevent dissent later on in the cave if such a situation does occur. The trip leader should also be made aware of any medical problems of the party members.

First and foremost, cardio-respiratory arrest (cessation of heartbeat or breathing) is life threatening and must be treated immediately. Before any other action is taken, all victims must be breathing and have a heartbeat. Only then can care be administered for shock, wounds, fractures, and other injuries. In a cave, the situation is hampered by the darkness, the cold, the uneven passage, and often by the long and difficult route to the entrance.

In an accident situation, keep in mind the following:

1. The accident scene must be secured for the safety of the victim and the rescuer and to prevent any further injury. If life-threatening hazards cannot be eliminated, the victim MUST be moved from further danger, regardless of the injuries or his condition.

2. The most knowledgeable, medically-trained individual should take charge of the victim.

3. The most experienced and best-trained first aid or rescue person should take charge of the situation. This individual may not be the trip leader or a doctor. (A doctor would be #2 above.) He can then delegate duties to other trip members.

4. Look for a Medic Alert tag on the injured person.

5. Look for the instrument or the cause of the injury, as this may give a better clue to the type of injury sustained.

6. If there is more than one victim, make a quick check of each person before beginning treatment. Quickly classify the severity of the injuries to your best ability. After checking a victim, assign someone to stay with the person and to inform you immediately of any adverse change in the condition.

7. Evaluate from the head and work down.

8. If the victim is conscious, ask him to describe his pain and sensations, and to give an evaluation of his own injuries. At this time, get a good history of the accident or injury.

Evaluation Checklist

Before caring for an accident victim, you must make a full assessment of his condition and injuries. This chart will help you to determine the most immediate hazards to him and to establish priorities in treatment

FUNCTION	METHOD OF ASSESSMENT	OBSERVATIONS	POSSIBLE CAUSES
Respiration	Watch and feel chest for rise and fall; listen for breathing; check skin color	No respiration, cyanotic, ashen, or general deathlike appearance	Respiratory arrest—begin mouth-to-mouth resuscitation immediately, check for airway obstruction if resuscitation is not effective
		Deep, gasping, labored, choking breathing	Airway obstruction, heart failure
		Rapid, shallow breathing	Hypertensive crisis, hyperventilation, pain, hypovolemic shock, cardiogenic shock, pulmonary embolism
Pulse	Check carotid and femoral arteries	Absent	Cardiac arrest, death—begin CPR immediately
		Rapid, bounding	Fright, hypertension, hemorrhage, septic shock
		Rapid, weak	Cardiogenic, hypovolemic shock, hemorrhage
Level of consciousness	General observation history	Brief periods of unconsciousness	Simple fainting, concussion
		Confusion	Concussion, slight blow to head, psychiatric disorder, hysteria, alcohol or drug use or overdose, cerebral insufficiency
		Stupor	Concussion, brain damage, skull fracture, severe blow to the head, diabetic shock, hysteria
		Deep coma	Severe brain damage, poisoning, drug overdose, diabetic shock, diabetic coma, hysteria

Evaluation Checklist

Ability to move	Ask conscious victim to move extremities, to describe any sensation; perform Babinski test on unconscious victim	Inability to move arms, hands	Injury to spinal cord in neck.
		Inability to move legs and feet	Injury to spinal cord in lower back
		Limited use of any or all extremities	Pressure on spinal cord or in brain
		Paralisis limited to one side	Stroke, head injury with brain damage, or hemorrhage
Skin color	Check extremities and fingernails; in dark pigmented victim, check fingernails, lips, and palms of hands	Red skin	High blood pressure, septic shock, carbon monoxide poisioning, heart attack, skin burn
		White skin	Cardiogenic, hypovolemic shock, heart attack, fright
		Blue skin (cyanosis)	Asphyxia, anoxia, heart attack, poisoning, electrocution
Skin temperature	Place back of hand on victim's forehaed	Hot, dry	Heat stroke, high fever, dehydration, septic shock
		Cold, clammy	Cardiogenic, hypovolemic, insulin shock
		Cool, dry	Long exposure to cold
Pain	Query victim, observe general reaction of victim to gentle pressure	General pain at injury site	Injury to body but probably no injury to spinal cord
		Localized pain in extremities	Fracture, torn muscles or ligments and tendons, hematoma
		No pain but obvious injury	Spinal cord injury, vicient shock, excessive use of drugs or alcohol, hysteria
Pupil reaction	Lift victim's eyelids and check response to light	Dilated	Unconsciousness, cardiac arrest, brain damage, drug use, shock
		Constricted	Disorder of the central nervous system, drug overdose or use
		Unequal	Head injury, stroke
		No pupil response to light, eyes rolled back in head	Death, coma, cataracts in older person

Refer to victim's history of the accident and other medical problems.

9. NEVER move an unconscious person or one with a spinal injury unless his life is immediately threatened.
10. Always treat the worst-suspected injury first.
11. Never attempt to administer any liquids by mouth to a semi-conscious or unconscious person.
12. Respect the modesty of the victim.
13. Always be honest but positive with the person. Explain what you are doing and why.
14. Continue to check his condition until trained personnel take over.
15. If in doubt about a person's injuries or the proper position, keep him flat.
16. Insulate the person from the cold ground—shock hastens hypothermia.
17. At least one person should stay with the victim while two others go for help.
18. The decision to move the victim is an individual one. It depends on the victim's condition and the ability of the trip members to handle the situation. The nature and location of the cave as well as the availability of rescue personnel will dictate what will be done.
19. Always anticipate some degree of shock and hypothermia with any injury.

Above all, stay calm. Psychological reassurance of the victim and other party members is just as significant as any first aid that can be administered.

The environment of the cave offers potential of injury to those who are ill prepared or careless. It also presents a unique challenge for first aid and rescue. The responsibility for preparedness is an individual one. A good rule of thumb is to be prepared for the worst injury on any caving trip. It usually won't happen. If it does, you can be assured that you have prepared and acted to the best of your ability.

References

American National Red Cross (1981) *Advanced First Aid and Emergency Care*, 2nd Edition: Doubleday & Company, Inc., Garden City, NY, 318pp.

American National Red Cross (1979) *Standard First Aid and Personal Safety*: Doubleday & Company, Inc., Garden City, NY, 268pp.

Bangs, C. C. *et al.* (1975) — "Winter Trauma: Help for the Victim of Hypothermia" *Patient Care* 11(21):46-57.

Boericks, P. H. *et al.* (1975) Emergency! Part 2, "First Aid for Open Wounds, Severe Bleeding, Shock, and Closed Wounds" *Nursing* 5(3):40-47.

Clarke, C., M. Ward, and E. Williams, (Eds.) (1976) *Mountain Medicine and Physiology*, Proceedings of a symposium for mountaineers, expedition doctors, and physiologists sponsored by the Alpine Club, London, 1975: reprinted by Mountain Safety Research, Inc., Seattle, Washington, 143pp.

Committee on Injuries, American Academy of Orthopedic Surgeons (1978) *Emergency Care and Transportation of the Sick and Injured*: George Banta Company, Inc., Menasha, Wisconsin.

Darvill, F., (1985) *Mountaineering Medicine*: Wilderness Press, 11th Edition, Berkley, California.

Fear, G. (1972) — *Surviving the Unexpected Wilderness Emergency*: Survival Education Association, Tacoma, Washington, 192pp.

Lathrop, T. (1975) — *Hypothermia: Killer of the Unprepared*: Mazamas, Portland, Oregon.

Mitchell, D. (1972) — *Mountianeering First Aid*: The Mountaineers, Seattle, Washington, 96pp.

Paton, B. C. (1975) — "Cold, Injury, Hypothermia, and Frostbite" *Summit* 21(12):6-13.

Wilkerson, J., (Ed.) (1975) — *Medicine for Mountaineering*: The Mountaineers, Second Edition, Seattle, Washington, 309pp.

Chapter 16

SINGLE ROPE TECHNIQUE

Vertical Caving

William Storage
NSS 16901

I leaned back in the pose shown in the book.

"Yeah, that's the way they show it," Pete said, "a hot-seat rappel." Around my chest was a second rope, a belay for safety, manned by two friends who had it wrapped around a tree and were letting me down slowly.

"O.K., here goes," I said. Leaves and dirt fell into the pit as I inched backward over the edge.

"More rope, more rope," I begged, as I got below the lip of the pit and felt the extent of the pain in my right thigh and left shoulder from the friction of the rope.

Soon I was on the bottom. There were no passages leading from the pit bottom. I could barely hear the muffled voices of my friends some fifty feet above. "O.K., pull me out!"

As the rope dug into my armpits, I left the ground in short jerks. I would go up five feet and then back down one. The higher I got, the slower my five friends pulled. Finally I was at the top. Here I had to climb hand over hand over the lip while my buddies tugged.

"Never again," I swore. "I am going to learn how to do it right!"

This was veteran caver Bill Steele, describing how he survived his first trip into a vertical cave. Bill and his friends were aware of cable ladders, commonly used in caving; but they were attempting a ladderless technique they had just heard about. Later Bill joined the National Speleological Society and learned safe ropework techniques for descending pits and returning to the surface painlessly. In the years that followed Bill became one of the world's foremost vertical cavers.

Ascending and descending pits without ladders is generally known as single rope technique, or SRT. It is now practiced almost exclusively by serious vertical cavers around the world. Single rope technique was used here and there in Europe in the 1940s and 1950s, but ladders and winches were generally favored worldwide. In the 1960s cavers in the United States, led by Bill Cuddington, began using mountain climbing techniques in caves.

Cuddington started with the painful and dangerous hot-seat rappel, and then progressed to rappel spools and carabiner rappels.

In 1961, he first descended the newly discovered 437-foot Surprise Pit, in Fern Cave, Alabama. By 1967 American cavers had successfully descended the 1,094-foot-deep entrance pit of Sótano de las Golindrinas in Mexico. To rappel they used John Cole's invention, the rappel rack, (Figure 1) now used widely in the United States. News of Golindrinas went around the world, and a slightly different brand of single rope technique began to evolve in Europe and Australia.

While Europeans had been pushing caves deeper and deeper over a few decades, single rope technique opened the door to more efficient vertical caving, and provided an alternative to endless ladder ascents. In Europe and the United States, mechanical ascending devices were becoming widely accepted. After Golindrinas the lure of deep caves in the western hemisphere drew many inno-

Figure 1—The six-bar rappel rack descending device. Rope runs across top bar, not against rack. Braking hand cradles rack to control descent. Bars at left squeezed together to stop. Center, bars spread for descent. Right, rack being locked off for resting. (photo David McClurg)

vative cavers who developed specialized equipment and techniques.

In the last 20 years or so, single rope technique has allowed cavers to explore many deep, multiple-drop caves in the southeast, as well as a few in the Rockies, California, and New Mexico. Exploration of Lechuguilla Cave, in Carlsbad Caverns National Park, has shown it to be over 1,500 feet deep.

American cavers have likewise explored caves in Mexico to depths over a thousand meters (3,300 feet), most reaching this depth in scores of successive pits. Nita Nanta, a wet cave in southern Mexico requires negotiating about 100 drops to reach its bottom.

Like Bill Steele's description of his first vertical cave, many of us originally learned to do pits from illustrations in books. This is perhaps the *worst* way to go about it! Vertical skills cannot be acquired by reading a book; an experienced instructor can point out mistakes and give pointers after seeing you practice—a service not provided by literature. Many chapters of the National Speleological Society (called grottos) regularly hold training and practice sessions, where newcomers can benefit from the collective experience of trained vertical cavers. Useful sessions are also held at national conventions of the National Speleological Society.

The following casual look at vertical techniques is intended only to serve as a brief glimpse of topics that need to be mastered on the surface, in the presence of experienced cavers. I say cavers, as opposed to mountaineers or others skilled in ropework, because an understanding of the underground environment—darkness, low temperatures, falling water, slippery mud, and loose rocks—is so important.

Negotiating vertical caves requires many skills. While we can't teach them with this chapter, we

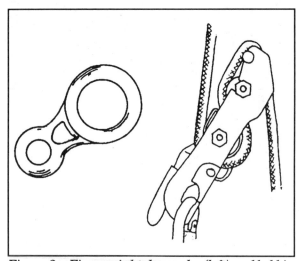

Figure 2—Figure-eight descender (left) and bobbin (right).

can provide a brief look at some of the methods used, to give readers some insight into single rope technique.

Descent

The topic most interesting to newcomers is rappeling. To descend into a pit you must be able to attach a rappel device to a rope, descend vertically, stop descent while on rope, and pass a knot or intermediate tie-off.

The hot seat rappel, using no mechanical descending aids, as described by Bill Steele, is rarely used these days. This makes sense, since it is as dangerous as it is painful. Fortunately, mechanical descenders have been developed.

The rappel rack is probably the most commonly used descending device in caving. It is also the most versatile. The rappel rack is attached to the caver's harness and then the main rope is threaded through it. By adjusting the number of brake bars contacting the rope, and the spacing between them, the caver can adjust the amount of friction, thereby controlling the rate of descent.

Other descending devices used in caving include the bobbin and the figure-eight descender (Figure 2), although neither allow adjustment of friction. When using these descenders, speed is controlled only by the braking force applied to the rope below the descender; therefore, they are usually used only for short drops—100 feet or so.

The amount of tension below the rappel device can, as a backup, be controlled by a person at the bottom of the pit. This technique, called a bottom belay, is often used as a precaution against loss of control by the rappeller. The bottom belayer must stand in a location well away from the rock fall zone.

While rappeling is very easy, practice above ground is necessary. And of utmost importance is knowing how to lock off the devices in mid-rappel and the procedure for passing knots and intermediate anchors. These techniques will vary, depending on the actual equipment used. Detailed instructions are beyond the scope of this chapter but can be found in several texts available from the National Speleological Society (Warild 1988, Padgett & Smith 1987, Meridith & Martinez 1986).

Ascent

The earliest method of ascent in single rope technique was developed by Dr. Karl Prusik. Cavers often use the term "prusiking" to mean any type of rope ascent, although Dr. Prusik's method involved knots which could slide up the rope and then grip the rope as weight was applied. Today, cavers know how to use Prusik knots (Figure 3) as

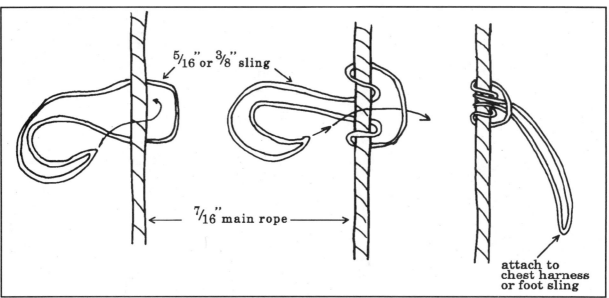

Figure 3 — *The Prusik knot, an emergency ascender.*

an emergency backup. Too clumsy to serve as a primary ascending method, the knots have a habit of moving when they are supposed to grip, and then jamming tight when you want them to slide. For-

tunately, as with descent, more convenient means have been developed.

Mechanical ascenders (Figure 4) are made in a variety of shapes by a number of manufacturers. All of them involve a cam which jams the rope, allowing the ascender to slide on the rope in only one direction. Small teeth on the cam provide a slight grip on the rope. As more weight is applied the cam squeezes tight against the rope, allowing large loads to be applied without damaging the rope. Some ascenders use springs to keep the cams in light contact with the rope. Several different lever arrangements are also available. Deciding on the best style for you depends on many things—whether a handle is needed, the method of rope loading, rope size, and so on. Minor differences in strength are of no concern.

An ascending system includes two or three ascenders, allowing one to be weighted as another is moved up the rope. A number of different systems can be used safely. Most cavers in the world use the frog system (Figure 5). This system is probably the least complex and is popular where complex rope rigging is encountered. While it is simple, many find it tiresome and inefficient. The Texas system, used by Americans in the deep caves of Mexico, is somewhat similar to the frog in advantages and disadvantages, but can be converted to the Mitchell rig, a system that allows the climber to take steps, thus avoid-

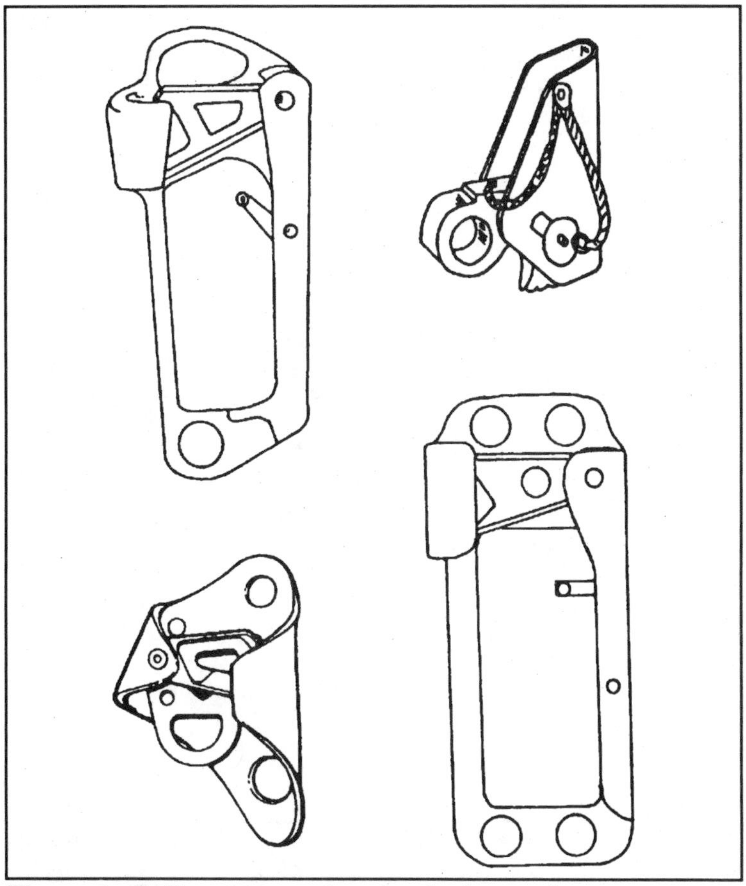

Figure 4 — *Different types of mechanical ascenders.*

Figure 5—The frog ascending system. From On Rope, *©National Speleological Society.*

Small variations in the arrangement of the ascending rig will also make a huge difference. For example, if a chest harness is a bit too loose, the amount of work done by a climber's arm will increase dramatically. A variety of equipment adjustments will be needed after a first practice session.

Rigging

When your life depends on a single rope, it simply cannot be allowed to fail. That means the rope must be rigged so that there is no chance of knots coming loose and so that it cannot be cut. If a pit is at the cave entrance, as is common in the southeast, a sturdy tree provides a great natural rigpoint. In other cases large, stable boulders can be used. Sometimes, artificial anchors, common in rockclimbing, are the only choice. All artificial anchors, and many natural ones, are less than perfect and require a backup for safety.

Because of the environment of caves may involve flowing water or slippery mud, knots appropriate for other activities may not be suitable for caves. In caves, knots must be strong, easy to see that they are tied properly, and easy to untie. Fortunately, even the most advanced rigging problem can be handled with a few basic knots (Figure 7).

The bowline knot is used for forming a loop in the end of a rope, for attaching to a tree, a carabiner, or anything else. While the bowline is still in

ing the sit-stand approach of frog and Texas methods.

A complex and heavy but efficient method of ascent is termed the "ropewalker" (Figure 6). This technique requires three ascenders, two of which are connected directly to the feet. It allows a natural walking type of motion, completely eliminating arm strain. With this system in gymnasium races, cavers have climbed 100 feet in less than 30 seconds. Despite its efficiency on rope, long rigging and removing times have steered most cavers away from the ropewalker in deep multi-drop caves. Detailed descriptions of all these ascending systems can be found in the references listed at the end of this chapter.

Except for elevators, which are rarely found in caves, all methods of ascending tend to produce fatigue. It is sensible to start with small pitches, on the surface, and then work your way up to multi-drop caves. Pacing is important. A short rest after each stroke is far better than long breaks between sprints.

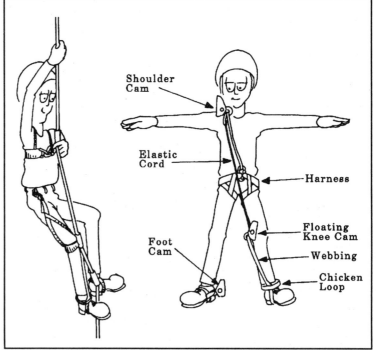

Figure 6—The rope walker ascending system, showing its components. From On Rope, *©National Speleological Society.*

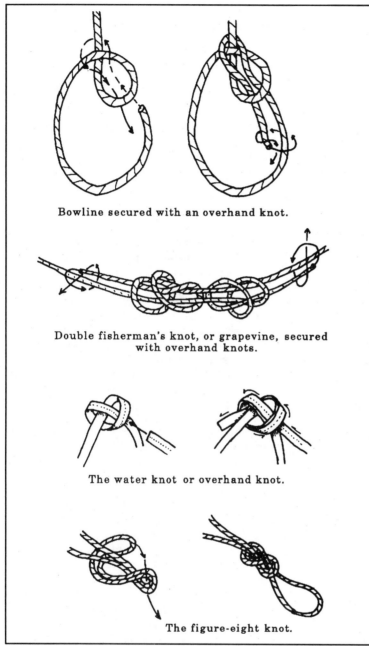

Bowline secured with an overhand knot.

Double fisherman's knot, or grapevine, secured with overhand knots.

The water knot or overhand knot.

The figure-eight knot.

Figure 7 — Basic knots used in caving.

sharp ledges and falling rocks. The rope must be rigged in a place where a rappeller will not dislodge anything. Pits that do not allow a free hang can present advanced rigging problems. Although uncommon in the United States, sometimes an intermediate anchor may be necessary to avoid severe rub points.

Safety Considerations

In addition to good rigging, single rope technique involves consideration of reasonably likely potential problems. From reading novels about caves, you might conclude that bat attacks, snakes, and ropes breaking as you climb hand-over-hand are real concerns. While in reality, ropes must be rigged to avoid cuts and abrasion, these are far more likely causes of problems in single rope technique.

Many accidents have occurred, for instance, because inexperienced riggers allowed a rope to hang in the flow of a waterfall. This is a minor concern during a rappel, which has a very short duration. But ascending—particularly with Prusik knots, or with a poorly "tuned" ascending system—could leave you hanging in the cold for half an hour or more. Without proper equipment that could be catastrophic.

In the dim light of a carbide lamp, several cavers have rappelled right off the end of rope that didn't quite reach the bottom of a pit. A knot in the end would prevent free-fall, and practice and planning would allow a caver in this predicament to return gracefully to the top.

Space does not permit a thorough listing in this chapter of all of the potential hazards and "Plan B" backup procedures associated with single rope technique. But with prior training and practice sessions, thousands of cavers are able to enjoy relatively risk-free vertical caving.

common use, many cavers are switching to the figure-eight knot, which has the same applications. The figure-eight has the advantages of being more easily verified to be correct, and not needing to be backed up with an overhand knot to prevent accidental untying. The water knot (doubled overhand) is generally used for attaching ends of flat webbing together. The double-fishermans knot is used to join two ropes. It has the advantage of working well even if the two ropes are of different diameters.

Serious accidents are possible if rope is allowed to come in contact with sharp edges. This includes

Bibliography

Meredith, Mike & Dan Martinez. 1986. *Vertical Caving*. Dent, Cumbria: Lyons Equipment. 80 pp.

Padgett, Alan & Bruce Smith. 1987. *On Rope*. Huntsville, Alabama, National Spelelogical Society. 341 pp.

Warild, Alan. 1988. *Vertical*. Sydney, Australia: The Speleological Research Council Ltd. 128 pp.

Chapter 17

CAVE CONSERVATION

Mark Laing
NSS 27874

In the last half of this century cavers have started to look upon themselves as stewards of the caves they love. There is no other sport where you can leave a automobile and be in total wilderness within a matter of minutes.

The first time you enter a cave you can either be overwhelmed by its beauty or horrified by the destruction that has been done. Usually the first cave you enter is a heavily traveled one. The effect of this overuse is quite obvious. There is graffiti on the walls and formations are usually broken. The floor may be littered with beer cans and broken glass. Still, most new cavers are fascinated by it and want to learn more about caves and caving.

Here are a few words on the need for conservation and a few ways you can practice these skills.

NSS Conservation Policy

The National Speleological Society is an organization that is dedicated to the exploration, study, and conservation of caves. Many concerned members feel that conservation should be the foremost priority.

On December 28, 1960, the Board of Governors of the Society adopted this policy:

"The National Speleological Society believes: That caves have unique scientific, recreational, and scenic values; That these values are endangered by both carelessness and intentional vandalism; That these values once gone, cannot be recovered; and that the responsibility for protecting caves must be assumed by those who study and enjoy them.

"Accordingly, the intention of the Society is to work for the preservation of caves with a realistic policy supported by effective programs for: the encouragement of self-discipline among cavers; education and research concerning the causes and prevention of cave damage; and special projects, including cooperation with other groups similarly dedicated to the conservation of natural areas. Specifically:

"All contents of a cave-formations, life and loose deposits-are significant for its enjoyment and interpretation. Therefore, caving parties should leave a cave as they find it. They should provide means for the removal of waste; limit marking to a few, small and removable signs as are needed for surveys; and, especially, exercise extreme care not to accidentally break or soil formations, disturb life forms, or unnecessarily increase the number of disfiguring paths through an area.

"Scientific collection is professional, selective, and minimal. The collection of mineral or biological material for display purposes, including previously broken or dead specimens, is never justified, as it encourages others to collect and destroys the interest of the cave.

"The Society encourages projects such as: establishing cave preserves; opposing the sale of speleothems; supporting effective protective measures; cleaning and restoring over-used caves; cooperating with private cave owners by providing knowledge about their cave and assisting them in protecting their cave and property from damage during cave visits; and encouraging commercial cave owners to make use of their opportunity to aid the public in understanding caves and the importance of their conservation.

"Where there is reason to believe that publication of cave locations will lead to vandalism before adequate protection can be established, the Society will oppose such publication.

"It is the duty of every Society member to take personal responsibility for spreading a consciousness of cave conservation to each potential user of caves. Without this, the beauty and value of our caves will not long remain with us."

Conscientious cavers, over the last few years, have developed the "Cave Softly" ethic. No longer is the saying, "Take nothing but pictures; Kill nothing but time; Leave nothing but footprints," appropriate. We must develop the concept that we are interlopers in a cave and that when we leave it, it should be in better shape than when we entered. The next party into the cave should never detect that you were there.

The geology of a cave is a slow process, taking hundreds of thousands of years. The formations you see have withstood the test of time. The destruction of speleothems can undo 10,000 years of growth in a matter of moments.

When traveling inside a cave we should be aware of what's around us. Formations can be broken accidentally by our hardhats because we may fail to realize what's over our heads. Many times caving requires our full concentration to safely negotiate the passage, but we still need to focus attention on the fragile environment around us.

Another hazard to the cave is the touching of still growing formations. The oils left on the formation from your skin can hinder the deposition of calcium carbonate leading to a ruined speleothem. Muddy handprints are not only damaging to formations but also ruin the esthetic beauty that we seek. Sometimes cavers will remove their boots to keep from spoiling the pristine floors they must cross while exploring the cave. Another thing that can be done is stay to a path. Footprints all over an area can be unsightly. Unique speleothems such as calcite rafts, gypsum flowers, angel hair, and cave pearls will have less chance for damage with traffic routed around them.

When laying out the path for the first time, a good idea is to use small pieces of reflective tape on popsicle sticks or pieces of flagging tape on nails. These can be inserted into the dirt on the floor of the cave and still be seen by cavers who follow. Reflective tape can be seen a long distance in a caver's headlamp.

Another consideration is to what extent and what type of hardware is used in a cave. Heavily visited pits where vertical gear is used may have a large number of unnecessary bolts placed in the walls. If possible, use a natural anchor or a bolt that is already placed. Please note that the use of old bolts can be risky; they should be thoroughly inspected before using them.

When placing a rope, be careful to set it so you don't dislodge rocks into the pit. This can damage the cave as well as injure cavers who are below.

Caves contain a unique and rare biological ecosystem. Some of these animals can be readily seen such as bats and cave crickets, others are more elusive and some are not visible to the naked eye. Unknowingly we can destroy the life in the cave.

Bats are usually the most noticeable animals in a cave. Many of them, such as the Myotis Sodalis (Indiana bat), are on the federal endangered species list. Caves that contain colonies of these species should not be entered while the bats are present. Also, some caves have bat hibernaculums (winter hibernation colonies), which should not be entered while the bats are hibernating. When a bat is awakened it uses its stored energy more rapidly and may not survive until spring. Hibernation generally takes place from early September to the end of May. Special care should be taken in caves with maternity colonies where young bats are born and reared in the spring and summer months. Disturbing these colonies can have fatal consequences to the young.

The ecosystem of a cave is very fragile. Dumping carbide and leaving trash can be extremely harmful to the life found inside the cave. Spent carbide is a strong chemical and contains arsenic as an impurity. It is poisonous to cave insects. Trash can upset the balance of the food chain and cause problems. If you carry carbide and food into the cave; you can carry it out. Please don't leave it outside for the owner to clean up either. Take it home and dispose of it properly.

Caves may contain archeological and paleontological artifacts. Early man used the entrances as shelters. A record of his day to day living can be buried in the sediments. Large amounts of bone from the Pleistocene era can also be found in caves. The preservation of this bone is due to the constant climatic conditions found in the cave. While buried, these artifacts can be protected from the footsteps of cavers overhead. Bone and artifacts seen in caves should never be disturbed. If you should happen upon an artifact it should be left where it is found. Record or remember where you saw it and report it to the nearest university or museum. Under no circumstances should you remove the artifact. The relationship of it to others can give clues to the scientist that would be lost if it is disturbed.

In many eastern and southeastern caves, historical artifacts are found. The best example are saltpeter works. These were usually troughs and pipes made of wood used in the making of saltpeter for gunpowder. This wood is usually rotten and could crumble if touched. It's best to view these works from a distance so as not to disturb them. Names written on the walls are considered artifacts by some unthinking people. Age does not change vandalism from graffiti to an artifact. Never write your name on the cave wall hoping that someday it too will be considered historic.

To protect caves you must take an active role in conservation. There are many ways this can be done. Grottos (local chapters of the National Speleological Society) sponsor special projects. These projects include cave clean-ups and restoration trips. Many times, if the cave is heavily damaged, more than one grotto will join in the task.

Many states now have laws to protect caves. A sign at the entrance of a heavily visited cave may help deter vandalism. The sign should spell out the law and the penalties if caught. If your state doesn't have a law, you and your grotto can work on having a law written.

Direct confrontation, while difficult, can have quick results. If, while in the cave, you see an act of vandalism, try to talk to the persons involved and explain how they are hurting the cave. If that doesn't work leave the cave and contact the nearest authorities if your state has a law protecting caves.

The best way to protect caves is through education. This approach may not be quick but in the long run the results will be much better. There are many slide shows and lectures that can be obtained from the National Speleological Society. By educating the public we can change the attitudes they have about caves. Local schools are very receptive to cavers coming in to give a lecture and slide show to their students. Children are the future stewards of our caves.

In conclusion, conservation should be a state of mind, practiced and adhered to in our daily lives. We should know the problems and how to counter them. If the answers are not known, write to the National Speleological Society Conservation Committee or the Conservation Section, they will be glad to help.

Remember: **Cave Softly**.

Chapter 18

LANDOWNER RELATIONS

Bill Tozer
NSS 4955

Most cave trips start with the question of "Where do we go today?" Should we go vertical, horizontal, wet, dry, and oh yes, will the owner let us into his cave? All caves are controlled by someone, whether a state or federal government or a private landowner. The procedure is the same regardless. Often a direct contact the day of the trip is all that is needed. However many government agencies require an advance written request and then a direct interview on the day of the trip. Some private landowners also like notice in advance of the trip, especially if the group is large.

So how do you find out who is the owner? The best approach is to get as much information as possible beforehand. Ask fellow

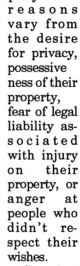

cavers or grottos about the status of the cave. If you know nothing, then ask people near the cave about the ownership. Most owners live at the cave property and absent owners often have their neighbors watch the property. They can give you information about the cave status. Always have alternative caves so your trip won't be ruined if you don't find the owner or fail to obtain permission.

So you found the owner, now what do you do? Well of course, you ask permission to visit HIS cave.

You must persuade him that:

1. You will take care of his property, including the cave.
2. You will not be injured or killed in his cave.
3. He will be assuming NO responsibility for your health and safety when visiting his property.

This is no easy task in just a few minutes. And the actions of previous visitors may have already

influenced him. Why should he take on these problems? It is easy just to say NO!

Contrary to the above, most cave owners will allow you to visit their caves. They are friendly, like to talk about their cave, and are happy that people think their cave is important. Many of these landowners grew up on farms and naturally welcome strangers. Yes, you do run into some who absolutely do not want anyone on their property. Their reasons vary from the desire for privacy, possessiveness of their property, fear of legal liability associated with injury on their property, or anger at people who didn't respect their wishes.

So what is a person supposed to do? Ask permission . . . The worst that could happen is they will say no. Thank them for their time and accept it. On one particular trip the owner gave the "Absolutely NO!" answer. And his wife shouted, "If you go into the cave, we will call the sheriff." Not a pleasant experience but just down the road was a friendly reception. "Come in and have something to drink before you go to the cave." So be polite regardless of the pressure, the next owner will surely be more friendly.

If you get the "No" answer in a friendly way, then all is not lost. Depending on his reasons and your behavior, you may still get into the cave sometime. So continue to be polite and respectful for there will be another day.

Of course if you get a "Yes," then ask where would be a good place to park the car and remember: you need to get away from the house to change clothes. Most people do not like to see cavers in their underwear in the yard. So be respectful; park where he directs and if necessary carry the clean clothes into the woods for changing. Never block a gate unless directed to do so by the owner. He may change his mind and need access, so try to keep the gate open regardless. Ask the best way to the cave. The owner will usually direct the route of least peril for livestock, fences, and cavers. He may even allow you to drive back to the cave.

The rules for gates are simple. Leave them **exactly** as you find them. If open, keep them open; if closed, keep them closed. Crossing fences should be done with **NO** stress on the fence. Slipping between barbed wire strands does little damage — but climbing on wire fences will destroy the wire. If it breaks because of many cavers, then someone must do the work of replacing it. The landowner may tire of the trouble and close the cave.

Let the owner know about how long you will be in the cave and estimate on the long side in case you find that "new discovery." He may want you to stop by on the way out or he may wish to be left alone. Talk to him about it and follow his lead. If, on leaving, you see him then be sure to tell him how much you enjoyed the visit and thank him. A little public relations now will make it easier to get into the cave in the future.

When you leave his property be sure to take everything with you. Nothing should be left behind, not even a scrap of paper or carbide residue. The National Speleological Society's Motto: "Take nothing but pictures, leave nothing but footprints, and kill nothing but time," applies on the surface as well as in the cave. The cave, the path, the area around the car, the fences, and anything else you can think of should be in the same condition when you leave as it was when you arrived. Some little thing you think won't make any difference may be important to the owner.

Keys to Success

How do you successfully obtain permission? Some owners will give permission to anyone, regardless. However, most are particular when it comes to giving permission. They look at you and your party and try to decide if you are responsible, careful, and considerate. They don't have much information other than what they see and hear as you talk to them. Their past experience with cavers certainly does influence their decision.

The key is to have everything possible on your side. That means to remove any potentially offensive factors. You need to make yourself neutral. Maybe he wouldn't care if you are still muddy from the last cave, or you swear at his dog, or you toss your drink cans in his yard. And maybe he would . . .

So dress in clean, respectable clothes and comb your hair. If the dog barks at you, talk to it in a friendly tone. Remember the owner will judge you by what you say, even to his dog. Speak clearly, don't look at the ground and mumble. Eye contact is important. Look at the owner and smile. It pays to be humble, but the owner wants to see confidence, sincerity, and honesty. These are best transmitted by a friendly smile and eye contact.

Timing is also important. Choose a reasonable time to approach the owner, especially if you don't know him. Avoid early Sunday morning or any day after sunset.

Sometimes little things can trigger a negative response. For instance, sunglasses seem to be hiding the eyes. Don't wear them. Don't wear a hat down over the eyes either. Cigarettes in the pocket may mean nothing to some people but a non-smoker may be turned off by it. The people in the car are not out of the picture either. Turn off radios and music. This portrays an image which might offend the owner. The passengers in the car should keep to quiet respectful conversation.

Alcohol should neither be displayed nor consumed on the owner's property. More than tobacco, alcohol implies drunken people and the associated irresponsibility. An owner tells how he went down there and they were drinking! The alcohol immediately implies an irresponsible, careless, and undesirable person. It makes no difference if there is only one beer. The image is there. Don't display or drink alcohol on the cave property.

Generally, it is best to send just one person to talk to the owner. Two or three people can be overwhelming. Knock on the door and step back. This is less threatening and helps the people relax. (Some people will not answer the door to a stranger. So make it easy and safe for them.) If someone is outside, approach them calling "Hello" before you get too close. This alerts them to your presence, eliminating any surprise.

Once contact is made, start slowly. Give them your name and start a conversation. You might begin like this:

"Hello, my name is (＿＿＿＿＿＿). I'm interested in a cave over there (indicate the direction). I understand the cave is on your property."

(It is important to get some response from the owner in order to gauge how he feels about this. If he is friendly, then ask about the cave. If he talks then you have started the friendship which could well lead to permission. If his response is short then you need to start building his confidence in you.)

"I understand the cave is very pretty. (Or that it goes a long way to a big room.)"

(Still little or no response. Then you need to come out and ask directly for permission.)

"I was wondering if it would be alright to go into the cave?"

(Most likely he will start talking if your answer is no. Most people will say they "don't want anybody to go in the cave." then proceed to give some reason, such as safety.)

"I understand your concern. I assure you I have no desire to do anything dangerous. I've been caving for some time and have visited many caves in the area."

Be honest and don't brag. If the cave is vertical, talk about your equipment.

More than once, an owner at first said "No." Then after talking a little changed his mind. Each situation is different and there is no set speech to follow. Just be friendly and talk. If you get them to talk then follow their lead. Address their concerns and assure them you will follow their wishes. **And of course follow their wishes to the letter!** Some people have things to do and don't want to talk for an hour. If they seem to be busy, then come directly to the point and don't belabor the conversation. If they want to talk a little, then talk.

And never assume the man is in charge. Talk to both men and women with equal respect. One owner heard the word "cave" and went into a cussing and shouting rage then stomped out of the room. His wife was so embarrassed she apologized for him and started to talk. Shortly, she went into the other room and retrieved him. After a little friendly exchange and two return trips to his home with some pictures, he gave permission to visit the cave.

If this all seems to be directed to the private owner, remember, you must deal with **people** at the state and federal properties. The same rules apply. Public land does not mean you are automatically entitled to visit the cave. Some caves on public land don't require permission. However, many require permission to enter and others are permanently closed. The government managers are entrusted to do the same thing that private owners do—protect the property, including the caves, and ensure that the people entering the caves can do so safely. They ask the same questions and you need to answer them. Do not assume you have a right to enter the cave because it is on public land.

Some negatives for owners are the people who go into the cave or onto the property without permission. They also point to the downed fences and litter along the road or near the cave. The lost glove or sock was not intended, but it sure looks bad lying on the ground. Many owners are seriously concerned about damage to the cave and formations. Even owners who never enter the cave are concerned. They also are very sensitive to the question of legal liability.

Show caves present another challenge. It is easy to obtain permission to take the guided trip; just pay your money. However that is about all you can expect. The liability risks are great for the commercial cave owner, which prevents exploration on your own. If you take the tour, leave the guides alone. They entertain by telling some "interesting stories" for their visitors. Don't feel you need to set them straight. Doing so will only create hard feelings. Many commercial cave guides are cavers too. A friendly conversation **after** the tour could yield information on other caves of the area.

Why are landowner relations a "Caving Basic"? The cave you are going to visit has been visited by countless people before you. You are able to visit the cave because most of these people have practiced good cave owner relations. You have the responsibility to promote the same good relations so that you and others can continue to visit this cave. We have little to offer the cave owner other than full cooperation and lots of appreciation. Offer him some pictures of the cave or send him a thank you card. If you offer pictures, **send them!** At least one cave has been closed because a caver forgot his promises. Some grottos and cavers regularly send Christmas cards to cave owners, a small but appreciated thank you.

There are many caves who don't really think of the landowner. They contribute to the problem of landowner relations. We can't control these people but maybe we can do a little extra. Pick up some trash you didn't leave and help the landowner if you can.

Don't practice good owner relations and the angry owner may dynamite the entrance, gate it, or greet you with threats of a shotgun and arrest. Take good care of the landowner and he will take good care of you!

Remember: **One owner crossed up, One cave crossed off.**

Chapter 19

RISK MANAGEMENT
FOR CAVERS AND CAVE OWNERS

Joel B. Stevenson
NSS 14246

Civil liability for personal injury and wrongful death is a complex subject. This chapter attempts only a general discussion of the theory and the application of such liability in contemporary American law. The discussion is necessarily both general and superficial. It is intended for an audience of nonlawyers spread across the fifty American states, each of which has its own distinct jurisprudence. The law in each of these fifty separate jurisdictions is subject to change, sometimes to drastic change, at each session of the state legislature and on each day that the appellate courts sit for the dispatch of their business. This chapter can, in no way, serve as a substitute for a lawyer or legal advice. It can, only at best, help you recognize situations of potential liability and furnish you with the components of a system to help manage those situations.

In Appendix B are found several forms, including releases, that can be reproduced and used in attempts to reduce and control potential liability. These forms are strongly worded and make their intent as clear as language will allow. They have been adapted from various forms that have been developed and used in various parts of the United States over the past ten years. Although these forms are designed to afford the maximum protection to the caver and to the landowner who seek to avoid liability, you must remember that no legal document is entirely and universally effective and the use of these forms does not guarantee the avoidance of liability. They may or may not be effective under the law of your particular jurisdiction, and the advice of counsel is advised in regard to the use of any of the appended forms.

Contemporary America is a society that litigates. Our courts, over the past 30 years, have expanded the scope of civil liability for personal injury, and the awards of juries have increased at least as sharply as has inflation. Although the scope and the cost of liability has expanded, and despite the fact that there are differences, sometimes substantial differences, among the fifty American jurisdictions, the basic principles upon which liability is imposed have remained the same for generations. The branch of law that deals with claims for wrongful death or injury to persons or property is called the Law of Tort. The concept of tort is so general that no inclusive definition has ever been successfully fashioned by any court; but, for the purposes of this discussion, a tort can be defined as:

A civil wrong, arising from a breach of duty, for which the law will provide a remedy.

In the following pages, we will examine the basic rules of tort liability and will discuss how they can be used as guidelines for the reduction or elimination of civil liability in the context of cave exploration and cave ownership.

Liability in tort can be based either upon intentional acts or omissions or upon negligent acts or omissions. Intentional torts, such as assault or defamation, are outside the scope of this chapter, which is concerned only with the liability that can be incurred for negligent acts or omissions.

There is no rigid or specific definition of "negligence" in its legal sense. Legal negligence is simply the failure to use reasonable care to avoid causing injury to someone to whom a duty of reasonable care is owed. In any situation, if you can determine what constitutes reasonable care and if you can ascertain to whom a duty of reasonable care is owed, you will have analyzed that situation from a standpoint of potential tort liability and you will have identified those things which you need to do to control or eliminate the potential for liability.

In order to be fair to all, the law must have consistency from one case to another. This requires a uniform standard which can be applied in any conceivable case and which will produce predictable and replicable results. There is an infinite possibility of different fact situations and a policy of pigeonhole categories and specific rules would be unworkable because of size and complexity.

The solution that has been developed by the courts is a fictitious standard against which all conduct is measured. This fictitious standard is known as "the Reasonable Man of Ordinary Prudence." The Reasonable Man has been described as "a model of all proper qualities, with only those human shortcomings and weaknesses which the community will tolerate on occasion." The Reasonable Man is not infallible, but his only errors are those unavoidable by careful planning.

The standard to which each of us is held is simply to act as the Reasonable Man would act under the circumstances as they appear to him at the time. The standard has the flexibility to fit any case which might arise. The conduct of the Reasonable Man will vary with the circumstances with which he is confronted. If the Reasonable Man has superior knowledge or training, he will be required to utilize that superior knowledge or training in conforming his actions to the circumstances. Likewise, if the situation involved increased danger or risk of injury, the Reasonable Man will conform his conduct to that greater risk of danger. If the Reasonable Man is aware of an unguarded elevator shaft he will give warning. If he is involved in blasting operations he will remove people from the area, post lookouts, and take other steps to prevent injury or damage. If the Reasonable Man is aware that children are in an area he will increase his lookout, decrease the speed of his automobile, or take other steps to compensate for children's known propensity to not take care of themselves.

If a danger is not reasonably foreseeable, the Reasonable Man is not required to anticipate the danger or to guard against it. For example, the reasonable proprietor of a motel in which there has never been a criminal assault is not required to foresee that there might possibly be one. If, however, the motel had a history of multiple criminal assaults on guests, the Reasonable Man would take steps to increase security.

This does not mean that ignorance of danger is a universal defense. Intentionally remaining ignorant, as for example, by failing to investigate land for hidden dangers (when there is a duty to warn) would be no defense in an action for failure to warn. In cases involving enhanced risk there is a duty to acquire the knowledge necessary to recognize the dangers involved. It has been held, for example, that the operator of a Ferris wheel cannot successfully defend an action brought after the wheel collapsed by pleading that he had no knowledge of the phenomenon of metal fatigue.

It is the duty of the landowner or land manager or the leader of an organized cave trip to provide against dangers which can, in the exercise of reasonable care, be discovered.

The courts and the commentators speak separately of "duty" and "foreseeability." These are merely components of the Reasonable Man standard, not separate or additional standards to which a manager is held.

Duty can arise in two ways. It may arise by operation of law, that is, through the enactment of statutes or by the decisions of courts. Duty can also arise when it is voluntarily assumed. The act of undertaking to fence the edge of a precipice, for example, is the assumption of the duty to provide a reasonably safe and secure fence.

If the duty is discharged with the perfection of the Reasonable Man (nothing else appearing) this will constitute an absolute defense to an action at law.

Foreseeability is that element of tort law which keeps liability within acceptable bounds. In general, if a consequence is not reasonably foreseeable, it does not give rise to liability. In other words, if the Reasonable Man would not foresee injury, there is then no legal duty to provide against such injury. Conversely, if the Reasonable Man could foresee the injury, the fact that a conscientious and competent manager fails to foresee it offers no defense. The warning here is that courts, judges, and juries have 20-20 hindsight.

The duty that will be owed will vary with the circumstances. The more important circumstances include the legal status of the person involved, whether or not children are involved, the nature of the danger to be guarded against, and what is physically (and, to a far lesser extent, economically) reasonable.

In the context of caving, we are concerned with three situations, each of which has its own distinctive liability potential. We are concerned with the liability which can arise from cave ownership, that which can result from organized caving activities, and with our own potential liability as cavers ourselves. The basic concepts discussed in this chapter are equally applicable to each situation.

Traditionally, in the common law, the ownership, use, or management of land gives rise to certain duties that are owed to those who come onto the land. The legal status of the person coming onto the land will therefore define the minimum duty owed by the landowner to that person.

The first classification is that of the trespasser. The duty owed to a trespasser is simply the duty not to willfully injure him. This duty not to willfully injure includes a duty not to set traps which would cause injury to the trespasser. There is no duty to warn the trespasser of dangerous conditions existing on the land and there is no duty to modify the land in order to make it safe for trespassers. There are, of course, exceptions to these broad rules. Frequent known and tolerated trespassers may be owed the same duty as licensees. For example, where trespassers wear a trail across a portion of land and no steps are taken to prevent continued use of the trail, some additional duties may become due to those trespassers and it would be prudent, for planning purposes, to look upon them as licensees. In the states which still recognize the doctrine of attractive nuisance, children attracted onto the land are not, strictly speaking, treated as trespassers.

The second classification of persons entering onto land is that of the licensee. A licensee is one who enters land with permission of the owner but not for benefit to the owner. There is a duty to warn licensees of known dangers on the land. There is no duty on the part of the landowner to inspect the land and discover unknown dangers in order to warn of them. There is no duty on the part of the landowner to modify the land and put it in safe condition for the benefit of the visiting licensee. The permission to enter which confers the status of licensee can either be direct or implied.

The third class of persons who enter onto the land of another are invitees. Invitees are those who enter with the permission of the owner for purposes beneficial to the owner. A paying tourist in a campground would be an invitee as would a customer in the business of a park concessionaire. It is possible that one who enters a wild cave on park land for the purpose of mapping the cave could be an invitee, if the park authority receives the benefit of the resulting map.

The duties which the landowner owes an invitee include the duty to warn of unsafe conditions, the duty to use reasonable care to inspect and discover dangerous conditions, and the duty to take reasonable steps to put the land in safe condition.

Children, whatever their legal classification while on the land, are owed a higher duty than is owed to adults. The reasons for this are twofold and obvious. Children cannot be expected to appreciate danger with the same discernment as adults and children are neither physically nor mentally as able to take care of themselves as are adults.

Because of the special and peculiar circumstances which children present, the courts developed the doctrine of attractive nuisance. The doctrine was developed to allow recovery by children who were injured while trespassing on the land of another. The theory conclusively presumes that the child is attracted by something on the land. Originally, this had to be something created by the landowner, the classic examples being quarries, railroad turntables, and artificial farm ponds.

Most American jurisdictions have abandoned the doctrine of attractive nuisance in favor of an even broader new rule which is based upon foreseeable consequences. Basically, this rule affirms that children can be expected to meddle, to use poor judgment, and to explore. The fact that a child is involved in the particular circumstance makes special dangers foreseeable. The standard of the Reasonable Man is then applied and acceptable conduct is determined to be that conduct in which the Reasonable Man would have engaged under similar circumstances involving like children.

The traditional distinctions of trespasser, licensee, and invitee are, to some extent, being blurred by the courts. More and more often, especially in cases where strict application of the traditional approach would lead to a harsh result, courts are applying the Reasonable Man standard to the acts and omissions of landowners. Undoubtedly this trend will continue and little, if any, reliance should

be placed on defenses that depend solely on the status of the injured party, especially if the injury was reasonably foreseeable.

As the courts develop this approach, the distinctions of trespasser, licensee, and invitee will tend to become more an element of foreseeability and not the controlling element of the case. The prudent owner or manager can no longer rely solely on traditional distinctions of status.

The duties and the potential liability of the owner of an unimproved wild cave for which admission is not charged is sharply different than the liability of a commercial cave operator. The potential liability of show cave operations is beyond the scope of this chapter. Duties and liabilities arising from the exploration of the "wild" portions of commercial caves are substantially the same as for unimproved caves.

There is no way that a landowner can totally avoid all possible liability, Even if he simply forbids entry into a cave, a trespasser could enter, receive injury, and demand compensation. Blasting the entrance shut, or putting a gate on it does not guarantee that entry will not, nevertheless, be made. It is not far fetched to imagine a scenario where rescue efforts could be hampered or injury made worse by such modifications. Probably the best solution to the liability enigma from the landowners' point of view is a simple management plan which would include some policy for limiting use of the cave, a means of informing cave users of known dangers, and the requirement of the reading and signing of a strongly worded liability release by all visitors.

A release, sometimes called a waiver, is basically a contract where the caver, in exchange for the right to enter the cave, sells to the landowner the caver's right to sue for injury received in the cave. The most important thing to remember about a release is that it is not always effective, although several recent cases have upheld well drafted releases and thereby barred recovery for SCUBA related diving injuries. As indicated, a release is a contract and it must, therefore, be supported by consideration. The consideration should not be money because, in most jurisdictions, that could constitute the caver an invitee and would place the landowner under a higher duty to him. The consideration in exchange for which the permission is given should be the release of the right to sue and nothing more. In some jurisdictions it may still be necessary to recite a nominal consideration, usually one dollar.

A simple blanket discharge for any and all negligently inflicted injury would probably not be effective if it became the subject of a court challenge. It is imperative that the release contain language indicating that the landowner has advised the caver of specific known dangers, that the caver is aware of these dangers and of the general dangers involved in caving, that he understands and accepts those dangers, and that he is knowingly exchanging his right to sue for injury for the right to legally enter the cave.

If a release has any significant chance of being enforced by the courts, it must be clearly written and it must appear, from the document itself, that the parties agreed and understood their transaction at the time it was made. The document will be construed against the party drafting it, usually the landowner, and it is to that party's benefit to avoid any ambiguity in the language of the release. At all costs "legalese" should be avoided entirely.

Because a release is a contract, it can only be effective if it is entered into by a person who is capable of contracting. A release signed by a minor (in most jurisdictions, anyone under 18 years of age), or by one who is mentally incompetent, will have no legal effect. Whenever it is necessary to obtain a release from a minor, the release should be signed by both parents of the minor or, in appropriate cases, by the guardian of the minor. The signature of one parent may or may not be sufficient to effect a release of possible claims. This will vary from jurisdiction to jurisdiction and will also vary with the facts of the individual case. The better practice therefore, is to require the signatures of both parents when attempting to release the rights of a minor.

Usually, in situations involving a minor, the courts, if they are called upon to construe a release, will view the language of the release very narrowly and will, wherever possible, interpret the document to allow recovery by the minor. For this reason, careful draftsmanship, which is always important, is absolutely imperative for documents which may be executed on behalf of a minor.

The signature of the minor should also be required on the release. Although the signature is of no contractual effect, it can be used to show that the minor was actually aware of the risks and dangers involved in cave exploration and this can, in many cases, furnish a defense—contributory negligence or assumption of the risk—in the event that a claim is made.

It bears repeating that, as in the case of any other release, the parents or guardian of a minor and the minor who signs the document, must all be required to read the document they are signing and it is absolutely imperative that the document be drafted so as to be understandable. No release will be legally effective if it is not understood by the parties entering into it.

The effectiveness of any release can be greatly improved by including additional legal theories. The theory of joint venture has been utilized in the context of caving related releases for a number of years. Members of a joint venture enjoy a degree of immunity from liability to one another. The legal theory is that each member of the venture is the agent of the other and that the negligence of each is imputed to each. In most jurisdictions four elements are necessary to constitute a joint venture. First, it must arise from a contract. A release, properly worded, would be a sufficient contract. Second, all of the members of the joint venture must have a common purpose. The purpose of exploring a given cave, or engaging in a given caving trip or cave project, would be a sufficient common purpose. Third, there must be what the courts call a "community of interest." This means that each of the members of the joint venture must have some real stake or interest in the outcome of the joint venture. Fourth, there must be an equal right of control, that is, each member of the joint venture must be given the right, whether it is exercised or not, to have a voice in all decisions.

Clearly, members of a cave trip or of a survey project can meet the four requirements of a joint venture. Whether or not a landowner can, unless he becomes a caver, enjoy this additional protection is not as obvious. The requirement of a "community of interest" is where this problem would usually arise. In most instances, the landowner will not engage in the cave exploration and will not have any great interest in the exploration of his cave. If it can be shown that there is a legitimate interest on the part of the landowner, such as an interest in learning about possible water resources, then the "community of interest" requirement could probably be satisfied. It would seem that the requirement of an equal right of control could be met in the average situation where the landowner always has the right to forbid further entry into the cave and where the cavers are not subject to being dispatched into the cave against their will by the landowner.

The joint venture theory can, in some situations, increase rather that reduce exposure to liability. For example, if a landowner is included in the joint venture, he may incur liability of some sort to third parties for acts of the other members of the joint venture. Although the inclusion of a joint venture theory may greatly enhance the effectiveness of a release, it should never be utilized without the advice of an attorney familiar with the laws of the jurisdiction in which the release will be used. The risks of unintended consequences are simply too great to attempt to use this device without qualified legal advice.

Another legal doctrine that can afford additional protection against potential liability is the doctrine known as assumption of the risk. The basis of this doctrine is that when someone assumes for himself a specific risk he thereby relieves others of the duty to protect him from that risk and they then owe him no duty as to the risk that is assumed. In any situation where no duty is owed, there is no liability consequence because the element of duty is essential to the existence of liability.

To cause an assumption of a risk, the parties must recognize an identifiable risk to be assumed and that risk must specifically be assumed by the party who undertakes it. The assumption of the risk should be supported by consideration. It would, under most circumstances, be sufficient to simply refer to the consideration for the release.

Other principles, which are of lesser value, but which may nevertheless afford some additional protection, include a covenant not to sue and an agreement for indemnification. The covenant not to sue is not a release. It is contract not to bring an action in the event of injury. It discourages litigation because the plaintiff may be liable for the costs of the defense of the liability lawsuit in a separate action for breach of contract. Because the covenant not to sue is a contract, it must have a specific reference to consideration.

The concept of indemnification is also borrowed from the law of contracts. It is a contract to pay damages recovered by a third party. If "A" contracts with "B" to repay "B" whatever amount of damages "C" might recover in a lawsuit, "A" has entered into a contract of indemnification with "B." Like any other contract, a contract of indemnification would require specific consideration. Obviously, a contract of indemnification is of no value if the agreeing party is not solvent.

At common law a tort claimant was required to be free of fault in order to obtain a recovery. This concept is known as the doctrine of contributory negligence and it bars any recovery as a matter of law if there is any negligence, no matter how slight, on the part of the claimant. Because of the harsh results that often resulted from application of the doctrine of contributory negligence, it has been abandoned by the overwhelming majority of American jurisdictions. It has been replaced by the concept of comparative negligence in which a claimant's recovery is reduced by the proportion of fault attributable to him. In some jurisdictions the doctrine of comparative negligence has been held to have abrogated or modified other defensive doctrines, such as assumption of the risk.

The concepts discussed here can be of great value in managing the risk of liability, but the primary tool of the land owner, manager or caver who wishes to limit liability exposure to acceptable levels must be the implementation of the Reasonable Man standard into the cave management or cave trip plan. Some specific suggestions follow, but no listing can be complete. In the final analysis the manager and the caver must develop the attitude and the outlook of the Reasonable Man their interaction with the cave.

The landowner or trip leader should never require the caver to demonstrate his ability, as in requiring him to demonstrate his ability to rappel, or to place artificial aid. If the cave manager or trip leader engages in judging such demonstrations, he is, if effect, judging the competence of the caver to perform the demonstrated activity and is passing judgment upon whether the demonstrated level of skill is sufficient for safe traverse of the cave. The liability potential of this should be obvious. The prudent manager will require the caver to demonstrate experience and will probably want to take a written history from the caver in order to avoid, as much as possible, passing judgment on skill levels, The manager should adopt written criteria for cavers wishing to enter the cave. These should be simple, non-judgemental and realistic. A manager with responsibility for a vertical cave might develop criteria that would include, for example, three years of vertical caving experience and the successful completion of ten vertical caving trips involving pitches of 70 feet or more. If the manager goes beyond a general screening criteria such as this, he runs the risk that he can be found to have certified the competence of the caver.

Likewise, neither the manager nor the trip leader should give an opinion regarding specific caving gear. A specific brand or generic type of gear should not be recommended or required. At the other extreme, the manager cannot allow a caver to enter the cave with obviously inadequate gear, or with gear that is clearly worn to the point of unreliability. This is an area of fine distinctions and the manager must develop not only a real understanding of the Reasonable Man concept, but also a genuine expertise about technical caving and climbing gear. The successful manager will know what types of equipment are generally considered to be unsafe or inadequate. He will then require those whom he allows to enter the cave to use gear which generally falls within the class of gear that is accepted in the caving community. As in the case of caving skills, the manager should never allow himself to certify the adequacy of cave equipment.

As a general rule, artificial climbing aids should never be provided by the manager or owner. If an artificial anchor or similar aid is provided and if it fails, causing injury, a lawsuit is almost inevitable. For this reason, artificial climbing aids or rigging anchors should only be provided when the risk of injury from not providing them is high. As example of this would be a situation involving a deep pit where there are no good natural anchors and there are numerous unsafe natural anchors. In that situation, the best risk management decision might well be to provide the best possible artificial anchor system, design sufficient redundancy into the system, and to inspect it carefully and regularly. Except for such extreme situations, artificial climbing and rope-rigging aids should not be provided. In this respect, when artificial anchors are provided by cavers who are not associated with the cave owner or manager, there is very little risk to the owner until the aid has been in the cave long enough to have become generally accepted by visiting cavers. At that point, the manager may have unwittingly adopted the artificial aid and may be responsible for its maintenance. For this reason, a strict prohibition against the placing of permanent anchors is probably a wise rule.

In summary, a landowner, in determining who will be allowed to enter his wild cave, should never pass judgment on the question of whether or not the caver is competent. The landowner should not, in any way, indicate that the caver has the ability to attempt the exploration of the cave. Rather, he should require that the caver demonstrate that he has the requisite skill or experience to enter the cave. The landowner should never certify the caver, but should make the caver certify himself to the landowner.

The leader of a caving trip will generally not be in a position to take this approach. He will, in all probability, know the skill level of all members or the party, and if he does not, then he is almost surely in violation of his duty to the party. He will owe a special duty of care to inexperienced members of the caving party. The trip leader must limit his liability by being willing to prohibit participation in a trip by cavers who clearly do not have the required skills, by clearly explaining the nature of the trip and the inherent risks during the early planning stages, and by insisting that the grotto or other organization have a proper training program.

In general, a landowner or cave manager should avoid any modification to the entrance or to the passageways of a so-called "wild" or unimproved cave. Anytime a modification is undertaken, a duty arises to see that the modification is done with all reasonable care. If a modified entrance collapses causing injury, the liability situation is probably much worse than if an unmodified entrance had collapsed. Any modifications that are done should not be done haphazardly, but with due consideration for the engineering principles that are involved. If the owner or cave manager does not have access to the expertise needed to make modifications in a sound manner, then the modifications should not be attempted. These considerations would also apply to individual cavers.

There are two primary exceptions to the prohibition against modifying the cave. One is for situations where there is obvious danger from the natural situation. If, for example, there is a large, unstable boulder over the entrance, prudent management policy would require removal of the boul-

der. The cautions given in the preceding paragraph to consider the engineering principles involved would, of course, still apply.

The second situation would be modification of the cave entrance, or of a specific passage, by the erection of a gate. A gate, properly designed, can be an effective tool in limiting liability. Gates present many potential liability problems and no gate should be erected without giving consideration to all of the potential liability problems that can flow from such a modification. The gate must be securely anchored to the cave walls so that it cannot be pulled loose to fall on a trespasser who is trying to breach the gate. The bar spacing must be proper so that the risk of a child becoming stuck in the bars is avoided. The door to the cave gate must be of sufficient dimension to allow passage of a litter in the event of an injury requiring evacuation.

Impediments meant to retard entry must be carefully considered and usually should be avoided altogether. If they are going to be effective, they will probably fall into the category of traps, the liability consequences of which are obvious. For this reason, industrial fences, or fences of any type, should be considered only as a last resort as a means of controlling access to caves. The standard industrial fence has barbed wire at the top to impede entry. The barbed wire can be considered a trap or an instrument intended to injure and can have serious liability consequences. If no barbed wire or other impediment is at the top of the fence, then the fence is so easily breached that its value is questionable. Generally, when access should be restricted, it should be restricted by a full orifice gate. State of the art information regarding cave gating practices can be obtained from the Conservation Committee of the National Speleological Society.

The responsibility borne by cave owners and cave managers in regard to potential liability cannot be delegated or transferred by them. If, for example, a cave owner turns over the management of a cave to a group of cavers, he does not thereby escape liability. From a management point of view, there are numerous advantages to including the caving community in the management of wild caves, but from a liability standpoint, the owner or the manager must retain the ultimate direction of the outside group in order to retain control of the risk management duties discussed in this chapter.

These concepts of risk management have been employed in industry for decades. Potential liability is an aspect of land ownership that is not unique to cavernous lands. All lands carry the potential for liability, and all lands, including cave and karst lands, can be safely and productively used with a minimum of risk if a comprehensive management plan is used to assess and address situations of potential liability.

Chapter 20

READING CAVE MAPS

Langford G. Brod, Jr
NSS 5329

Introduction

Cave maps are somewhat like road maps in that they depict a geometrical arrangement of routes and features in a cave. Some cave maps will show a single passageway, much like a highway traversing a sparsely-populated area; other maps of more complex caves will show multiple interconnections, somewhat resembling a network of city streets. All of these maps give some idea to the reader of how the explorer can travel through the cave, what routes he can follow. However, only a small percentage of cave maps are made with the express purpose of displaying a route and most of these maps have been prepared for commercial caves. Most cave maps are produced by unpaid cave surveyors for their own purposes.

Probably the greatest number of cave maps are prepared specifically for the purpose of determining the relationship of rooms and passages with each other and with surface features. Such maps will reveal potential connections between adjacent passages or even between separate caves, assuming both caves have been mapped and the relative positions of their entrances is accurately known. There is a thrill and a sense of discovery associated with the map preparation. First in seeing the skeletal development of the survey lines as they are laid out line by line, next in seeing the fleshing out of the map as walls and details are added, and finally laying this completed segment on the main map and properly orienting it. Suddenly, that large,

blank area on the main map is no longer blank; there is now a passage in that space, filling in the blank area with unforeseen detail. Your just-completed large side passage isn't at all heading in the direction you thought it was going. No, it's heading more easterly, nearer the main passage. You check the alignment to see if the segment has shifted. No, it's good; the alignment is correct. Suddenly, you see a verification: the previously-mapped, tiny side passage with a small stream is only a few feet away from the terminal room of your just-completed side passage—that's where the waterfall runoff is going! You have a sense of satisfaction; two previously unrelated hydrologic features are now united and you know the map is right. This insight is the payoff, the reason that cave surveyors labor under cold, dirty, poorly lighted conditions for no pay to survey a cave, to make a map.

Thus, in reading a cave map, one must bear in mind that the map is, for the surveyor, a highly personal creation and, within the limits of permissible variation allowed by the cave map format, is a product of his own personal creative biases. Features of little general interest may be shown, while other information of more importance may be omitted. Alternatively, such additions and omissions may not necessarily reflect the surveyor's bias, but may represent a regional standard followed by all the mappers in a certain locality. Names of features in the cave, of little or no significance to the casual reader, may evoke deep feelings in the surveying crew and others familiar with the cave, especially if the cave is a challenge. To these cavers, the names bring back memories of campsites; crises; pinnacles of achievement; milestones of penetration; or, in less frequent instances, a breakthrough into virgin passage. Notable exceptions are provided by those cases where the map is accompanied by an account of the exploration and surveying, such as in the case of Jewel Cave (*The Jewel Cave Adventure* by Herb and Jan Conn) and the Flint Ridge-Mammoth connection (*The Longest Cave* by Roger Brucker and Richard Watson). There is a growing number of such publications and, hopefully, many of the larger caves will be similarly documented in the future.

In addition to the personal bias of the surveyor, there are a number of drafting styles. Despite the restrictions imposed by the cave map format, individual styles and techniques are evident. Furthermore, there is a great variety in the quality of the maps, depending on various factors such as the size of the cave, its complexity, the surveying difficulties encountered, and the survey leader. As a consequence, maps range in quality from rough sketch maps to precise and highly detailed cave cartography. It should not be inferred that less detailed or less accurate maps are necessarily inferior. There is no formal standard of excellence to which all maps must comply. Whether or not the map pleases the reader is a secondary consideration; the primary question is: did the map serve the purpose intended by the person who drew it? All cave maps should be observed with this question in mind rather than a critical appraisal of style or technique.

The Various Views

Cave maps are drawn in three principal views: the "plan view," the "profile view," and the "cross section" (Figure 3). If we imagine the cave to be a straight horizontal tube, the plan view will correspond to an outline of the cave in the horizontal plane, as viewed directly from above. The profile view is an outline of the cave in the vertical plane as viewed from the side, while the cross section is an outline of the cave passage viewed end on. Thus the three views in this case correspond to three slices taken through the cave in three mutually perpendicular planes.

Actual caves are much more complex and are seldom linear or horizontal; consequently, the maps differ from the simplistic explanation given above. Though not horizontal, many caves dip at low inclination angles and are approximately horizontal. Rather than showing an outline along the actual floor, the plan view in this case is a projection of the cave passage onto the horizontal plane and tilted features are slightly foreshortened.

Similarly, profiles may consist of projections of the cave passage into a vertical plane generally parallel to the passage. Frequently, because of bends in the passage, it is impractical to project into a single vertical plane; in this case, the profile is made up of a series of short profiles strung together to form a single profile. The bends where the profile segments join may be marked or unmarked, depending on the preference of the map draftsman. In some instances, the profile is not a vertical projection but a trace of the ceiling and floor along a particular plane, most often along the station line which serves as the skeleton upon which the plan view measurements are made. Frequently, there is little difference between the two methods; in cases where there is a difference, features out of the plane are shown with dashed lines. Some mappers show entering side passages in a quasi-pictorial style on the profile, with the actual side passage shape shown in solid black. Of course, the profile can be drawn from either side of the main passage and the correct view must be chosen so that the side passage appears in the background.

Section views are generally shown as an outline formed by the intersection of the cave passage with an arbitrary section plane. The section plane is generally vertical and is usually roughly perpendicular to the axis of the passage, but not always. Cave passages in some cases are so irregular that an axis is undefinable. In other cases, such as a large room, it may be more feasible to take the section along the length of the room, similar to a profile view. In general, however, sections are taken across the passage, more or less perpendicular to the long dimension.

The alignment of the section plane is shown on the plan view by a line, either continuous across the passage or broken in the middle. In most cases, this line is broken where it crosses the plan view so that it does not interfere with plan view details. This line is either connected to the section view by an auxiliary line or is marked with letters corresponding to identifying letters on the section. Section views are usually drawn at the same scale as the plan view, but in some cases it may be necessary to enlarge some or all of the section views. In that event, the enlargement factor is indicated somewhere on the map or adjacent to each enlarged section.

Section views may be taken across pits, in which the section plane is horizontal or nearly so. These section views should complement a profile view. The pit may exhibit unequal development in different directions, so that two or even more profiles may be required to show the configuration, as shown in Figure 9. The profile planes are usually, but not necessarily, vertical. The alignment of the profile planes is indicated on the plan view by linear line segments, exterior to the wall outline, identified by appropriate letters or numbers, as in the case of the cross sections. If the profiles are not vertical, the line segments indicate the alignment of the profile plane at floor level.

Types of Maps

The Rough Sketch Map. The rough sketch map depicts only the most significant relationships in a cave. There has been no attempt to depict dimensions and directions in their true relationships and the map is frequently distorted. The primary utility of this map is to depict the sequential arrangement of rooms or other interesting features, which are frequently named on the map. Thus, this type of map is often accompanied by a verbal description or a written description and loses some of its utility without this information. The rough sketch map is frequently used to describe a new find or to plan an exploration or survey trip.

The Detailed Sketch Map. The detailed sketch map is similar to the rough sketch map in that it is simply a sketch and is not based on surveyed dimensions. However, greater care has been devoted to its preparation. The map is roughly to scale and has approximately the correct alignment. This map is usually intended to illustrate some particular detail or relationship.

The Compass and Pace Map. The compass and pace map is similar to the detailed sketch map, except that it incorporates a very crude survey technique which provides rough measurements of distances and directions. This type of map is used principally to find out how far and in what direction a passage extends. A relatively large amount of effort in relation to the useful data is required for a map of this type, so it is not often made.

The Line Map. The line map, Figure 2, consists of a sequence of straight-line segments corresponding to the surveyed distances and directions (station lines) between consecutive survey points (survey stations) in the cave. The line map does not depict any features such as the width of the cave, but it does give some idea as to the size of the cave and the direction and orientation of its passages. Unless specific features are named on the map, it cannot serve as a guide. The map is as dimensionally accurate as a fully detailed map and thus can provide directional and distance data between various cave features if they are noted on the map. Because of their limited utility, line maps are not frequently made as a specific end product. One principal exception to this general rule is the case of the computer-generated stereo maps in which two maps generated in different colors are viewed as a stereo pair with appropriate colored glasses; this arrangement provides a visual three-dimensional view of a complex cave developed on multiple levels.

Line maps are most frequently encountered as intermediate stages in the survey of large cave systems, where they are produced by computers using the survey data. The computers are programmed to correct for closure errors produced in surveying around a complete loop of cave passage; the error is apportioned among the survey measurements so that the loop closes. The computer-generated line map then serves as a skeleton upon which the walls and other cave features are manually drafted.

The Solid Outline Map. The solid outline map, Figure 4, is somewhat similar to the line map; but, in addition, the cave walls have been included. The entire cave passage is depicted by a solid black line of varying width. Solid outline maps are generally prepared when the cave is large compared to the size of the passages. In that case it would be difficult and probably confusing to show the adjacent cave walls by two separate lines; thus, the space between the cave walls is completely blacked in. This type of map is much superior to the line map as the size of passages and rooms are readily apparent. Dimensions and directions are to scale, so that significant rooms may be ascertained without additional captions. A variation of this type of map shows white cave passage on a black background representing the enclosing rock. In this type of map, features can be symbolically or pictorially depicted in the white region representing the interior of the cave.

The Detailed Map and Symbols. The detailed cave map, Figure 7, is the most sophisticated of all cave maps in that it depicts significant features within the cave as well as the walls. Both the features and the walls are dimensionally to scale so that anyone reading the map can obtain a fairly accurate idea of what the cave is like. The various features are illustrated symbolically and some symbols are shown in Figure 1. The National Speleological Society has published a list of standard map symbols (by the standing Committee on Cave Map Symbols, Cave Geology and Geography Section, NSS) for caves in *NSS Bulletin*, V 41, No 2, 1979, which is available from the NSS Bookstore.

These symbols should be used in the preparation of cave maps. The cave walls are shown by lines—either solid, dashed, or dotted—depending upon whether the lines portray the main passage (solid), an underlying passage (dotted), or unsurveyed passage (dashed). Ceiling heights are shown by numbers inside circles; the number generally represents height in feet, but may represent height in meters. Breakdown, which includes blocks of rocks fallen from the cave ceiling or tumbled in from the entrance, is pictorially depicted with angular, block-like outlines to resemble a rock. Larger blocks are usually illustrated with a shaded or blackened edge on one side, giving the block a three-dimensional appearance. Larger blocks may be drawn to scale, while smaller rocks are simply

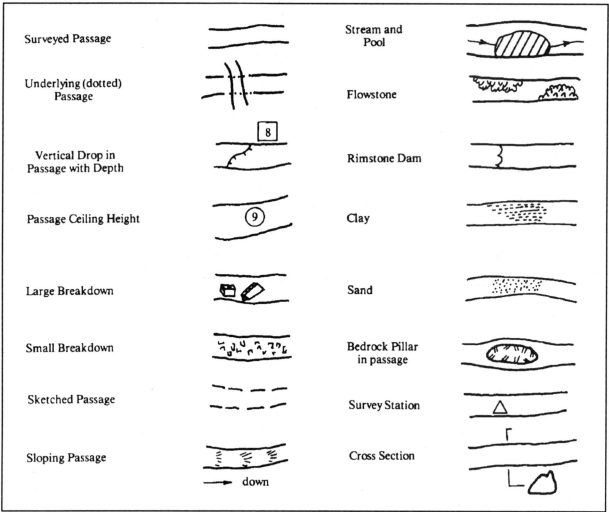

Figure 1—Common cave map symbols from the 1976 NSS Standard Map Symbols in The NSS Bulletin, *V. 41, No. 2, April 1979, pp 35-48*

illustrated. Slopes, whether of clay, silt or talus, are shown by sets of radiating lines, with the divergence pointing in the downward direction. Ledges and drops are symbolized with the hachured line, a primary longer line representing the ledge edge with short line segments (tick marks) perpendicular to the primary line attached at closely spaced intervals. The tick marks point to the drop-off side.

Pools and streams are represented in several different ways. Probably the best symbolism is one in which the pool outline is drawn to scale and the interior region is shown by finer lines at an angle to the general passage. Flowstone and speleothems, where of significant size, are depicted by a series of small circular segments arranged so that the end of one segment joins another segment partway along its length. This connected series of circular segments represents the outline of the feature. That part inside the outline is represented by isolated circular segments with the area density

of the segments being roughly proportional to the surface slope of the feature. An older symbol used for small speleothems is a small, black, arrow-shaped triangle. The symbol for rimstone dams consists of a series of very small, semi-circular line segments joined at diametrically opposite points to form a chain of semicircles. The convexities point in the downslope or downstream direction.

Different symbols may be combined to illustrate composite features. For instance, the flowstone symbol and the breakdown symbol may be combined to show flowstone-covered breakdown. Talus can be shown by combining the slope symbol with the symbol for small rocks. Flowstone-covered ledges can be shown by drawing tick marks on the flowstone symbol.

Conventional plan view maps are often supplemented by profile and section views. Symbolism is less frequently used in these views, and the primary objective is to depict the actual physical out-

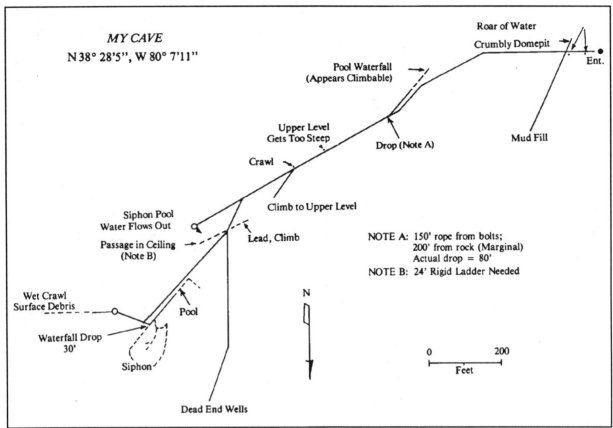

*Figure 2—Map of My Cave, West Virginia. [*The Potomac Caver, *V. 9 No. 1 (1966), p 6. Copied from the 1966 Speleo Digest, p 1-135.]*

line of the cave chamber lying on or close to the profile plane or the section plane. These views are used to supplement the symbolism on the plan view and to clarify relationships not readily apparent on the plan view.

Once the symbolism is understood, it should be possible to read a cave map with some fair degree of comprehension. Problems arise, however, when the cave is complex. In that case, the only recourse is to study the map in great detail to distinguish the different levels and sublevels. In some complex caves the configuration has been clarified by depicting different passages in different colors. Thus, all passages at a single level are shown in a single color, overlying passages of a different color, and underlying passages of a third color. Unfortunately, this color technique cannot be duplicated by most types of reproduction equipment, so the technique is found exclusively on special one-of-a-kind maps.

Title Block

The symbolic representation of the cave is accompanied by the title block, which includes the name of the cave, the political province in which it is located, the names of the surveying crew or the group responsible for the map, and the date of the map. Other information is sometimes included, such as a precise location of the cave, the total surveyed length, and the survey accuracy. Underneath the title block or in some convenient position is the bar scale, a line or a narrow linear strip of alternating black and white spaces marked off in feet and/or meters at the same scale as the map. A distance measured on the map with a ruler or a pair of dividers can be placed on the bar scale and the length in feet or meters can be read directly from the scale. On maps of small caves, the bar scale may be an appreciable part of the length of the cave or even greater than its length, whereas on maps of larger caves the bar scale is only a small fraction of the cave length. On some maps, a scale factor, such as 1 inch = 50 feet, is included. It is only necessary to measure the distance on the map in inches (or whatever unit is used) and multiply by the scale factor to get the actual distance. This scale factor only applies to full-scale maps which have not been reduced (or enlarged) and therefore should be used with caution.

On the subject of reduction, it happens that cave maps are sometimes copied by Xerox® copiers or similar machines. The copies are not only enlarged slightly but also are enlarged at slightly different factors along different axes. Thus, the map is distorted slightly, not enough to significantly alter the appearance of the map but enough to preclude accurate measurements.

A north arrow is included at some convenient place on the map, usually more closely adjacent to the plan view if a profile view is included. In some instances, the north arrow will point to magnetic north rather than true north. If so, the north arrow should be indicated as magnetic north.

In addition to the title block, bar scale, and north arrow, cave maps sometimes include a list of symbols with an appropriate description for each symbol. This list explains the use of unusual or nonstandard symbols, or clarifies the usage for standard symbols as used on that particular map.

Some map draftsmen include small human figures in their cross section or profile views; such figures, while not standard symbolism, are universally recognizable and provide handy references for passage size and shape.

Using the north arrow, it is possible to align the map with surface features and determine the relationship of those features with the cave passages. If the map fortuitously happens to be at the same scale as the topographic map of the area, the cave map can be directly laid upon the topographic map for comparison. The cave entrance (or entrances) on the cave map can be superimposed on the entrance location plotted on the topographic map; the cave map can then be rotated with the entrance as a pivot point until the north arrows on both maps are parallel. The maps can be transilluminated

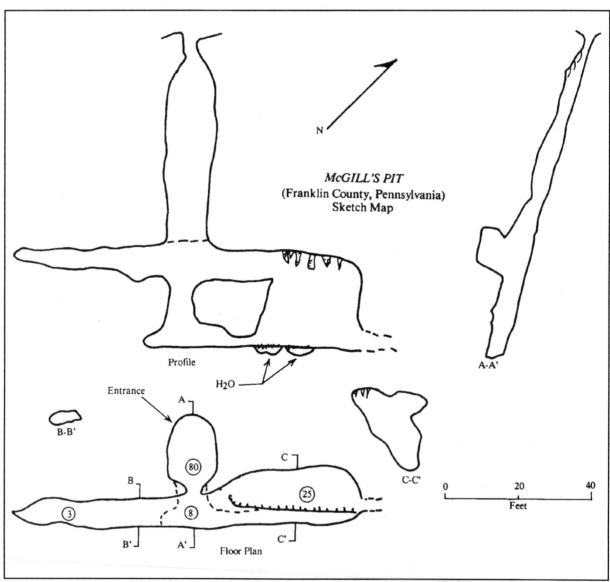

Figure 3—Map of McGill's Pit, Pennsylvania (Copied from the 1962 Speleo Digest, p 1-71.)

with a strong light to view the cave and surface features together. It is, of course, necessary to mentally supply the missing third dimension by imagining the cave lying underneath the surface features, as if the earth were transparent and were viewed from a height.

Usually the scale of the cave map and available topographic maps are greatly different, with the cave map scale factor much higher than the topographic map. To illustrate the relationship of the cave to surface features, some cave maps include surface topographic contours and/or surface features enlarged from standard topographic maps or independent surveys.

The topographic additions illustrate the relationship of the cave to surface drainage routes, valleys, highways, mines, quarries, and so on. The site of potential new entrances can be studied and the feasibility of digging a new entrance can be evaluated. The possibility of a connection between adjacent caves or the possible extension of a terminated cave can be ascertained from the topographic data.

Despite the quality and accuracy of a map, people are disappointed when a map fails to describe a cave in terms which convey the "feel" of the cave. A map, however, by its very nature, is a double abstraction: it reduces features to dimensional relationships and it portrays only two dimensions in any one view. This double abstraction is not a defect of the maps; it is, in fact, a deliberate objective so that dimensional relationships may be shown in a clear and unambiguous manner. It is possible, if desired, to abandon the three mutually perpendicular (or almost perpendicular) plan-profile-section views and combine the data into a single quasi-perspective (isometric) view which simulates a three-dimensional view of the cave. In doing so, the draftsman provides an illustration which may be more understandable in certain respects, but only at the price of deleting or obscuring other relevant data.

It should always be remembered that a map is, first and foremost, a scale drawing illustrating geometric relationships of the cave, usually in the three principal planes. Maps cannot and will not convey to the reader the majestic grace of a cathedral-like chamber or the yawning blackness of a deep pit. These visual impressions are better left to artistic renditions, cinematography, or still photography.

Discussion of Cave Map Examples

Figures 2 through 9 show eight cave maps. A discussion of each map follows.

Map of My Cave, West Virginia, Figure 2

This map is a line map of a moderately large cave in West Virginia. It is not clear from the map whether the lines are actual survey lines or merely average alignments. In any event, several lines are about 300 feet long and probably represent several individual measurements, even though the several station lines may have the same direction. Regardless of such details, the end result is a line map, which of course corresponds to a plan view of the cave. The map includes no passage details, no symbolism, no profile, and no cross sections. Significant features are denoted by captions. The title block is the utmost of simplicity, including only the cave name and the latitude/longitude location. The bar scale, 0 to 200 feet long, is subdivided into 100-foot increments by a midpoint marker.

The map is not intended as a finished product, but rather as a schematic diagram for the accompanying article in the original publication. The article discusses eight potential places where the cave may possibly be extended. Despite the limitations of the map, it serves its intended purpose and clearly demonstrates the size and directional trend of the cave. Furthermore, the preliminary map could serve as the basic planning document for a more detailed survey, if one has not already been done.

Map of McGill's Pit, Pennsylvania, Figure 3

This map of McGill's Pit is a well-drawn sketch map, a fact which is noted in the title block. The name of the draftsman and the source publication have, unfortunately, both been omitted, and there is no accompanying report. The map includes the plan view, two profiles, and two cross sections which adequately define the major aspects of the cave's configuration. The plan view includes a ledge (shown with the hachured line), a breakdown block and four ceiling heights. The primary profile view shows two pools and a group of stalactites. This same profile also illustrates the cave's horizontal development along two principal levels, an aspect not apparent in the other views. The secondary profile, shown as section A – A', depicts some stalactites near the entrance and shows the tilted nature of the entrance pit. Whether this view is treated as a profile or a section is immaterial; the draftsman has chosen to show it as a section. Sections B – B' and C – C' show the cross sections of the horizontal extensions.

There is so much detail here that one might think that the pit had been surveyed if the map were not specifically called a sketch map. In all probability, the explorers made at least one compass reading at the bottom of the pit to ascertain the primary alignment and estimated a number of pertinent dimensions, as implied by the north arrow and the bar scale. This relatively small cave is well suited to such a sketch. The technique is more difficult to apply in the case of a more complex cave.

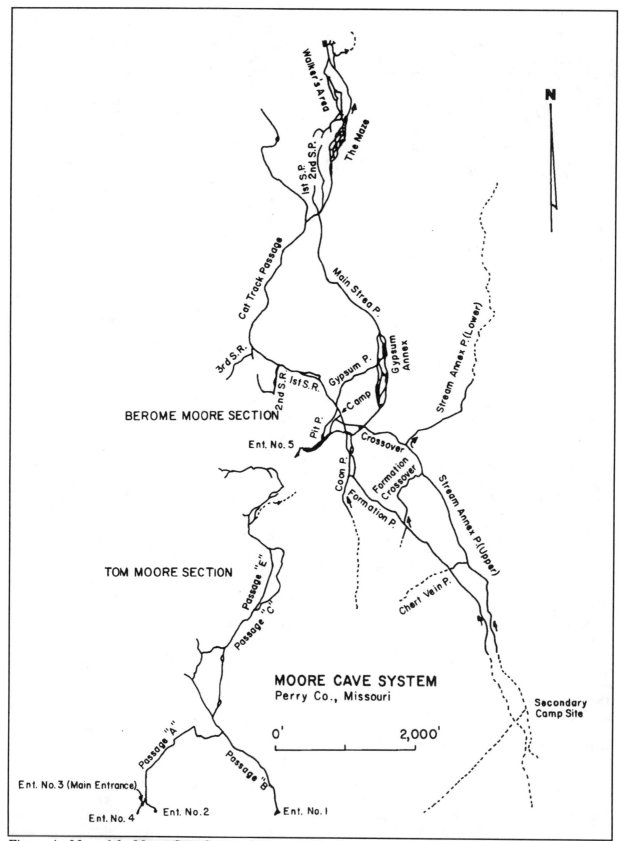

Figure 4 — Map of the Moore Cave System, Missouri. [The Underground, V. 11, No. 2 (1968), p 32a. Copied *from the* 1968 Speleo Digest, *p 1-80.*]

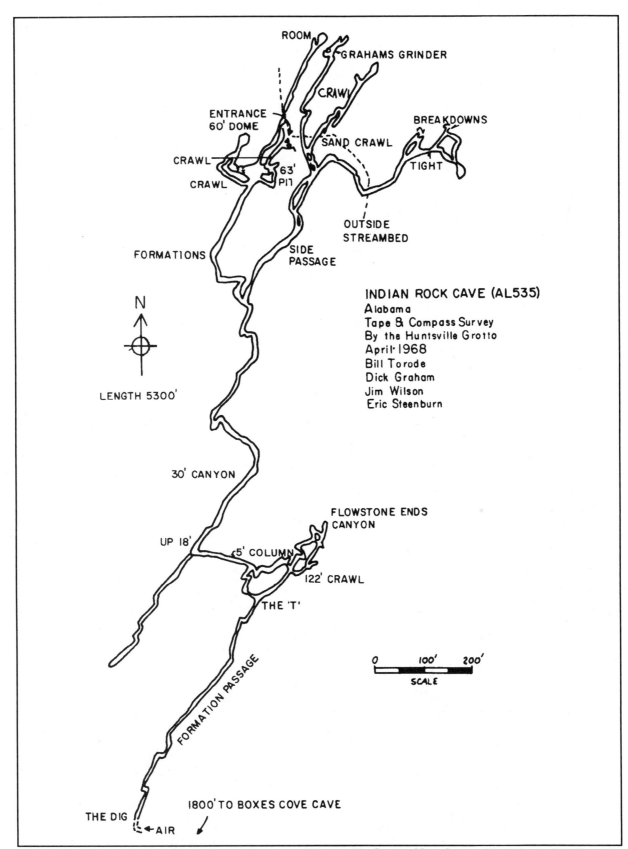

Figure 5 — Map of Indian Rock Cave, Alabama. [Huntsville Grotto Newsletter, *V. 9 No. 5 (1968), p 72.* *Copied from the 1968 Speleo Digest, p 1-8.]*

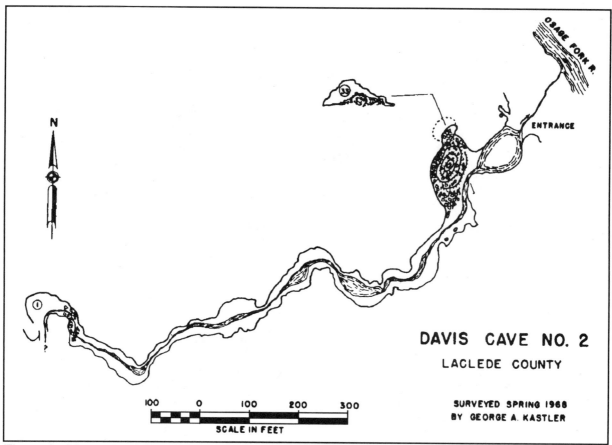

Figure 6—Map of Davis Cave No. 2, Missouri. [Missouri Speleology, V. 13, No. 1 (1973), p 14]

Map of the Moore Cave System, Missouri, Figure 4

This map depicts the plan view of two large caves considered to be segments of a single cave system. The map is an example of a solid outline map, where the cave passage is shown in solid black. The scale of this map, about 1,200 feet per inch, is such that passages 15 to 20 feet wide are proportional in width to the width of an inked line. Some wider passages are indicated by a corresponding increase in the width of the passage shown on the map. Unsurveyed passages are shown by the small arrows. With these two exceptions, no other symbolism is employed. No cross sections and no ceiling heights are shown. Significant features are denoted by captions.

The primary objective of this map is to illustrate the geometry of the two caves, the relationship of the two caves to one another, and the position of notable features in the caves. The map is a reduction from a more detailed map drawn at a scale of 160 feet per inch, which in turn was prepared from map notes and detailed map segments at a scale of 16 feet per inch.

Map of Indian Rock Cave, Alabama, Figure 5

This map of Indian Rock Cave, Alabama, Figure 5, shows only a simplified plan view of a long and, in places, apparently complex cave. The map is fairly typical of the maps of long caves appearing in grotto newsletters, where the lack of sophisticated reproduction equipment and the restriction to an 8½ × 11-inch size format preclude showing much detail. Thus, this map is just about the simplest detailed map which can be found. There is no profile, no cross sections, and no specific ceiling heights. One symbolized mud slope is shown. The lack of symbolism is partially compensated by the use of captions which indicate significant features in the cave. Interestingly, the name of the county in which the cave occurs is not listed in the title block information. The AL535 in parentheses is a unique serial number assigned to this cave for purposes of identification by the Alabama Cave Survey. The length of the cave is listed under the north arrow as 5,300 feet, a large amount of passage to show on a single page. Despite its limitations, the map clearly shows the geometric relationship of its

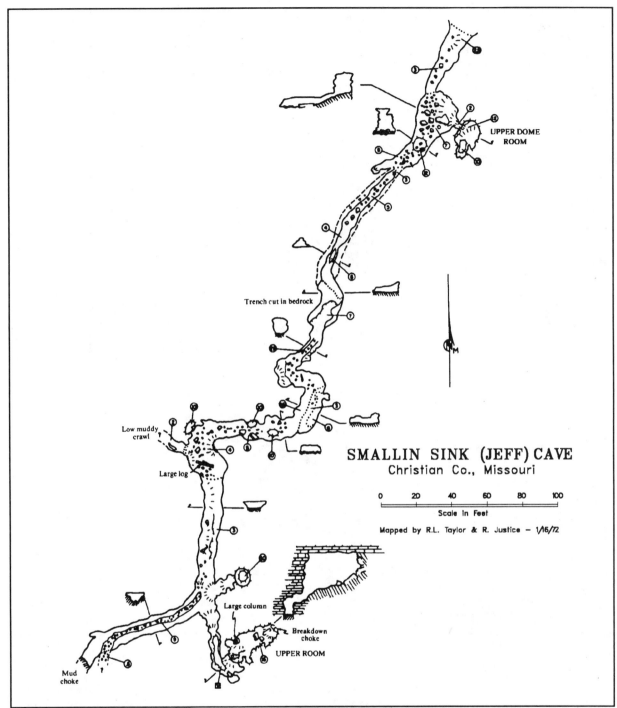

Figure 7 — Map of Smallin Sink Cave, Missouri. [Missouri Speleology, V. 15, No. 4 (1975), p 21.]

passages and salient features to one another. Note the three interesting captions at the bottom of the map, implying the distinct possibility of a connection to a cave 1,800 feet away, or at least the possibility of finding another entrance. This map is probably a simplified version of a larger, more detailed map.

Map of Davis Cave No. 2, Missouri, Figure 6

Figure 6 shows a cave of moderate size (1,460 feet shown) in Laclede County, Missouri. The map consists of plan view and one section, and it is fairly simple for a detailed map. Two ceiling heights are shown, one of which is included in the section view, rather than the plan view which is customary. The

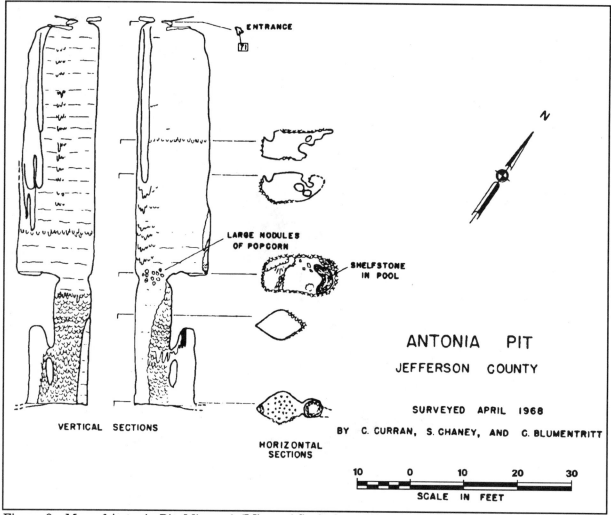

ENTRANCE

LARGE NODULES
OF POPCORN

SHELFSTONE
IN POOL

VERTICAL SECTIONS

HORIZONTAL
SECTIONS

ANTONIA PIT

JEFFERSON COUNTY

SURVEYED APRIL 1968

BY C. CURRAN, S. CHANEY, AND C. BLUMENTRITT

10   0   10   20   30

SCALE IN FEET

Figure 8—Map of Antonia Pit, Missouri. [Missouri Speleology, V. 12, No. 2 (1971), p 36.]

use of symbols is limited to three on this map: breakdown, the hachured line for ledges, and the symbol for streams and pools. A stream is shown running the length of the cave and forming a pool at the entrance with an arrow indicating the flow direction. In addition, the stream is shown exiting the cave and running overland a short distance to the Osage Fork River, thus showing the relationship of the cave to surface drainage. The stream is shown entering the cave via a low extension with a question mark beside it, indicating that the stream was not followed farther and that the continuation is unknown. An accompanying report (not included here) states that this extension is a water crawl. Another extension leading to low, unsurveyed passage is indicated by a second break in the wall line adjacent to the water crawl.

The title block information omits the state name, a common omission in maps published in *Missouri Speleology*. The north arrow indicates the true north direction. The map can be somewhat

misleading if the reader does not pay close attention to the bar scale. The average width of the cave is 30 feet, and there are several places where the width exceeds 70 feet, reaching 100 feet at one point. These large widths cause the cave to appear more like a shorter, narrower cave at first glance.

Map of Smallin Sink Cave, Missouri, Figure 7

This detailed map shows a moderate size cave (about 625 feet long) in southwestern Missouri. The map consists of the plan view and ten sections; no profile is included. The wealth of detail shown on this map permits the size and nature of the cave to be readily assessed. Note the use of breakdown symbolism, slope symbolism, and hachured lines for ledges and domes. The drip line at the entrance has been depicted by a dotted line and dotted lines are employed further back in the cave to show abrupt changes in ceiling elevation. Ceiling heights, shown by the circled numbers, are scattered throughout the cave. Decimal points on some ceiling heights have become obscured by photographic reduction from a larger original map; fortunately in the ambiguous cases the ceiling heights can be deduced from adjacent heights. The plan view is supplemented with several names and explanatory captions, and the caption of a large log points to a scale drawing of the log in its actual position. The large section view at the bottom of the map, actually a profile of the terminal room, includes symbolism showing the horizontally-bedded limestone which forms the walls of the cave. The title block lists both the primary name and an alternate name of the cave. The bar scale, included here in the title block, is simply calibrated from 1 to 100 in 20-foot increments. The north arrow shows N_M, indicating that the specified direction is magnetic north, not true north. Judging from appearances, the map has been photographically reduced by a factor of about four to five.

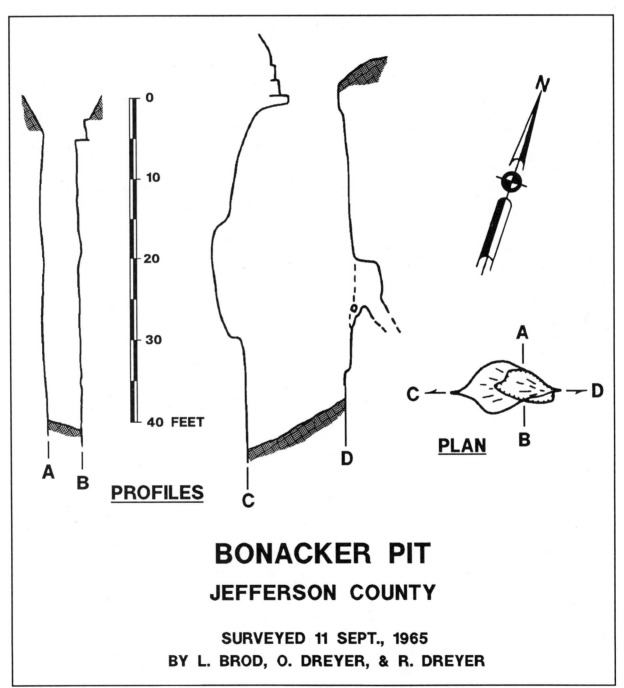

BONACKER PIT

JEFFERSON COUNTY

SURVEYED 11 SEPT., 1965
BY L. BROD, O. DREYER, & R. DREYER

Figure 9—Map of Bonacker Pit, Missouri. [Missouri Speleology, V. 12, No. 2 (1971), p 40.]

Map of Antonia Pit, Missouri, Figure 8

This map shows a pit 71 feet deep with a small entrance opening. Contrast this map with the map of Bonacker Pit, Figure 9, in the same county. The map of Antonia Pit shows two profiles, termed "vertical sections" on the map. The two profiles are not taken perpendicular to one another as in the case of Bonacker Pit but instead are two views of a single profile with the background details of the two halves of the pit included in each profile. The profile plane is taken across the larger width of the pit. Note the extensive use of flowstone symbolism, especially in the lower part of the pit. The map is interesting for its display of horizontal sections, of which there are six, including the floor plan. The uppermost horizontal section, taken through the entrance, shows the numeral 71 enclosed in a square; this figure denotes the depth of the pit, a standard symbol on cave maps. Pool symbolism is shown in the fourth and sixth section, and the corresponding pool surfaces are shown as straight, thin, horizontal lines in both profile views. The bar scale in this map is horizontal. Note the ten-foot section subdivided into two-foot increments at the left side. In using the bar scale, this ten-foot section should not be included in the 30-foot length.

Map of Bonacker Pit, Missouri, Figure 9

Figure 9 shows a small, almost featureless pit about 40 feet deep. Because it had developed along a joint (Shown by half-arrows pointing toward C and D), it exhibits unequal development along the joint and across the joint, and it is in these two directions that the two profile views are drawn. Both profiles pass through the entrance, which is shown by the hachured line in the plan view. A small alcove is shown in profile C–D about 15 feet above the floor, but the alcove is not shown on the plan view. Thus, the plan view is only the floor plan of the pit with the entrance opening superimposed upon it. On this map, soil and talus are shown by a non-standard symbol consisting of small, cross-lined squares. This symbol is used to show soil at the lip of the pit and the talus covering the pit floor. The bar scale is drawn vertically, parallel to the longest dimension of the cave, but it obviously also applies to the plan view. The state name has been omitted in the title block; however, as the map was published in Missouri Speleology, there should be no problem arising from this omission.

Remember: **Make your mark the right way, make a map.**

Chapter 21

READING TOPOGRAPHIC MAPS

Tom Rea
NSS 5683

Introduction

A map is a representation of an area from the viewpoint of exactly overhead. Looking at a map is similar to looking at the area through a hole in the floor of an airplane as it flies over. There are many different kinds of maps. State highway maps are useful for traveling by car from city to city. Nautical charts are designed to aid in piloting a boat. Aeronautical charts are necessary when flying an airplane. City maps not only help you find your friend's home but also help utility companies, fire departments, and police agencies plan their services for the city. When searching for caves, most cavers rely on "topographic maps."

Topographic Maps

The name "topographic" comes from the Greek *topos*, place, and *graphein*, draw—a drawing of a place. Practically the entire United States has been mapped and topographic maps published by the U.S. Geological Survey. Several sources of topographic maps are listed in Appendix D.

Scale: The scale of a map is a mathematical representation of the relationship of the size of features on the map compared to the size of the actual feature on the ground. The most common topographic map seen in use by cavers is the 7½-minute quadrangle. These maps are published at a scale of 1:24,000. What this means is that a measurement of one unit on the map (a unit can be an inch, a foot, a millimeter, or any other linear measurement) corresponds to 24,000 of the same units on the ground. You may also see the scale presented as one inch equals 2,000 feet. One inch on the map equals 24,000 inches, or 2,000 feet, on the ground. Topographic maps are also available in scales of 1:62,500 (15-minute) and 1:250,000. Fifteen-minute quadrangles are uncommon but are available for some areas. The entire United States is covered by the 1:250,000 series. However for caving purposes they are little more than fancy highway maps.

Name: Each individual topographic map, called a "quadrangle," is named for a prominent feature on the map, a city, lake, mountain, or other location. The name of the map is printed in the upper right corner of the map margin along with the state and, the county (if the map is all in one county). This name is also repeated in the lower right corner. When you order topographic maps from a dealer, you order them by quadrangle name, state, and scale. At the middle of the "neat line" (edge of the map portion) on each side of the map is the name of the adjoining quadrangle. At each of the four corners of the neat line the diagonally adjoining quadrangle is designated. These adjoining maps are the ones you will need if your travels take you over the edge of the map you are using. State index maps are published by the Geological Survey showing the names and locations of all the quadrangles superimposed on an outline map of the state.

Date: Beneath the name in the lower right corner of the margin is an important piece of information often overlooked by casual map users, the date the map was published. Sometimes you will see, in addition to the original publication date, a revision date. This publication date lets you know how closely to expect the map to match what you find in the field. In developed areas, a map 20 years old will not show many of the man-made features you will find. The publication date is shown on state index maps so you can know if your map is the latest version. In the lower left corner of the map you will usually find the date of the aerial photography on which the map is based and the date the map was field checked.

Boundaries: Where, exactly in the world, is the area that is represented by your topographic map? In the lower margin of the map is a small outline of the state with a black square indicating the location of the quadrangle. This is a pretty rough location but will sometimes answer the question satisfactorily. If you want to be more precise, just outside each of the four corners of the neat line you will find the latitude and longitude of that corner. For a complete discussion of latitude and longitude as it relates to topographic maps, see the Chapter 22, "Locating Caves on Topographic Maps."

Map Symbols: Map makers have devised a set of "symbols" to represent the things you will find in the field. It is not practical to draw a tiny picture of a house, a barn, or a power line on the map. Whoever invented the map symbols used on topographic maps made an effort to make the symbols look like the things they represent. For example a tiny black square represents a house. A black square with a cross on it represents a church. A black square with a flag represents a school (See Figure 1). You will find many more map symbols when you examine an actual topographic map. All of them are described and illustrated on a sheet,

Topographic Map Symbols
(Representative Sample)

Primary highway, hard surface (red)	————	Building (dwelling, place of employment, etc.)	▪ ■ ▌ ▌ ▨
Secondary highway, hard surface (red)	———	School, church, cemetery	▲ ▲ [†] [Cem.]
Light-duty road, hard or improved surface	═══	Building (barn, warehouse, etc.)	▫ ▭ ◪ ▨
Unimproved road	··········	Power transmission line	—·—·—·—
Dual highway, divider exceeding 25 feet (red)	▬▬▬	Telephone line, pipeline, etc. (labled)	– – – – –
Trail	------------	Wells other than water (labeled)	○Oil ○Gas
Perennial stream (blue)	∿	Tanks: oil, water, etc. (labled only if water)	● ● ● ◑ Water
Intermittent stream (blue)	∿·∿	Open pit, mine, or quarry; prospect	✕ ✕
Water well and spring (blue)	○ ∿	Shaft and tunnel (cave) entrance	◪ Y

Figure 1—A sample of symbols used on U. S. Geological Survey topographic maps.

"Topographic Map Symbols," available free from the Geological Survey (See Appendix D).

For caving purposes, you are mainly interested in four types of symbols, each with its own distinctive color: man made features called cultural features, water features called hydrographic features, vegetation, and elevations.

Man-made Features: Man made features include things that we have built for ourselves. This includes, among other things, homes, schools, factories, roads, bridges, and power lines. Also included are political divisions such as state and county lines, city limits, property lines, and fence lines. Cultural features and names are printed in black. Important roads are emphasized with red to distinguish them from less travelled roads. Public land survey section lines, land grants, and field and fence lines are also shown in red.

Cultural features are usually printed much larger than they actually are. In built-up urban areas, only the landmark buildings are shown. There are too many structures to show them all. These areas are overprinted with a pink tint to indicate that abbreviated information is being presented.

Water: Lakes, rivers, canals, glaciers, swamps, ponds, and other hydrographic features are shown on topographic maps in blue. Very few cave entrances are shown on topographic maps. When they are, the symbol resembles a small black letter "Y." Springs are represented by a blue circle with a wiggly blue line leaving it. Permanent streams are shown by a single thin blue line; rivers by a broader blue band. An intermittent stream, one that does not have water in it all year long, is shown by a series of dashes and dots (See Figure 1). Caves are often indicated by intermittent streams (or permanent streams for that matter) that just end with no apparent reason. A normal stream flows to a bigger stream, and a bigger stream yet, and a river, and finally to the sea. A stream that just stops in the downhill direction may flow into a cave.

Vegetation: Vegetation is shown on topographic maps in green. Woodlands or forest is shown by a solid green overprint. Orchards, vineyards, and scrub are shown by distinctive green symbols. Vegetation is the most variable and easily changed feature on the map. Carefully consider the publication date of the map when trying to correlate vegitation shown on the map with what you find in the field.

Elevations: A distinctive feature of topographic maps (the feature tham makes them "topographic") is the representation of elevation by the use of "contour lines." Contour lines are shown on your map in brown. Contour lines are not intuitive and are the least understood, but perhaps the most valuable, information on the map.

A contour line is an imaginary line which, if it were drawn on the ground, would everywhere be at the same elevation above sea level. Starting at zero elevation, every fifth contour line will be drawn with a heavier line. The heavier lines are known as "index" contour lines and will have the elevation above sea level printed on them (in feet on U.S. maps). The interval between contour lines will be given in center of the bottom margin of the map. Areas with slight relief may have a contour interval of ten feet. More mountainous areas will have an interval of 20 or 50 feet. Supplementary dotted contour lines, at less than the regular interval, are used in selected flat areas. This means as you travel along the ground, each time you cross a contour line you have changed elevation by the contour interval.

The spacing of the contour lines will show the relief or ground shape. Knowledge of the relief is essential to finding your way in a strange area. Caves are often found at the contact between two different geologic formations. These contacts usually occur at a given elevation across a wide area. Following the proper contour line is one of the best ways to locate new caves in such an area.

Where contour lines—

—Are evenly spaced and wide apart it indicates a uniform, gentle slope.

—Are evenly spaced and close together, a uniform, steep slope is indicated. The closer together the contour lines are spaced, the steeper the slope.

—Make a closed loop or loops, a hill exists.

—Make a closed loop with ticks, a depression or sinkhole is shown. The ticks are *always* on the downhill side of the contour line.

—Are "U"s with the open end pointing toward high ground, a ridge is shown. A ridge has no definite shape and many extend for miles including dips and rises.

—Are a series of "U"s in successive contour lines, a spur exists. Unlike a ridge, a spur has a continuous slope. The open ends of the "U"s point toward higher ground.

—Are roughly paralleling a stream and represent elevtions lower than those farther from the stream, a valley is shown.

—Form a series of "V"s in successive contour lines it indicates a draw. The points of the "V"s point toward higher ground.

—Converge into one line, a cliff is depicted. Contour lines never split nor cross but their representation on maps may cross in the case of sheer or overhanging cliffs, escarpments, or quarried areas.

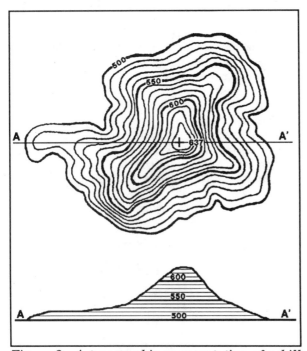

Figure 2—A topographic representation of a hill and a cross section of the hill along line A — A'.

Figure 2 shows a topographic representation of a hill and the cross section of that hill along a line, A — A'. Of course, if the line A — A' were rotated to a new position, the cross section would appear completely different.

In addition to the contour lines, bench marks and spot elevations are used to indicate points of known elevation. Bench marks are usually symbolized by a small triangle and the letters BM. Spot elevations are shown by a cross (see Figure 2). These elevations are usually found at the tops of hills and at road inersections but other locations are also used. The number indicates the elevation.

Revisions: Office revisions made from aerial photographs are shown in purple. These changes have not been field checked. The date of the purple revision is shown in the lower right corner of the margin of the map.

Directions: Just looking at a map will show you the relative direction between two points. You can see that the sinkhole is west of the barn or the spring is south of the small pond. However if you need to walk through the woods for a considerable distance to find the sinkhole, you need to know the actual direction to the sinkhole as related to the north and south of the landscape. To do this you need to know what is north and what is south on the map as a whole.

When you look at a topographic map with the words in the margins upright, you can be pretty sure that north is at the top of the map. To be sure, look in the bottom margin for the "north arrow." You will find a small diagram of an angle with one leg marked "TRUE NORTH" and the other leg marked "MAGNETIC NORTH." The true north line should run parallel with the lines that frame the east and west boundaries of the map. The magnetic north line indicates the magnetic "declination." This measurement acknowledges that the earth's magnetic pole is not directly under the north pole but is actually somewhere in northern Greenland. Thus, your compass, which points to the magnetic pole, misses the north pole by the declination angle. On some compasses the compass scale can be rotated so that when the compass needle is pointing to magnetic north, the compass scale is pointing to true north.

To find the actual direction from where you are to the sinkhole in the woods, first you must "orient" your map. There are many different types of compasses in use by cavers and each works in a slightly different way. Rather than give exact step by step directions for one type of compass, we will assume you know how to use your particular compass, or have instructions for it, and give directions for how to handle the map. All compasses have a "lubber line" which is the line used to indicate the direction the compass is pointing. Set off the declination on your compass scale if it amounts to more than one

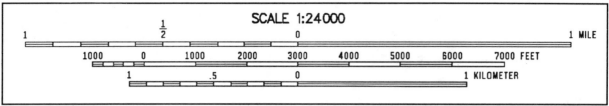

Figure 3 — The three graphic scales on a 1:24,000 scale topographic map.

or two degrees. Place the map on level ground or some level, non-magnetic support (not the hood of your car!) and align the lubber line with the east or west margin of the map (and thus the true north arrow). Turn the map (and the compass along with it) until the compass needle is indicating north. Now, north on the map is aligned with north in the world. This basic maneuver is necessary any time you want to compare the map with the terrain around you. Now draw a real or imaginary line from where you are to where you want to go. Move the compass so that the lubber line is parallel with this line. Read the compass needle and it will tell you the direction you have to walk to reach your destination.

To actually walk to the destination, pick the compass up and sight along the lubber line while holding the same direction on the compass needle. Pick a prominent object on your line of sight that you can recognize when you reach it. Walk to that object and take another sighting, picking another object closer to your destination. By carefully repeating this process and checking your progress by comparing the terrain you are crossing with your map, you will surely reach your goal.

If you don't have a compass, you can still use the topographic map to find your way, if you have some idea of where you are on the map. Orient the map by "inspection," rotating the map until the roads, rivers, houses, hills, valleys, or other features match what you see around you. With the map properly oriented you can walk in the direction of your goal, checking your progress by comparing the map with the terrain as you cross it. If you have a "catcher" landmark such as a road or river that runs perpendicular to your course and near to your goal, you can be sure of finding your goal by traveling until you intersect the catcher landmark and then turning in the direction most likely to lead you to the goal. Carefully check the map as you walk

along the catcher landmark to be sure you turned the right way.

Distances: We have already discussed the scale of your map, but how do you use the scale to determine the distance between two points. If you know the scale of your map is 1 inch = 2,000 feet, you can simply measure the distance on the map in inches and multiply by 2,000 to get the number of feet. Better still, most topographic maps have three "graphic scales" in the center of the bottom margin. These scales are marked in feet, miles, and kilometers. Usually zero on the scale is not at the left end but some distance from it. The part of the scale to the left of zero is subdivided into finer increments than the rest of the scale to allow easy measurement without cluttering the scale (see Figure 3). To use the graphic scale, mark the distance you want to measure along the edge of a scrap piece of paper, or cut a match stick, small twig, or pine needle to the exact length. Transfer the marked measurement to the graphic scale and align the right edge with the division point that allows the left edge to fall in the subdivided area left of the zero. The measurement will be the division point number plus the fraction indicated left of zero (see Figure 4).

Practice: Topographic maps are fun. Order a few maps of your favorite caving area. When they arrive, spread them out on the table or the floor and relive your travels over the area by locating familiar landmarks. See if there are any surprises in what the land looks like compared to what you thought it looked like. Take the map with you on your next caving trip and follow along on the map as you drive and walk to the cave. See how the terrain is depicted by the contour lines on the map. Pick an interesting feature on the map and see if you can walk to it. Soon you will be an expert with map and compass.

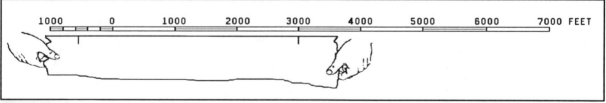

Figure 4 — A measurement of 3,550 feet on one of the graphic scales shown in Figure 3 by use of tick marks on a scrap piece of paper.

Chapter 22

LOCATING CAVES ON TOPOGRAPHIC MAPS

Tom Rea
NSS 5683

Introduction

Early in your caving career you will be introduced to topographic maps. Almost all cavers use topographic maps to find their way to caves, to discover areas likely to contain new caves, or to describe the location of caves to their fellow cavers. Reading the symbols on a topographic map and using a compass and topographic map to find you way to a particular point, a skill known as "orienteering," could be the subject of a book all by itself and several excellent books on orienteering are available. The subject of this chapter is the specialized use of some orienteering, engineering, and military techniques to describe the locations of caves in a concise manner that can be understood by other cavers.

This chapter assumes you know where you are on the map when you discover a cave or you can get to a given spot on a map if the spot is there. (A big assumption!) Everyone has said something like, "Meet me at Third and Vine," or "Come to 2351 North Main Street." This method of describing a location depends upon a system of "coordinates," in this case a city with named and identified streets. Very few caves are found in the city, however, so we need a similar system of coordinates useful in the forest, the desert, or anywhere else on the surface of the earth. For locations accurate enough to find an unknown cave opening our system should have the following characteristics:

1. Does not require a knowledge of the area.
2. Does not require landmarks.
3. Applies to all map scales.

Many such systems exist. Three of the more common ones are presented here. One should be just right for you.

Geographic Coordinates

The oldest coordinate system for describing locations, "geographic coordinates," is based on two imaginary lines. One, known as the equator, runs east and west half way between the north and south poles. The other, known as the "prime meridian," runs north and south from pole to pole. The location of any point on earth can be described by giving its distance north or south of the equator and east or west of the prime medidian.

The distance a point is north or south of the equator is known as its "latitude." The distance a point is east or west of the prime meridian is known as its "longitude." The lines which describe latitude are known as "parallels of latitude" or simply "parallels" and the lines that describe longitude are known as "meridians." Meridians run at right angles to the parallels but meridians themselves are not parallel because they all converge at the poles (see Figure 1).

The unit of measurement used with geographic coordinates is the degree, which is a measure of angles. A full circle is divided into 360 degrees (°), each degree into 60 minutes ('), and each minute into 60 seconds (").

Starting at the equator, the parallels for latitude are numbered from 0° to 90° both north and south. Since a parallel can have the same numerical value on either side of the equator, the direction, N or S, must also be given. Starting at the prime meridian, longitude is measured both east and west around the world. The meridian opposite the prime meridian on the other side of the world is either 180°E or 180°W. Once again, the direction, E or W, must be given. The prime meridian that most western countries use is the one passing through Greenwich, England.

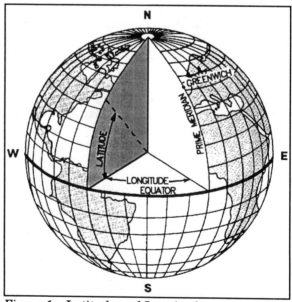

Figure 1—Latitude and Longitude

Since distance is almost always measured in linear units rather than angular units, it may be more meaningful to compare the angular measurements of geographic coordinates to a linear unit. The ground distance between one degree of latitude is about 69 miles. One second of latitude is about 100 feet. One degree of longitude is about 69 miles at the equator, but the meridians converge toward the poles so the measurement decreases as one moves north or south until it becomes zero at the pole. At the equator one second of longitude is about 100 feet but at the latitude of Washington, DC, it is about 78 feet.

The most common topographic map used by cavers, the 7½ minute map, is called that because its dimensions are 7′ 30″ of latitude by 7′ 30″ of longitude. The actual latitude and longitude is in-

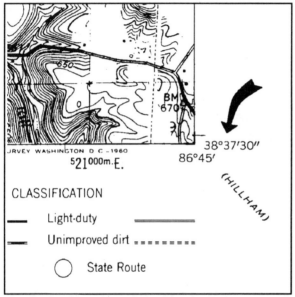

Figure 2—A portion of the Shoals, Indiana, quadrangle. The arrow shows the latitude and longitude of the southeast corner of the map. The false easting of the first UTM grid tick is also shown.

dicated at each of the four corners of the map (with the N, S, E, or W deleted) (see Figure 2). All latitudes in the United States are North and all longitudes are West. There is a black "tick" (short line) along the "neat line" (edge of the map portion) every 2½ minutes. These ticks are labeled with the minute and second value.

To describe the location of a point on the map, carefully connect the ticks for the two parallels and the two meridians which enclose the point in a 2½ minute square area. To find the latitude, the problem now is to find the proportion of the 2½ minute distance that lies below and that which lies above the point. Finding the longitude is exactly the same but the measurements are made east and west instead of north and south.

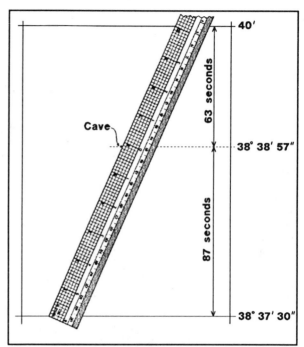

Figure 3—Method of calcuating the latitude of a point on the map by proportional parts.

Obtain a ruler with the inches divided in tenths instead of eighths. Such a ruler is available at most engineering supply stores. Place the ruler on the map with the zero mark exactly on the southern parallel and the ten mark (not twelve) exactly on the northern parallel. (The ruler will not be running north and south but will be slanted toward the east or west.) Slide the ruler east or west until the point you want to describe is just touching the scale edge of the ruler. Read the scale at that point (see Figure 3).

Now you must use a little mathamatics. Suppose the reading on the ruler at the point is 5.83 inches. This means that the point is 58.3% of the way from the zero mark to the ten mark. The 2½ minutes between the zero mark and the ten mark is equal to 150 seconds. 58.3% of 150 seconds is 87 seconds (rounded to the nearest second) or 1′ 27″. Since the southern parallel in Figure 3 is 38° 37′ 30″, add 1′ 27″ to this measurement giving 38° 38′ 57″ for the latitude of the point.

Finding the longitude of the point is exactly the same except that the measurements are made east and west instead of north and south. You would place the zero on the eastern meridian and calcuate the percentage toward the western meridian.

If you are given the location of a cave in geographical coordinates and want to spot it on your map, you must work the above problem in reverse. Using the same map as in Figure 3, assume you are told the cave is at 38° 39′ 10″ N latitude. 38° 39′ 10″ is 100 seconds north of southern identified parallel. This is 66.7% of the way from the southern parallel to the northern parallel (150 seconds). Place the ruler with the zero mark on the southern parallel and the ten mark on the northern parallel. Mark a point at 6.67 inches (66.7% of the way from zero to ten). Now move the ruler sideways, keeping the zero point and the ten point at the identified parallels. Make another mark. Make these two marks as widely spaced as possible. Draw a line across your map through the two points. This line is the latitude of the cave. Mark the longitude of the cave in the same manner. Where the latitude and longitude lines cross is the location of the cave.

A problem can occur with this method when the point is near the edge of the map. In this case, securely tape a piece of paper to the bottom side of the map to allow extending the lines you draw outside the boundaries of the map.

Public Land Survey

In many areas of the country, topographic maps are marked off showing the units of the public land survey. Since these units are printed on the map and do not have to be extended by pencil work, many cavers use the public land survey to describe the locations of caves.

The present system of government land surveys was adopted by Congress on May 7, 1785. This system has been used to describe all lands surveyed in the United States since the date of adoption. This amounts to all of the land except the original 13 colonies and Texas. That is why you do not find this system in use in Kentucky and Tennessee. They were part of the original Virginia Colony.

In the public land survey all distances are measured from two lines set at right angles to each other. These lines are known as the "principal meridian," running north and south, and the "base line," running east and west. The intersection of the principal meridian and the base line is known as the "initial point." The principal meridian is established by carefully observing the North Star through a transit and referring to a table of its exact position for any date and time. Each principal meridian has its own base line and these two right angle lines form the basis for the surveys of all land inside the territory which they control.

For purposes of illustration, the survey of Indiana will be used as an example because the author is familiar with it.. All of the land in Indiana except that in the Clark Military Grant around Charlestown, the French grants about Vincennes, and a few scattered Indian reservations was surveyed in the public land survey. The state falls into two areas for surveying purposes. The part of the state east of a line known as the

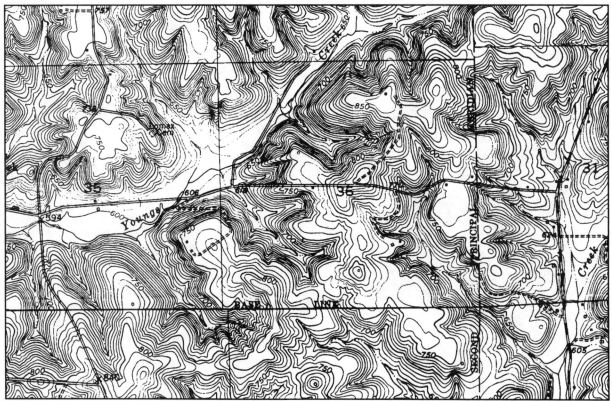

Figure 4—A portion of the Valeene, Indiana, quadrangle showing the intersection of the Second Principal Meridian and its base line.

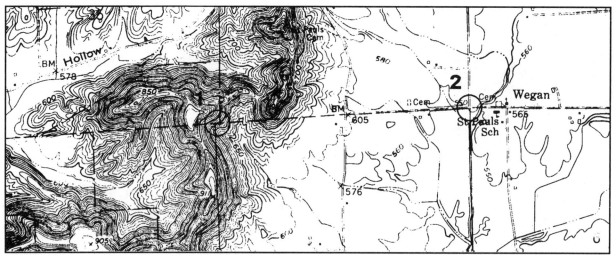

Figure 5—A portion of the Vallonia, Indiana, quadrangle showing a "jump" (at 1) and a "bend" (at 2) in range and township lines used to correct the size variation in townships as the survey moves north.

Greenville Treaty Line, whose direction can be determined by the western boundary of Dearborn County, was surveyed from the First Principal Meridian (the Indiana-Ohio boundary) and a base line in Kentucky. This survey is commonly known as the Ohio Survey. The remainder of the state is surveyed from the Second Principal Meridian, just west of the middle of the state, and from a base line about 24 miles north of the Ohio River, crossing south of Paoli in Orange County. (see Figure 4)

The Second Principal Meridian was laid out in 1804 by Ebinezer Buckingham. The survey of Indiana was completed in 1840. Indiana became a state in 1816.

The next step in surveying the land, after the principal meridian and base line are established, is to lay out tracts approximately 24 miles square. Since the earth is a ball, the north-south boundary lines of these tracts (known as range lines) con-

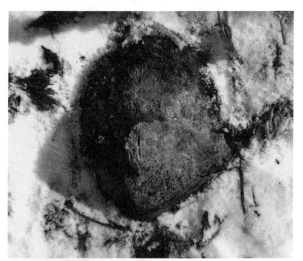

Figure 6—A section corner stone marking the author's property in central Indiana. (photo Tom Rea)

verge toward the north. The east-west boundaries (known as township lines) are always at right angles to the range lines so they are curved lines. This is corrected when the tracts are laid out causing a "jump" in the range lines and a "bend" in the township lines. (see Figure 5) These tracts are next divided into six mile square areas known as congressional townships. Congressional townships are different from the more familiar civil townships which are political divisions and have names. The surveyor runs north-south lines (range lines) at intervals of six miles to the east and west of the principal meridian. The six mile strips between them are called ranges. Ranges are numbered upward starting at the principal meridian. Ranges east of the principal meridian are designated Range 1 East, Range 2 East, etc; those on the west are designated Range 1 West, Range 2 West, etc.

Next the surveyor runs east-west lines (township lines), again at six mile intervals. The numbering of townships is similar to the numbering of ranges: Township 1 North, Township 2 South, etc. Originally ranges were numbered with Roman numerals and townships were numbered with Arabic numerals. More recently Roman numerals have been discontinued in favor of Arabic numerals for both townships and ranges.

The range lines and township lines cross forming six mile squares. These are the congressional townships. In the description of a township it is necessary to refer to both its range and township; for instance, the township in the northwest corner of the crossing of a principal meridian and its baseline would be Township 1 North, Range 1 West, or, as it is abbreviated, T.1-N, R.1-W.

In order to further subdivide the township, the surveyor locates what are known as section lines. Section lines run at intervals of one mile north and south and east and west. They divide the township

6	5	4	3	2	1
7	8	9	10	11	12
18	17	16	15	14	13
19	20	21	22	23	24
30	29	28	27	26	25
31	32	33	34	35	36

Figure 7—Numbering of sections in a township

into 36 sections, each one mile square. Finally the surveyor divides each section into four equal parts known as quarter sections. Each quarter section corner is marked in the field, usually by a large stone (a "three man" stone) with a cross chiseled into it. (see Figure 6) These stones must be found today to complete an accurate survey. A perfect township contains 23,040 acres. A perfect section contains 640 acres. All sections do not contain exactly 640 acres for two reasons. First, surveyors make mistakes; and second, since the range lines converge as they run north, townships vary more or less from 23,040 acres. Converging lines are corrected as described above. The original surveyor's errors are lived with and never corrected.

In the case where a section varies from 640 acres, the southeast quarter section is laid out exactly one half mile square and the error is distributed among the remaining three quarters.

In numbering the 36 sections that make up a township, the surveyor starts with Section 1 in the northeast corner of the township and runs west to Section 6 in the northwest corner. Section 7 is south of Section 6 and the numbers run east to Section 12 which is south of Section 1. They continue back and forth in this manner until they end with Section 36 in the southeast corner. (see Figure 7)

Any location in an area surveyed by the public land survey may be described by reference to the quarter-section, section, township, and range. For example: Northwest quarter of Section 29, Township 13 North, Range 1 East. This is usually abbreviated NW 1/4, Sec.29, T.13-N, R.1-E. For more definite locations quarter sections are often di-

vided into equal quarters and these smaller areas are again divided until the desired degree of exactness is reached. A quarter of a quarter of a quarter contains 10 acres which is quite a large area to search for a small cave opening.

The most common mistake cavers make in using the public land survey is to confuse the order of the quarters when reading or writing the abbreviated form of a location. Remember that the smallest area is stated first. For example NW 1/4, SE 1/4, NE 1/4, Sec.10 should be read as "The northwest quarter of the southeast quarter of the northeast quarter of Section 10." (see Figure 8) To avoid confusion, read "of the" for each comma in the description.

Many people have made plastic overlays the exact size of a normal section on a 7½ minute topographic map on which the quarter, quarter, quarter sections are carefully laid off. This template is very useful in writing the location after a cave has been spotted on the map. These templates may also be bought ready made. One may be available from a surveying or engineering supply store.

Universal Transverse Mercator Grid

Most 7½ minute topographic maps have one or more additional grid systems for locating or describing the location of points. The Universal Transverse Mercator Grid (UTM) is useful for locating caves. It has several advantages: The squares are all the same size and shape. You describe a point rather than an area. You make straight line measurements rather than angle

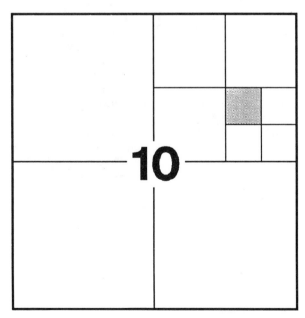

Figure 8—Naming of a subdivision of a section. The shaded area is NW 1/4, SE 1/4, NE 1/4, Sec 10

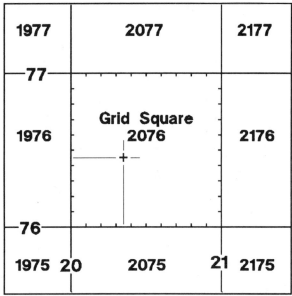

Figure 9–Division of a grid square and numbering of a point.

measurements. The system is not widely used and a person who does not know the system will not even know he is seeing a location when the cave description is right in front of him. The UTM Grid is indicated on the topographic map by blue ticks along the neat line of the map. There is a blue tick every thousand meters and the grid squares are 1,000 meters square.

Starting at 180°E the globe is divided into narrow zones six degrees wide and numbered 1 through 60. Each zone has one meridian known as the "central meridian" that passes through the center of the zone. Using the intersection of the central meridian and the equator as the origin any location could be described by measuring the distance east or west and north or south from the origin. This would involve the same inconvenience as geographical coordinates, however, the necessity of including N, S, E, or W in the measurement. This is avioded by assigning a numerical value to the origin that will produce positive values for all measurements in the zone. The value assigned to the central meridian is 500,000 meters with values increasing from west to east. This value is known as "false easting." In the northern hemisphere the equator is zero and values increase toward the north. In the southern hemisphere, to permit val-

ues to increase toward the north, the equator is given a value of 10,000,000 meters, with values decreasing toward the pole. These are known as "false northings."

The first grid line in each direction from the southeast corner of the map is labled with its false easting and false northing value. The grid interval on the 7½ minute topographic maps is 1,000 meters. Two digits of the value are printed in large type and are called the "principal digits". See the value $^521^{000m}$E. in Figure 2. It labels the tick between the "N" and "G" in "WASHINGTON" which is a blue tick on the original map. This is the false easting for this line and means that it is 21,000 meters east of the central meridian of the zone. The first tick north of the corner on this same map (which does not show in the figure) is labeled $^{42}76^{000m}$N. which means that this line is 4,276,000 meters north of the equator. The intersection of these two lines designates a point. The designation of a grid square identified by such a point always follows the rule, read RIGHT and UP. The coordinates 2076 identify the 1,000 meter square which lies to the right and up from where grid lines 20 and 76 cross (see Figure 9). A 1,000 meter square is too large to be of any practical use in locating a cave entrance, however. To locate the cave more precicely, the sides of the square can be divided into 100 equal parts. This gives a square ten meters on a side (about 33 feet). In Figure 9 the + lies in grid square 2076, 350 meters (35%) east of line 20 and 450 meters (45%) north from line 76. The coordinates of the point would be 20357645. Grid coordinates are written as one number but they always contain an equal number of digits. The first half of the total digits refer to RIGHT and the second half refer to UP.

Given spots on the map can be located by proportional parts, exactly like the procedure given above for geographical coordinates. However, on a 7½ minute quadrangle, the UTM Grid squares are less than two inches across. If you understand the mechanics and mathmatics of the prior process, you can use the same technique with a metric rule and measure the proportion of five millimeters. A template, or overlay, that will divide the sides of a UTM Grid square into 100 equal parts is available, but it is much harder to find than one for the Public Land Survey. Perhaps you can find one in a military surplus store.

Chapter 23

ELECTRONICS IN CAVING

Frank Reid
NSS 9086

Many cavers are knowledgeable in electronics, and would like to combine their seemingly incompatible interests.

Electronic aids to caving are gaining popularity in the United States. "Cave radio" is a powerful mapping aid. Underground and surface communication is vital to cave rescue. Electronic instrumentation and telemetry are used in cave-related sciences—that is, hydrology and bat study. The small, affordable electronic navigation receivers now available have numerous cave-related uses. Caving electronics includes electric lights and battery-charging systems. (See Chapters 3 and 4.)

Computers are increasingly important in cave study. Cavers have developed software for computer-assisted survey data reduction, map plotting, and cave data management.

Cave Radio.

Magnetic-induction cave radios can communicate through a few hundred meters of rock. More important, however, is their ability to precisely locate the surface point above an underground transmitter and measure depth. The technique is well-developed and reliable. Besides mapping, cave radio is an aid to connection searches and rescue. It has located water-well sites for landowners, surveyed property boundaries at commercial caves, and found places to dig new cave entrances.

Most cave radios operate at very low frequencies. Some transmit voice, others communicate only by Morse code. Cave radios are not available commercially; plans have been published by the National Speleological Society's Communication and Electronics Section, one of many self-supporting special-interest groups within the Society.

An underground transmitter passes low-frequency current through a coil of wire, creating a magnetic field which is detected on the surface by a receiver with a similar coil antenna. To "home in" on the transmitter location, we use the directional properties of loop antennas—the received signal strength depends on the quantity of magnetic flux passing through the receiving loop. The nature of this dependence is shown in Figure 1; the abrupt disappearance (null) of the signal when the plane of the loop is parallel to the field tells us when the antenna is pointing toward the transmitter.

Note in Figure 1 that the null is much more sharply defined than is the direction of maximum signal.

If the underground coil is level, then the axis of the magnetic field is vertical and the geometry of the field is as shown by dashed lines in Figure 2 (from above) and Figure 3 (from the side).

When within range and receiving the signal, hold the receiving loop in a vertical plane and rotate it around a vertical axis until the null is found. The plane of the loop at the null contains "ground zero" (the center of the magnetic field) but the direction is ambiguous. Move to a nearby point and repeat this procedure. The intersection of the two planes so determined gives the approximate location of ground zero, as shown in Figure 2.

The ground-zero location can be refined to within a few centimeters by holding the loop in a vertical plane with its axis aimed toward the expected location, and tilting it backward or forward to find the null. In the side view of the magnetic field, we see that the magnetic lines slant away from ground zero as they emerge from the ground nearby. Ground zero therefore lies in the direction opposite the tilt of the loop when the null is obtained. Move toward decreasing vertical angles until the null is straight down. Rotate the loop 90 degrees horizontally, and again seek a straight-down null. Repeat the turn-and-seek process as necessary—ground zero is the one point where the null is exactly vertical, no matter which way the loop's axis is pointed. A spirit-level should be mounted on the loop to indicate when it is vertical.

This technique is extremely sensitive; the null plane will differ measurably from vertical when the base of the loop is 10 to 20 centimeters from ground zero, even when the transmitter is 50 meters below. The main limit to the accuracy of this method is the precision with which the transmitting loop can be leveled; a leveling error of ½ degree will produce a ground-zero location error of about one percent of the transmitter depth.

Measuring Depth

The following procedure is from *Caving Information Series,* article number 8501, published by the National Speleological Society. Since the closed curves of the magnetic field (side view) are ellipses, we cannot find depth by simple triangulation. The shape of the curves is well known, however, so we can still use this information to compute depth.

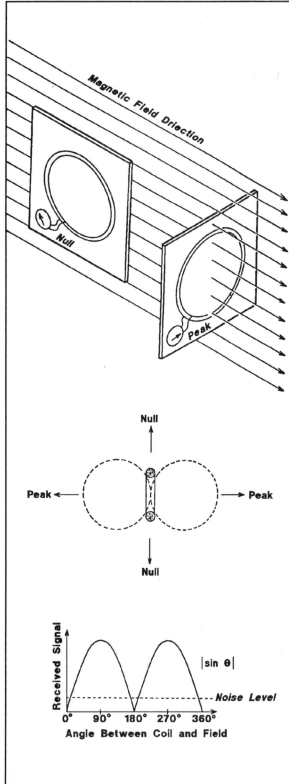

Figure 1—Principle of direction finding. The received signal disappears when the coil is parallel to the magnetic field. Nulls are more sharply defined than peaks, but with very weak signals, you may have to seek peaks not nulls.

Using a simple but adequate approximation to the shape of the field, we can write the relation

$$\text{Tan } \Theta = \frac{3LD}{2D^2 - L^2}$$

for the angle the field makes with the vertical at a distance L from ground zero when the transmitter is at depth D (the angle is measured in the plane containing ground zero). Figure 4 is a set of curves of D versus the angle, for various values of the distance from ground zero. Larger charts are included in references 1 and 2.

Having such a diagram available, stretch a measuring tape in a straight line away from ground zero in some direction where it can be made to lie fairly level. Pick a set of distances along the tape which correspond to curves on the diagram (in meters or feet—the chart works with any distance units). Measure the angles (Θ) (Figure 3) at these points. Do this by pointing the axis of the receiving loop toward ground zero, then tilting the loop forward or backward as needed to find the null in the signal. The resulting angle can be measured with an adjustable machinist's protractor or other inclinometer. Plot the data on the diagram as shown. The points should lie near a straight horizontal line corresponding to the depth of the underground station.

For best accuracy use enough points to give an accurate estimate of the best line; avoid parts of the diagram where the curves are steeply rising (Θ less than about 12 degrees); measure vertical angles to at least the nearest $\frac{1}{2}$ degree. If possible, take another set of depth data in the direction opposite the first.

The radio locating process has intrinsic error indicators. If the transmitting coil is unlevel, it will be impossible to find a unique ground zero; the receiver operator will keep searching around a small area. In such a case, check for proper alignment of the receiving loop's bubble level. If the problem persists, mark ground zero in the middle of the ambiguous area.

If the transmitting loop is unlevel or if ground zero has been improperly located, depth readings will have an increasing or decreasing trend as shown in the top half of Figure 5. The curved lines of points approach the true depth as the distance from ground zero increases. If data have been gathered in opposite directions from ground zero as suggested, most of the error will be removed by averaging the two sets.

A programmable pocket-calculator can be used to evaluate the above equation solved for depth:

$$D = \frac{L\left(3 + \sqrt{9 + 8\tan^2\Theta}\right)}{4\tan\Theta}$$

$$0° < \Theta < 90°$$

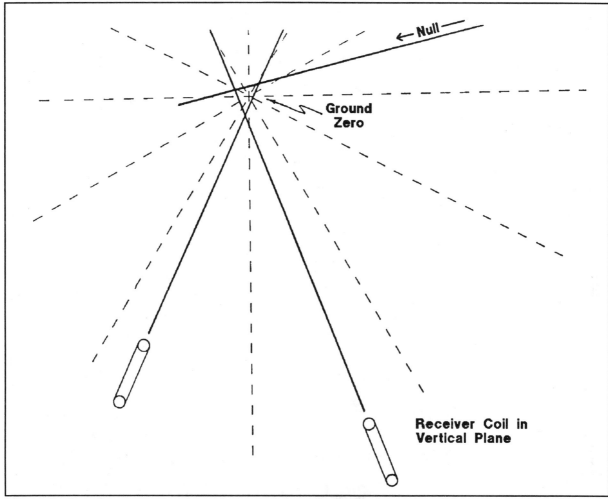

Figure 2—Locating approximate surface point above the transmitter, viewed from above. Dashed lines in Figures 2 and 3 are magnetic lines of force.

Depths calculated from several pairs of data should be averaged. The calculator method does not require a copy of the special chart, and data may be taken at any convenient distance along the measuring tape. The chart method is least expensive and makes more obvious the effects of the errors discussed above. It should be possible to determine the depth of the transmitter within three percent.

Conductive or magnetic ore-bodies which could distort the magnetic field seldom occur in limestone cave areas. (Cullingford, 1969)

Cave Communication

Long-duration underground camping expeditions, popular in many countries, are seldom used in the United States. Such expeditions require communication links with the surface for logistical support and weather warnings. Cavers, notably British Commonwealth and European, have developed sophisticated equipment for un-

derground communication by telephone and wireless means.

Pit Communication

Radio waves normally do not penetrate the earth, nor will they follow cave passages for an appreciable distance. Few radios can withstand the cave environment. Suitably-protected Citizens' Band (CB) and VHF radios have been used for communication in very deep pits. Even in line-of-sight conditions, radio waves reflected from walls may cancel each other, resulting in "dead spots." Inexpensive 49-megahertz "headset" radios have been used successfully in pits; their voice-activated transmitters provide hands-free operation.

Experimenters have achieved ranges of over 300 meters (1,000 feet) by holding CB and 49-MHz radio antennas near a wire strung through cave passage, such that the signal follows the wire. Any insulated wire will work. The "guide wire" should be strung through air as much as possible, minimiz-

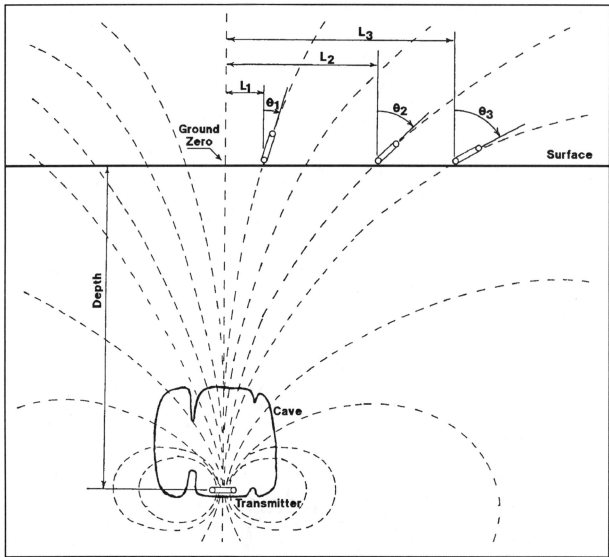

Figure 3 — Ground zero is the point where the field is vertical (see text). Distances (L) and vertical angles (θ) are used in calcuating the depth of the transmitter.

ing contact with walls or floor. Special ropes containing telephone wires should work well for conducting radio signals.

Rescue Communication

Communication is vital in cave rescue. Cavers crawling back and forth with messages waste time and create extra traffic and confusion. Cave radios are not widely available, therefore we rely upon military-surplus or other field telephones under ground. Radios and telephones provide outside communication. The National Cave Rescue Commission (NCRC) and the NSS Electronics Section have developed special equipment for rescue communication.

Communication, of course, is not electronic equipment but the exchange of ideas and information. Problems often occur when cavers and other rescue participants do not understand each others' terminology. Practice rescues should include communication with other emergency services (fire-rescue, ambulance, etc.) likely to be involved.

The easiest way to maintain clear and effective communication is to decide upon message content before speaking. Listen before you transmit. The worst communication problems occur when inexperienced or excited operators all try to talk at once. Talking too loudly causes distortion and decreases intelligibility.

A field-telephone circuit from the cave entrance to as near the patient as possible is the most critical link; it should be considered second only to getting the first medical team to the patient. This link expedites delivery of manpower and supplies, and will provide communication to a physician outside the cave. Phone and wire should immediately follow the first team if the patient's location is known, or as soon as the patient has been found.

Test all telephones before deployment! The first wiring team should carry two phones, in case of failure or for an intermediate station at a critical point between patient and entrance. A telephone talker should accompany the team moving the patient.

For planning purposes, phone wire should be considered expendable. In real rescues it often becomes damaged or hopelessly tangled during retrieval, or is abandoned if rescuers are too exhausted. Telephones or radios may link the cave entrance to a staging area (perhaps the nearest parking area or shelter). Ideally, the various communication links should be able to interconnect as desired. A log keeper should record the times and contents of messages to prevent loss of vital information and for later analysis of the rescue.

A long-range link ties the rescue site to the outside world (police, hospital, etc). This link speeds the dispatch of additional resources, and allows coordinators to activate or release the backup teams on standby. The longer distance "control" circuit usually requires a commercial telephone or an amateur radio link. Two-way radio

can establish communication between the rescue site and the nearest available telephone.

Rescue communications equipment should include telephone directories, and a portable, "Bell-compatible" telephone with a very long cord and various connectors. A telephone credit card allows charging long-distance calls to your home number when using another private or public telephone.

All phones and radios must be cleaned, dried, and tested soon after each rescue, else corrosion may do irreversible damage.

Radio Communication

All radios are delicate; treat them as you would cameras. Do not use radios underground unless there is no alternative. Tie portable radios to climbers and people near pits.

The most common type of 2-way radios are 27-MHz Citizens' Band (CB) sets. It is usually possible to acquire several sets of CB equipment on short notice. CB has serious limitations: Interference can make CB unreliable or totally unusable. CB radio traffic concerning a cave rescue may attract unwanted attention. CB radios are not sturdily constructed, and often fail under field condi-

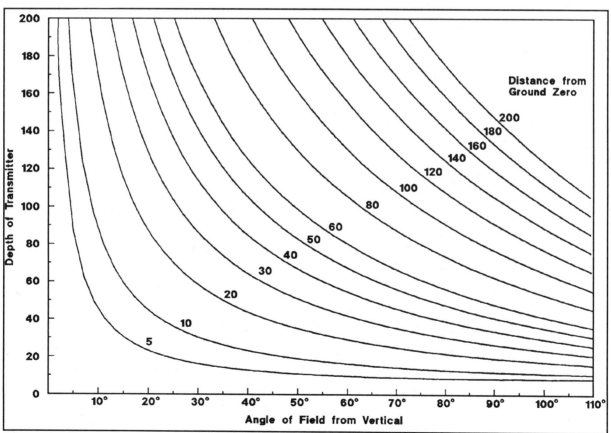

Figure 4—Cave radio depth gauge.

tions. If you must depend upon CB at a rescue, try to procure as many spare radios as possible.

The radio needs of each group will differ, depending upon group size, organization, operating area, and how the group interacts with other emergency services. There is presently no national standardization of 2-way radio for cave rescue. The reasonably-priced "frequency-agile" radios now available can meet a wide range of contingencies.

Radio Security

The news media and family should NOT be able to overhear cave rescue communications or discussions between rescuers, lest they draw incorrect conclusions from fragments of conversation. News agencies usually discover cave rescues by monitoring emergency frequencies. Crowds attracted by radio traffic can impede rescue efforts. The following procedures will minimize eavesdropping:
- Restrict unnecessary conversation.
- Use telephones instead of radios whenever possible.

- Avoid broadcasting names and locations unnecessarily.
- Avoid CB radio.
- Use earphones.
- Use tape to cover frequency readouts on radios.
- Use short range radios for local communication.

Interconnected Communication Links

Connecting the various systems together saves time and preserves message integrity by eliminating the need to relay messages. For example, the field-phone circuit inside the cave could be linked directly to a radio transceiver at the entrance, and by radio into commercial telephone. It is especially important to provide a direct voice link to a physician when medical treatment is required.

A phone patch connects radios and telephones together. Phone patches are available commercially, or can be home-built. Cave rescuers have designed a "universal" phone patch for linking field phones, commercial phones, and radios in any combination.

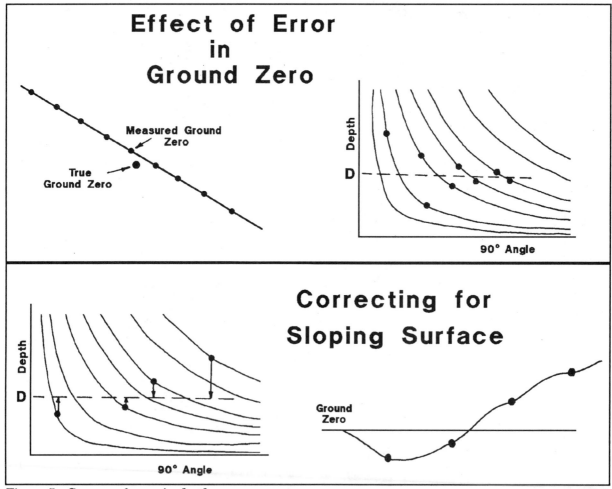

Figure 5—Sources of error in depth measurement.

"Acoustic patch" (holding a radio and telephone close together) is cumbersome and degrades voice quality but often works acceptably. It is worth trying when no direct-connect device is available.

VHF and UHF repeaters greatly extend the range of mobile and hand held transceivers by retransmitting their signals from high elevation at high power. Amateur radio repeaters cover most of the United States. Many have an "autopatch" feature, allowing access into the telephone system via a Touch-Tone® keyboard on the user's radio. Autopatch repeaters have proven invaluable during many cave rescues.

The NCRC has tested a voice-activated portable repeater made from field telephones, phone patches, and hand held radios. This system automatically links underground telephones to radios on the surface.

Amateur ("ham") radio operators (not to be confused with CB operators) freely offer valuable support during cave rescues and other emergencies. Hams can organize and man communication networks, freeing cavers to work underground. Cave rescue groups should contact a local ham-radio club and become familiar with their capabilities, which often exceed those of professional emergency services. These public service oriented groups build and maintain repeaters and emergency communication vehicles, conduct simulated emergency exercises, and hold training classes for people wishing to get amateur radio licenses. (The technician class license, which allows VHF and UHF voice operation, is quite easy to get and no longer requires a knowledge of Morris code.)

Future Caving Electronics

Portable earth-satellite communication equipment may become available for cave rescue operations. Rescue groups have experimented with biomedical telemetry (EKG) from cave to hospital via interconnected communication links.

Amateur-radio "packet" digital communication networks are being established which carry long-range, error-free, and relatively secure written messages. Their usefulness has been demonstrated in large-scale emergencies. Packet technology is also useful for transmitting scientific data from cave to surface; cavers have demonstrated microprocessor-controlled instruments for underground data-gathering.

Small, affordable receivers for the Loran-C and GPS electronic navigation systems are becoming available. These are useful for surface karst studies, mapping, guidance to unfamiliar caves and to specify locations for rescue helicopters.

There are presently no reliable ways of detecting caves electronically. Research in remote-sensing, geophysics, and antisubmarine warfare may someday yield useful methods.

References

Use of the Cave Radio in Mapping, Caving Information Series #8501, National Speleological Society., 5 pp

Mixon, W. and R. Blenz (1964): "Locating an Underground Transmitter by Surface Measurements," *Windy City Speleonews*, December 1964, p. 61., reprinted in *Speleo Digest*, 1964. A revised, condensed version by W. Mixon appeared with the same title in the *NSS NEWS*, April 1966, p 61.

Plummer, W (1964): "Depth Measurement with the Cave Radio," *Baltimore Grotto News*, August 1964, p. 259. This and other cave-radio articles by Plummer were reprinted in Speleo Digest, 1964.

Reid, F. (1984): "Cave Man Radio," *73 Magazine*, February 1984.

Drummond, I (1984): "Cave Radio Update," *NSS NEWS*, Dec. 1984, p 366.

The Radio Amateur's Handbook: Newington, CT, American Radio Relay League, revised yearly.

Cullingford, C., ed. (1969): *Manual of Caving Techniques*, Cave Research Group of Great Britain, Routledge & Kegan Paul, London, 1969.

Hudson, S., ed. (1987): Manual of U.S. Cave Rescue Techniques. (second edition), National Speleological Society.

NSS Communication and Electronics Section, PO Box 891, Camden, AR 71701.

BCRA Cave Radio and Electronics Group, c/o Dick Glover, 11 Gerard Ave, Morley, Leeds LS8 43X, United Kingdom.

LINDA HESLOP

Chapter 24

WHY YOU SHOULD JOIN
AN ORGANIZED CAVING GROUP*

David McClurg
NSS 4608

Organized caving clubs offer five things you can't provide for yourself—and for the most part won't be able to find any other place. Here's what they are:

- **They know how to cave and can show you how.**
- **They know where the caves are.**
- **They have ropes and other special gear.**
- **They go caving.**

And in most cases—unless you are a complete klutz . . .

- **They'll welcome you, whether you're a beginner or an experienced caver.**

Let's take these one at a time to see how important they are, both to the neophyte and to the old timer who has recently moved to a new area.

They know how to cave and can show you how. Experienced cavers, by definition, know how to cave. Just as vital, they know the caves in their area and know what's needed to explore those caves.

Whether they have a formal training program or just take you out to some easy caves on your first trip, this is the way to learn. You're with other cavers, so that meets the warning about not caving alone. And by following what they do and asking questions you can learn the basics much more safely than you can alone or with some other inexperienced recruits.

They know where the caves are. It doesn't matter what part of the country you live in, this is worth the price of admission all by itself. Every new caver soon finds out that the best way (sometimes the only way) to find a cave is to go there with some one who's been there before. Clubs have been there before. More on this later.

They have the specialized gear. This is why some groups got together in the first place. They wanted to share the cost of an expensive piece of equipment like a long rope, mechanical ascenders, or surveying equipment. One club I know passes the hard hat at every meeting to save up for new equipment.

They go caving. What this actually means is that they have regularly scheduled trips, probably once a month or more in good weather. Trips are often varied, some to horizontal caves, some to vertical, some for beginners, some more advanced.

Many clubs lay out the schedule in January for the whole year. This lets them make the most of holidays or three-day weekends. Also, members can plan their time off to go on a Christmas trip to Mexico or a June excursion to the annual caving convention.

So strongly do cavers prize their three-day weekends, that when my youngest daughter got married, she felt compelled to apologize to local cavers on two counts. Not only was she marrying a non-caver, she was getting married on Memorial Day Weekend. (It was the only time the college chapel was free.) Many cavers came anyway, three-day weekend or not. It only proves that all cavers worth their weight in carbide will never turn down free food and beverage!

They will welcome you (usually). As I said, unless you're a complete klutz, most caving groups will welcome anyone with a real interest in the sport. Now, I know of some exceptions that prove the rule—but by and large it's true. However, I'll give you this warning gratis—if you're shy, you may be completely overlooked at your first meeting. Don't be afraid to speak up. Tell the group who you are and why you decided to come to their meeting instead of staying home to watch your favorite TV show.

Some clubs have an official meeter and greeter who watches for new people and hands out membership applications or new caver information sheets. If you're lucky, you may locate this kind of group. If not, don't be put off at first by the inside jokes and comments about activities that seem completely foreign. Stick with it for a meeting or two even if it seems that you're being treated like an outsider.

Whatever you do, don't start out by asking for a complete list of local caves, or for detailed directions on how to find them. I guarantee you that this will not endear you to the group. Many cavers are super sensitive about conservation and very protective of local caves.

If you've been caving elsewhere but are a newcomer to the area, you can usually expect to be welcomed too.

By the way (if you'll pardon the commercial). this is one of the hidden benefits of being a member of the National Speleological Society. With an So-

---

* Adapted from the author's book, *Adventure of Caving*, ©1987, D & J Press.

ciety membership list in hand you can chart your course to locate kindred caving spirits all over the country. Many will invite you to their meetings or on a cave trip. If you're on the road, you might get lucky and be asked into their homes to talk caving or to stay, if you don't mind sleeping on the floor.

To sum it up, cave clubs offer fellowship and a framework for cave exploration. So the next question is how do you find a local club?

The National Speleological Society

As you might have guessed, a good place to start is to ask the National Speleological Society. It turns out that a lot of the action in the caving world takes place in and around the chapters and individual members of the National Speleological Society.

It has an active publications program designed to keep the membership up to date on developments in both the sport of caving and the science of speleology.

Besides grottos, the National Speleological Society has many special interest sections (geology, vertical caving, electronics, biology, photography, to mention a few) most of which have their own publications and sessions at the annual convention.

As of 1992, the Society has over 10,000 members and more than 150 local chapters, or grottos. Most are in the United States, but Canada has a number of members too, as well as a scattering throughout the rest of the world.

To find out if there is a grotto near you, address an inquiry to the—

National Speleological Society
2813 Cave Avenue
Huntsville, Aabama 35810-4431
Phone: (205) 852-1300

Since they get a lot of inquiries every month, a self addressed, stamped envelope would be appreciated even though it's not required.

The Society has some paid professionals in its Huntsville office, but the administration, committees, and local grottos are all run by volunteers. Be patient if things seem a little on the slow side.

Conventions

One of the most rewarding Society events is its annual convention, generally held in late June or mid-August. It rotates around the country, and is a tribute to the hard work and stamina of the local volunteers who put it on in their area.

The annual Society convention is the one time of the year when the Society really comes together—cave trips, meetings, fellowship, technical sessions, papers, more fellowship, slide shows, seminars, films, workshops, a banquet, and even more fellowship.

I've always felt it's the best thing the Society does by a long shot. You meet friends old and new and swap caving stories (some of them even true) during a week that's so full of activities that you just can't do everything you'd like to.

Regional Conventions

In addition to the summertime national convention, many Society regional organizations hold weekend caving meets in their part of the country. Some of these are quite venerable affairs, with over 25 or 30 years of tradition behind them. One is usually held somewhere each weekend in the summer, most popular being the three-day weekends like Memorial Day, July Fourth, or Labor Day.

Like the NSS Convention, many regional events have contests, papers, slide shows, and a banquet in addition to cave trips.

During the winter, a number of regions also sponsor educational seminars, sometimes called paper regionals or sessions regionals. These often take place on Washington's Birthday or around Easter, when many people have three-day weekends.

All of these meetings are great fun—a real chance to see old friends and learn some new skills.

They're all part of the many benefits—publications, caving trips, meetings, fellowship, and more—that you get from joining organized caving.

Pat Newby admires the spectacular formations in Three Fingers Cave, New Mexico. (photo Scott Fee)

Chapter 25

CAVE GEOLOGY

John E. Mylroie
NSS 12514
and William B. White
NSS 2237

Introduction

This chapter is intended to provide an introduction to the descriptive aspects of cave geology. It tells something about the patterns and shapes of caves, and about the features found inside caves. The chapter initially looks at all types of caves, but will eventually focus on caves formed by dissolution in limestone and related rocks. The origin of these caves will be reviewed in a general way, so that the reader will be able to view any dissolution cave in terms of how it may have developed. With an understanding of how dissolution caves form and change through time, the caver can more fully appreciate caves, and have a better chance of locating undiscovered cave.

The practitioners of cave geology usually operate from one of two viewpoints. They may be inwardly looking, concerned about some specific cave or cave system, its historical evolution in context of its geologic setting, the minerals it contains, or the detailed processes of growth and decay that are the fate of all caves. Alternatively, they may be outwardly looking, concerned with the regional flow of groundwater in an aquifer that happens to contain caves, with the chemistry of the dissolution process by which caves are formed, or with the evolution of entire drainage basins and how the caves can be used as clues to historical events. Examples of the current state of cave geology may be found in the textbooks cited at the end, to which this chapter may be regarded as an introduction.

What is a cave? Some writers insist that a cave is a "natural cavity beneath the earth's surface whose dimensions are measurable in feet, whose walls are bedrock, and usually extending to absolute darkness." Quite a bit is wrong with this definition. There are caves in the mountains into which daylight may penetrate for hundreds of meters. There are caves in unconsolidated sediments or in glacial ice whose walls are not in bedrock. How large a void must be to qualify as a cave depends on the observer. The Alabama Cave Survey requires 15 meters (50 feet); the New Jersey Cave Survey, two meters (six feet). Our favorite definition is: "A cave is a natural opening large enough to admit a human explorer and which some explorers, at least, chose to call a 'cave.'"

Caves and their geology are seen primarily from the viewpoint of the explorer, and as the definition above shows, it is almost impossible to separate our ideas of what a cave is and how it looks from our experiences in traversing the cave. Terms such as "crawlway," "stoopway," and "walking passage" reflect our preoccupation with negotiating caves. If the cave passage becomes too small, or fills with water, or is choked with sediment, we say the cave ends (Figure 1). The cave doesn't necessarily end under these circumstances, our ability to continue

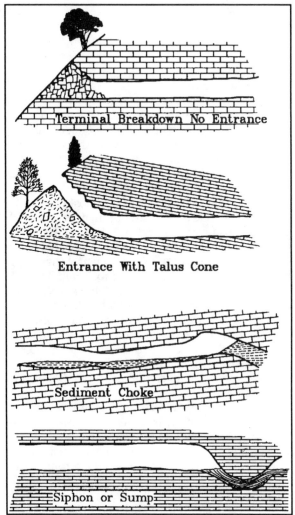

Figure 1 — Several types of cave passage truncations. (from White, 1976)

ends. Defining caves in terms of human accessibility is called "explorational bias," and this bias must be recognized when we think about the geology of caves. Explorational bias is inherent in all we do with caves, for without human exploration, we would know next to nothing about caves.

The Kinds of Caves

We separate caves into two broad classes: those that are formed by essentially chemical processes and those that are formed by mechanical processes. Within these two classes caves are listed by the major process which led to their formation.

I. Caves formed by mainly chemical processes:
   (strongly dependent on the type of host rock)
   1. Dissolution caves
   2. Lava caves
   3. Ice caves

II. Caves formed by mainly mechanical processes:
   (Essentially independent of the lithology of the host rock)
   1. Tectonic caves
   2. Eolian caves
   3. Sea caves
   4. Talus caves
   5. Suffosional caves
   6. Erosion caves

Dissolution caves are formed by the removal of bedrock by groundwater and/or by underground streams. The water transports the bulk of the rock material out of the cave in solution. In recent years, geologists have begun to differentiate the act of dissolving rock (dissolution) from the resulting mixture of water and dissolved rock (the solution), hence the term "dissolution cave." Most rocks, even the highly soluble ones, also contain a certain residuum of insoluble material which must be transported mechanically by the water. Most dissolution caves are in limestone. Less frequently they occur in dolomite, marble, gypsum, or rock salt. The only requirement is that the bedrock be soluble. Over long time periods in unusually stable environments, even rocks like granites and quartz sandstones can occasionally form dissolution caves. Limestone caves achieve the largest sizes and contain most of the interesting and attractive mineral deposits.

Lava caves form in fluid pahoehoe basalt lava flows and result from the draining of moving subsurface streams of lava after the surrounding lava has solidified. In many instances, an outlet permits draining of the tube and a conduit-like cave results. These can be of considerable length, such as Ape Cave in Washington which is more than three kilometers long, or of considerable complexity, such as in Lava Beds National Monument in California. Single conduits, anastomatic systems, and multi-level systems are common. These caves occur in most volcanic areas in the United States.

Ice caves are caves formed in ice. These occur in many glaciers throughout the world and form by the action of subglacial streams which emerge from the foot of the glacier. Once the cave is formed, air motion through the cave may also remove ice from the cave walls by sublimation, enlarging the cave further. Ice caves consist of long elliptical tube conduits often with delicately sculptured walls. Exploration of these caves is difficult since they are often completely flooded during part of the day by surface meltwater, and may be accessible only at night when the water freezes on the surface. Explorations of several kilometers have been conducted. Because glaciers are dynamic and move, and because they are vulnerable to variations in sunlight and snowfall, the passages can collapse, migrate, or disappear from summer to summer. An extreme example of ephemeral cave development is the formation of ice caves in thick seasonal ice that collects in the winter and melts away in the summer. Explorers can literally watch these caves grow and die within a few months.

Ice caves should not be confused with "glacieres" or freezing caves which are simply caves in bedrock of some sort which contain perennial ice. The term "ice cave" in most American writing refers to this type of cave.

Tectonic caves are formed by actual movement of masses of bedrock. They can occur in any type of rock (including limestone), but are usually associated with hard, insoluble rocks where they are easily distinguished from caves of other origins. The type of bedrock movement can vary. It might be slippage along bedding planes, parting because of intense folding, or sudden splitting due to faulting. The term "tectonic" implies that the caves developed as the rock was deformed, but in most cases it is later weathering of the deformed rock that allows separation of the rock under the influence of gravity to produce a cave. Tectonic caves are usually small, but examples are known that run into hundreds of meters of passage.

Eolian caves are formed by the abrading action of wind-borne particles. They are common to desert regions where soft sandstones often have caves carved into them. Caves which are apparently formed by wind action have also been reported in loess, a homogeneous deposit of silt. Eolian caves are generally small, usually a single chamber. They are common in the southwestern United States.

Sea caves (also called "littoral caves" in some literature) are formed by the milling of sea coasts by wave action. They occur in many coastal areas throughout the world. Some of the most famous caves known are sea caves, such as Fingal's Cave in the Hebrides Islands and the Blue Grotto on the Isle of Capri. While some sea caves have formed along the rocky New England coast, the mid-Atlantic and Gulf coasts of the United States are unsuitable for development of sea caves because of the low relief of the Coastal Plain. The coasts of California, Oregon, Washington, Alaska, and the Hawaiian Islands abound with sea caves in a variety of rocks. Some of these caves can reach lengths of more than 100 meters.

Talus caves are formed when masses of piled boulders or other rock debris arrange themselves in such a way as to leave negotiable openings beneath and between the blocks. Most boulder slopes have many openings, but they are rarely human-sized. When the blocks are unusually large, the openings between them are also larger and caves with big chambers and lengths of over a kilometer can be found. Talus caves are most common in mountain regions where glaciation has over-steepened cliffs, promoting cliff collapse to produce large piles of big boulders. The Adirondak Mountains of New York, and the mountains of New England, Colorado, and California all have large talus caves.

Suffosional caves are produced by a process called "soil piping" in which unconsolidated soils and sediments are transported through a material by rapidly moving water. Sudden flows of water in unconsolidated or poorly consolidated materials may flush out openings of human size. These caves occur frequently in badland topography where gradients are steep and there is little vegetation to protect the underlying sediments. Suffosional caves are usually small, but examples from southern California can exceed several hundred meters in length.

Erosion caves is the term used to describe minor openings formed by mechanical erosion of soft rock material. Most "rock shelters" have this origin, where a soft shale horizon has eroded back beneath a resistant sandstone horizon. Rock shelters are routinely considered caves by archaeologists and historians because of the human activity associated with them. They often appear on topographic maps and in neighborhood memories. Limestones are usually mechanically resistant, and often interbedded with shales, so they readily form rockshelters, as many a ridgewalker has learned after following a local's directions on a long hike.

The Shapes of Caves

Most caves appear complex when viewed either from inside or in map view. It becomes less difficult to understand this complexity if we use a building block principle to describe caves. Caves are made of passages and chambers. These passages and chambers have various shapes, various relationships to each other, and have formed at various times. Passages and chambers may be genetically related or only fortuitously connected.

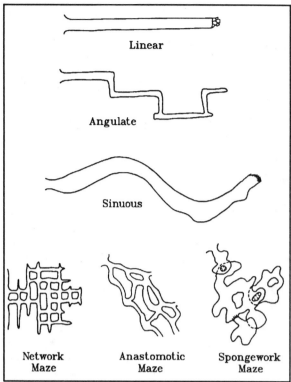

Figure 2—Plan view of several basic types of cave passage patterns. (from White, 1976)

Caves produced by chemical means tend to be the longest and the most complex, and they require interpreting of a variety of interconnected passage types and chamber configurations. Caves produced by mechanical means are often short, and the entire cave may be developed only as a single passage or chamber. However the cave formed, what is currently accessible to the explorer might only be a portion of a former larger cave system. To understand the cave, so that it may be explored completely and properly described, requires that the caver recognize the type of cave, and how much of it is currently accessible. Using simple geometric terms, cave passages and chambers can be described (Figure 2). Where a cave consists of only a simple geometry, it is considered a *fragment*. When the geometry is complex, the cave is considered a *system*.

I. Fragments
  A. Passages—isolated cave fragments without branches.
    1. linear—a straight reach of passage without bends.
    2. angulate—a passage that has several sharp bends.
    3. sinuous—a passage that has broad sweeping curves.
  B. Chambers—an isolated void or the local enlargement of a passage or intersection of passages.

Cave Type	Fragments				Systems			
	Passages			Chambers	Mazes			Dendritic
	Linear	Angulate	Sinuous		Network	Anastomatic	Spongework	
Cave Configurations								
Chemical								
Dissolution	X	X	X	X	X	X	X	X
Lava		X	X		X			X
Ice		X	X		X			X
Mechanical								
Tectonic	X	X		X	X			
Eolian				X				
Sea	X	X		X	X			
Talus	X	X		X			X	
Suffosion	X		X	X				X
Erosion	X	X		X				

Table 1 — Cave Configurations

II. Systems
    A. Mazes — a highly interconnected set of passages.
        1. network maze — angular grid of intersecting passages.

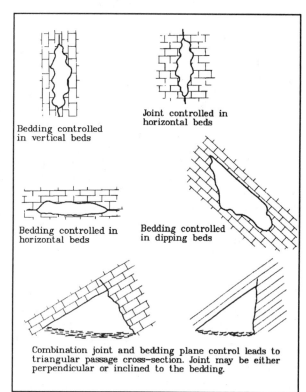

Bedding controlled in vertical beds

Joint controlled in horizontal beds

Bedding controlled in horizontal beds

Bedding controlled in dipping beds

Combination joint and bedding plane control leads to triangular passage cross-section. Joint may be either perpendicular or inclined to the bedding.

Figure 3 — Cross-sectional passage shapes which have been controlled mainly by the structure of the surrounding bedrock. (from White, 1976)

          a. on a single horizon.
          b. stacked on multiple horizons.
        2. anastomatic maze — curvilinear grid of passages; usually confined to a single plane.
        3. spongework — irregularly (and apparently randomly) interconnected cavities in three dimensions.
    B. Dendritic caves — collection of subsidiary cave passages and chambers focused on one or more central routes.

The geometric classification of caves presented above can be applied to the types of caves discussed earlier, as in Table 1. Note that chemical caves, especially dissolution caves, exhibit a tremendous variety of geometries, while most mechanical caves show only the simplest of the geometries. Mechanical caves produced by water transport, such as sea caves and suffosional caves, are among the most complex of this type. Some mechanical cave types are very simple because the process that forms them does not interact with the cave being formed, such as tectonic caves, eolian caves, or erosion caves. In other mechanical cave types, such as sea caves and suffosional caves, the formation of the cave is in part dependent upon the cave produced. There is a high degree of interaction and hence complexity. Chemical caves by definition form by interaction of the cave forming process with the cave produced, and the caves are therefore complex.

The geometric classification allows a cave system to be built from fragments. If a linear fragment is long enough, it will probably form a bend, in which case it moves up to angulate or sinuous

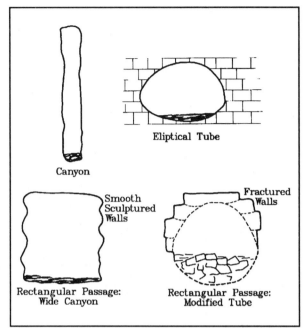

Figure 4—Several cross-sectional passage shapes that have been controlled mainly by flow hydraulics. (from White, 1976)

in nature. If many connections develop, the fragment becomes a system, the nature of the interconnections determining if the system is dendritic or a type of maze. With cave exploration branching out more vigorously in recent years—from traditional dissolution caves to lava tubes, suffosion caves, sea caves, and talus caves—it is important that there is a way to classify caves by geometry.

Passage Cross Sections

The cross sections of cave passages are the synthesis of the initial processes that formed the cave passage and the subsequent processes that modified the cave passage. In chemical caves, the interaction of a moving fluid with the cave wall produces the cross section. Initially this was a tubular cross section of some orientation. In mechanical caves, the initial passage cross section is more variable, depending on the type of cave. Eolian caves tend to be smooth and curvilinear chambers, while tectonic caves tend to be rough and angular passages. For many chemical and mechanical caves, cave development was initiated along some favored horizon that acted as a plane of weakness or an avenue of focused fluid flow. This horizon can be a fault, joint, or bedding plane (Figure 3). The subsequent passage cross section reflects the importance of this initial plane. Tectonic, erosion, sea, and dissolution caves tend to reflect this initial plane of weakness more than other cave types.

Lava and talus caves form in a novel way relative to the other cave types. Lava caves and talus caves are primary caves, in that they were formed

as the rock material was deposited (talus can become a type of rock deposit called a breccia or a conglomerate). The rest of the cave types are secondary, formed by modification of the rock material after it had been deposited.

In any cave passage, modification of the cross section can occur after the cave has developed to produce a composite cross section. Sediments may wash into the cave, minerals may form on cave walls, and the cave passage roof may break down, all changing the cross section (Figure 4). Through time, additional cave forming processes may modify the cross section. In a dissolution cave, this might be incision of a stream into the floor of a tube to produce a canyon (Figure 5). In a lava tube, a secondary flow might produce wall ledges or floor grooves. To understand the cave, and perhaps to locate new passage, it is important to recognize the information contained in a passage cross section. If the original cross section can be determined, the way in which the cave passage formed might allow the cave explorer to figure out where the passage continues. For example, secondary modifications like breakdown might reveal that the roof has migrated upwards and the original passage continues at a lower level.

Cave passages can have four types of cross sections, or a combination of these four types:
1. Tubular—oval to sub-oval cross sections.
2. Planer—pronounced orientation along a single horizon.
3. Rectilinear—void bounded by planer sides.
4. Chaotic—extremely irregular cross section.
   A. migrating
   B. three dimensional

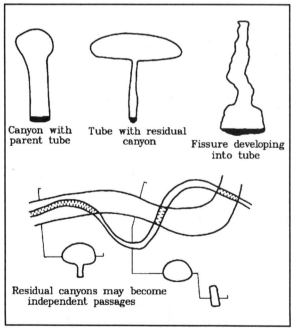

Figure 5—Composite passage cross-sections that form as a result of a combination of structurally controlled features. (from White, 1976)

	Cave Passage Cross Sections					
Cave Type	Cross Section Elements					
	Tubular (T)	Planer (P)	Rectilinear (R)	Chaotic Migrating (CM)	Chaotic 3-D (C3)	Combinations
Chemical						
Dissolution	X	X	X	X	X	T-P; T-CM; T-R; T-C3
Lava	X		X			T-R
Ice	X		X	X		T-R; T-CM
Mechanical						
Tectonic		X	X		X	T-C3
Eolian	X		X			T-R
Sea	X	X	X			T-R
Talus					X	
Suffosion	X		X	X		T-R; T-CM
Erosion		X				

Table 2 — Cave Passage Cross Sections

In limestone dissolution caves, the tubular and planer cross sections types often combine as water flow modifies an original joint or bedding plane into a more tubular shape. Subsequent passage collapse might convert the cross section into a rectilinear form. Lava tubes are usually tubular, evolving to rectilinear. Tectonic caves are usually planer or rectilinear. In limestones, a wandering canyon passage cut into the floor of a tube is an example of a migrating chaotic cross section. Talus caves and some spongework dissolution caves are often three-dimensionally chaotic. The type of caves and their common passage cross sections are shown in Table 2. Note again that dissolution caves have the greatest variety of passage cross section.

Pits

Caves are underground voids. To be underground, a cave must be lower than at least some portion of the land. Even apparently horizontal caves all have some vertical component relative to the overlying land surface. Some caves go deep beneath the surrounding landscape, descending in steps and/or slopes. Anytime this vertical descent is steep enough that careful climbing has to be done (often using ropes), cavers tend to say that the cave contains a pit. A pit, then, is a sudden change in the elevation of the cave. If the elevation change is configured such that it is easy to negotiate, cavers often don't record the elevation shift as a pit.

No matter how a cave has formed, if a hole develops in the cave roof, then a pit exists from the surface into the cave. Pits inside a cave can form during the development of the cave, or as cave collapse and cave deposits rearrange the cave's interior. Few mechanical caves contain many interior pits. Mechanical caves often have entrance pits formed by collapse. Chemical caves often have interior pits. The development of chemical caves produces abrupt changes in level, or pits, by the movement of fluid (lava or water) downward in the earth. Limestone dissolution caves commonly form entrance pits and interior pits, and most vertical caving is done in limestone caves. Figure 6 gives examples in which pits develop in limestone dissolution caves.

Limestone Dissolution Caves

Throughout this chapter, it has repeatedly been noted that limestone caves are abundant, have great length, are complex in passage type and configuration, and readily develop pits. The majority of caving done in the United States, especially in the east where volcanos are absent and sea caves rare, is in limestone caves. The remainder of this chapter will concentrate on the unique circumstances that produce limestone caves and the features we find within those caves.

Limestone is a unique rock. It is mechanically very strong, so that it tends to be resistant to mechanical erosive forces. The walls of the Empire State Building in New York City are built of Indiana limestone because of the rock's strength. In pure water, limestone is barely soluble. However, if the water can be made acidic, the mineral calcite ($CaCO_3$), which forms the limestone, will dissolve. The key to producing large and long caves in limestone is to make groundwater acidic. Nature does this in a variety of ways. Because limestone is mechanically strong, it persists on the earth's surface long enough for dissolutional processes to make caves.

Carbon Dioxide and Limestone

Carbon Dioxide, or CO_2, is a minor component of the earth's atmosphere. Rainwater picks up CO_2 and arrives at the earth's surface slightly acidic (this normal tendency to minor acidic behavior has been recently increased by industrially produced sulfur and nitrogen compounds to produce "acid rain"). This natural acidity alone is enough to produce caves. When rainwater infiltrates the soil, it encounters elevated concentrations of CO_2 because of biological activity in the soil. The increase in CO_2 makes soil water even more acid than rainwater. When this CO_2-charged water meets limestone, it dissolves the rock. As the water works its way down deeper into the rock, it dissolves out passageways that, through time, lead from where

the water sinks to a spring at some lower elevation. A negotiable cave may result.

The chemistry of dissolving limestone this way is interesting. The water does a lot of dissolving quickly, but then takes a long time to complete the process. This means the water gets deep into the ground and is still able to dissolve limestone. If the water could dissolve and saturate faster, only surface limestone would be dissolved and caves could not form underground. If the water dissolved limestone any more slowly, it would re-appear back on the surface without having carried away much limestone, and again cave development would be minimal. It turns out that limestone chemistry is just right for making long caves.

When limestone is dissolved by water, it produces a unique landscape called "karst." Karst landscapes are characterized by internal drainage (caves). This internal drainage results in the development of such common karst features as etched bedrock surfaces, caves, sinkholes, sinking streams, dry valleys, and springs. Careful analysis of where sinkholes, sinking streams, and springs are in a karst area will help locate new caves.

Most limestone caves are portions of the normal hydrologic cycle, taking rain water underground and passing it back to the surface at a lower elevation. In this way caves act like surface streams,

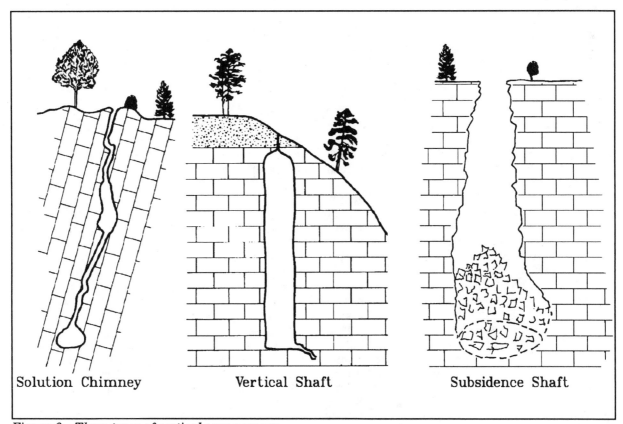

Solution Chimney   Vertical Shaft   Subsidence Shaft

Figure 6 — Three types of vertical cave passage

collecting water from many input points and forming a major underground stream carrying the water to lower elevations. This is called a "dendritic" pattern. The water moves from the surface down to the water table. The area between the land surface and the water table is called the "vadose zone." The area beneath the water table is called the "phreatic zone." In the vadose zone, groundwater moves under the direct influence of gravity, working its way downward by available paths to the water table. The resulting cave passages tend to be high, narrow passages with a migrating chaotic cross section called "vadose canyons." Abrupt vertical descents of the water produces cylindrical shafts called domepits (pits seen from above, domes when seen from below). Domepits form very quickly, from a geologic viewpoint, because of how the downward moving water coats the wall as a thin film. This film puts the maximum amount of water against the most rock surface, so domepits enlarge rapidly. Water in the vadose zone is constantly changing its route downward, and many cave systems develop complex patterns of vadose canyons and domepits. The vadose water may also take a tiny route long or slow enough that it picks up significant amounts of calcite. When this water enters a cave passage, the water chemistry may be such that instead of dissolution occurring, calcite is precipitated to form one of many calcite cave mineral forms.

When the water reaches the water table, it enters the phreatic zone. In the phreatic zone, its flow is governed indirectly by gravity through hydraulic pressure. The water will dissolve out what ever pathway provides the largest initial opening. In many cases, especially where the rock is deformed and folded, the water path will migrate in three dimensions beneath the water table following the best route for flow. Where rocks are flat-lying, the pathway tends to be more direct and closer to the water table. This flow pattern tends to produce oval and sub-oval tubular cross sections.

The nature of the dendritic pattern depends on the surrounding geology. If rain runs off of insoluble rocks like shale and sandstone, it will sink into the limestone as streams. The cave that develops is often simple in plan because the water has already been gathered on the surface by the insoluble rock. The water supply is said to be "allogenic" (from without). If instead, there is no adjacent insoluble rock, then the water falls on the limestone and sinks as many tiny inputs. This means the water must be gathered together in the underground. These caves tend to be very dendritic, and the water supply is said to be "autogenic" (from within). Autogenic caves are sensitive to small variations in the ability of the limestone to transmit the groundwater. Each flow path competes with its neighbors, only the

most efficient win and become the tributary streams to the main cave passage. This competition in passage development can add to the complexity of the cave passage plan. Allogenic caves, on the other hand, tend to flood easily, and contain dissolutional features produced by floodwaters. Some of these flood features include anastomatic and spongework mazes. Allogenic caves tend to have lots of sediment and organic material. Autogenic caves tend to flood more slowly and have fewer sediments and organics.

As these dissolution caves begin to mature, they capture available surface water and deliver it to springs through active cave passages. As the major surface river erodes its valley deeper, the adjacent cave systems respond by developing new passages at the new lower elevation, leaving previous passages dry and abandoned. Through time, caves may develop many levels, which if they stay connected, can produce caves of great length and complexity. Vadose water entering a mature cave will cut through the abandoned upper levels, connecting them to the active lower ones, and allowing the explorer to see more of the cave system. The process of draining passages results in the tubular passages in the phreatic zone becoming occupied by free-flowing streams in the vadose zone. The original tubular cross section is now modified with the migrating chaotic cross section of the vadose canyon as the stream incises into the tube floor. The abandoned upper levels undergo cross section modification by collapse and mineral deposition.

As the major surface river cuts deeper, its valley widens and deepens. The abandoned upper levels of the adjacent caves become breached by surface erosion, and new entrances form. This process can also truncate fragments of upper levels, or collapse and sediment can seal the passages. The cave explorer, by understanding how the cave formed, can make educated guesses as to where continuations of the cave might be hidden.

In some cases, because the geology is complex, the cave makes a trip deep beneath the water table. This portion of the cave system can only be entered by specially-equipped cave divers. In France and Mexico, caves of this type have been followed to depths in excess of 200 meters, beyond the limits of current technology. In some mountain regions, uplift has drained deep flow systems, and the explorer can walk dry in passage that was once under water pressures seen only in the ocean depths.

Caves with allogenic recharge often receive sudden bursts of floodwater. The floodwater comes rapidly from the surface, which means it hasn't had time to dissolve much limestone on the way into the cave. This water can dissolve more limestone inside the cave than can slower-moving water, and there is often quite a bit of it. Floodwater may also help abrade a cave passage mechanically, just like surface streams abrade their channels. Floodwaters are important in helping cave passages grow.

Situations similar to flooding can occur when the cave passages are constricted by sediment or collapse, and water ponds upstream. The increased water pressure can help develop new passages that bypass the obstruction. Floodwaters of any type may rise up into previously abandoned passages, rejuvenating them for short time periods.

When a cave passage is being abandoned because the cave stream is dropping to a new, lower level, the cave passage is alternately drained during low flow, and full during high flow. Even in autogenic systems, a cave passage in the transition to being abandoned is subjected to what amounts to a series of minor flood events. These events constantly subject the cave passage to drain and fill cycles, which can cause enlargement and alteration of the passage.

Special Cases

Most caves that are visited on a routine basis are similar to what was just described. Some caves, including famous ones like Carlsbad Caverns, Lechuguilla Cave, Wind Cave, and Jewel Cave formed under a different set of circumstances. Some special cases of cave development in limestone are presented next.

Diffuse Recharge Caves: When limestone is overlain by a porous rock like sandstone, the sandstone will deliver water to the limestone like a sponge. Because the sandstone limits the flow of water, no single passage in the limestone below can develop at the expense of its neighbors; all the passages develop about equally. In limestones that are well jointed, this will produce a series of cave passages in a maze pattern dissolved out along the joints, or a network maze. These maze caves can contain several kilometers of passage.

Another way in which network mazes develop is when a major river cuts into the limestone. Each time the river floods, floodwater is forced into the adjacent limestone banks. The situation is similar to the situation just described—each crack in the limestone gets all the water it can handle, no matter how inefficient it is in transmitting water. The result is a network maze dissolved out along joints and other available openings in the limestone.

Sea Water Mixing Caves: Where limestone is found in islands, as in the Bahamas, or in coastal areas, such as Yucatan, Mexico, unusual things happen in the groundwater. Freshwater from the land interior flows out to the coast, where it meets sea water encroaching inland. Sea water at shallow depths is usually saturated with calcite, and cannot dissolve any more limestone. The freshwater is also usually saturated with calcite. When the two waters mix; however, they become capable of dissolving more limestone. Caves develop that have an spongework pattern in more porous limestones, and a network pattern in dense, well jointed limestones. Complex maze and chamber caves over a kilometer in total passage length can result. Because cave development occurs as a result of mixing, cave development is restricted to where the two water types mix inside the limestone. The rock adjacent to the mixing area contains water that was saturated and could not dissolve limestone, as a result, the cave passages end abruptly, and have little relationship to the overlying land surface. Large caves in the Bahamas that have formed in only ten to fifteen thousand years demonstrate how potent mixed waters can be when making caves.

During the last two million years of earth history, a time period called the Pleistocene Epoch, unusual climatic events called the Ice Ages or "glaciations" have resulted in the advance and retreat of ice on high latitude continents. Ice advance stores water on the continents, and sea level drops, only to return when the ice melts and retreats. Sea level has changed many times during the Pleistocene over a range from about six meters above present to as much as 125 meters below present. Many coastal areas contain caves, now drained, that formed in a higher water table produced when sea level was higher. These caves are dry today and can be entered. Caves also developed at a whole range of elevations as sea level fell, and these are now drowned today. The big springs of northern Florida are reflooded cave systems, and the famous Blue Holes of the Bahamas connect to complex, flooded cave systems.

Hypogenic Caves: Caves that form as a result of water rising from deep in the earth are called "hypogenic caves." The rising water (hypogenic water) can form caves in two different ways, and the results are some of the most spectacular caves in America.

Thermal Caves: When water is deep in the earth, it is warmed by heat generated in the earth's interior. If the water is in limestone, it may be saturated with calcite, and not able to dissolve more limestone. As the water rises to the earth's surface, it will begin to cool. Calcite is more soluble in cool water than in warm water, and as the hypogenic water rises, mixes with shallow phreatic water, and cools, it can dissolve limestone. The water will be able to dissolve the limestone very effectively, and both efficient and inefficient flow paths are enlarged by solution. The result are large maze caves with little relationship to the land surface. The hypogenic waters may contain large amounts of dissolved minerals and dissolved CO_2, and as the water reaches the water table, the excess

CO_2 escapes, causing precipitation of calcite. The result is very large and complex caves with abundant and diverse minerals and crystal coatings. Wind and Jewel Caves in the Black Hills of South Dakota are superb examples of this type of cave formation resulting in network mazes.

H_2S Caves: Hypogenic water can carry a lot of dissolved material towards the water table from below. If organic materials, such as oil or natural gas are present, one of the materials carried can be hydrogen sulfide or H_2S. Hydrogen sulfide is what gives rotten eggs their unpleasant smell. Water rich in H_2S generally has no dissolved oxygen in it. When hypogenic water rich in H_2S rises to the top of the water table, it mixes with water coming down through the vadose zone. The vadose water is usually rich in oxygen, since the water has just come from the surface. The upper portion of the phreatic zone therefore is usually rich in oxygen. When hypogenic water rich in H_2S meets phreatic water rich in oxygen, the oxygen reacts with the H_2S to produce sulfuric acid or H_2SO_4, a potent acid. If this reaction occurs in limestone bedrock, large amounts of limestone are dissolved. The solution process occurs best in the area where the two water types mix. The resulting cave pattern is one of complex mazes and chambers. Dense, well-jointed rock produces network mazes, more porous rock produces spongework mazes many kilometers in length. In a manner extremely similar to that seen in the mixing of fresh and salt water, cave development is restricted to the area of mixing. As a result, cave passages end abruptly and have little relationship to the overlying land surface. The presence of sulfate (SO_4) from the oxidized H_2S and Calcium (Ca) from the dissolved limestone allow the development of large amounts of gypsum ($CaSO_4 \cdot 2H_2O$). Later on in cave development this will provide the raw material for numerous and abundant gypsum formations. The caves of the Guadalupe Mountains of New Mexico, such as Carlsbad Caverns and Lechuguilla Cave, are the result of this H_2S mixing process.

Sea water caves, thermal caves, and H_2S caves form in a manner that is mostly independent of the nature of the land surface above them. Unlike dendritic caves and diffuse recharge caves, these caves form by actions that occur inside the earth by thermal or chemical mixing. The mixing process results in caves that have little relationship to the overlying land surface, and cave passages that can end abruptly. The input and outlet points for dendritic caves allows the explorer (ideally) to follow the water into and out of the ground. This is not the case in mixing caves. Entrances for mixing caves are the result only of random intersections of the land surface and the caves by surface erosion. The cave chambers and passages occur only where the waters mixed in the past, the input and

outputs are diffuse flow, not conduits. To explore these caves, and locate new passages or entrances, requires understanding the unique way mixing caves form.

Geologic Structure and Caves

Dissolution caves are influenced by orientation of the limestone bedrock layers in which they develop, and by the type and distribution of fractures within the bedrock. Bedrock orientation and fractures are called "structure." Geologic structure interacts with surface geomorphology to produce the active and abandoned flow paths we see in dendritic dissolution caves. The orientation of bedrock layers is defined by "dip" and "strike." The dip is the direction and magnitude of the tilt of a bedrock layer. Rocks that dip less than five degrees are said to be gently dipping, more than five degrees produces steeply dipping rocks. The term strike refers to the direction perpendicular to the dip along which the there is no elevation change. A tilted board placed partway in a bucket of water will show the strike of the board as the water line. In dendritic cave systems, water tends to flow down the dip as long as it is in the vadose zone and under the direct influence of gravity. Subtle changes in the dip will control the path the water takes. Vadose canyons result. Once the water hits the water table, it tends to move laterally along the strike of the beds in the phreatic zone under hydraulic pressure. Phreatic tubes develop. Under these conditions the flow path is controlled by where the biggest initial openings are in the bedrock, so the path can migrate quite a bit in three dimensions. In rocks that have a gentle dip, the water may have to follow the dip for a long way before it hits the water table. If the dip is steep, then the water will flow quickly to the water table. In gently dipping rocks, there is much cave developed down the dip, but in steeply dipping rocks, most cave passage develops along the strike.

How water gets into and out of the limestone is controlled by where the limestone outcrops at high elevation for input, and where it exists at lower elevations for spring output. Caves tend to run from plateaus and valley sides to valley bottoms. If the limestone is underlain by an insoluble rock, and the surface valley has breached the limestone all the way through to the underlying insoluble rock, then the springs will be perched on the valley wall, and the cave may consist entirely of down-dip vadose passages.

If there is no valley incised down the dip, the water has two choices. It can migrate back upwards through the limestone layers and come out at the top of the limestone where it appears down-dip at a lower elevation. This pathway often produces many vertically-looping passages that contain deep sumps, as in Wookey Hole in the Mendip Hills of England. Or the water may travel along the strike until it reaches an outlet, a common situation in the folded Valley and Ridge province of the Appalachian Mountains. In gently dipping limestones with no down-dip valley, quite long cave systems develop as the water runs down the dip for a long distance to the water table, then a long way along the strike to a release point. The ten-kilometer-long, National Speleological Society-owned, McFails Cave system in New York appears to have developed this way.

Where the bedrock has been deformed from simple tilted planes into complex folds and faults, the situation becomes much harder to describe. Downward bent rock, or "synclines," tend to gather water from the surrounding sides of the folds down the dip and funnel it down the axis of the fold along the strike. The Butler-Breathing Cave System in southwest Virginia is a good example. Complex faulting can offset limestone blocks and make groundwater follow intricate pathways to get back to the surface, as in the Balcones Fault Zone of Texas.

Many cave geologists and cavers talk about caves being joint controlled, bedding controlled, or fault controlled. Joints are fractures in bedrock along which there has been almost no movement. They are common world-wide and provide initial groundwater pathways through the limestone if it is massive and dense. Bedding planes are the initial depositional layers of the rock, and as such are also good initial groundwater pathways. Faults are fractures along which there has been measurable movement. They can be thin cracks or thick zones of ground-up and pulverized rock. Depending on their characteristics, they can either facilitate or impede groundwater flow. Bedding planes tend to separate rock layers of subtle or gross differences, joints tend to be oriented along the regional strike and dip. Faults tend to cut through entire packages of rocks. It is not surprising that joints, bedding planes, and faults are widely used by groundwater to initiate cave development. But these features only provide the route by which the water flows. The over riding control of dendritic cave development, whether it is allogenic or autogenic, is where the surface landscape allows water into and out of the limestone. It is better to say a given cave is dip controlled or strike controlled. Individual cave passages and chambers are controlled in their morphology by joints, bedding planes, and faults, but overall dendritic cave systems are controlled by geomorphology.

Mammoth Cave, Kentucky, is an example of how the right landscape, bedrock, and structure can combine to form a great cave. Thick and relatively pure limestone is dipping very gently in a climate that provides lots of water and soil CO_2. The limestone is cut by a down-dip valley, a valley that has lowered in stages, so the cave contains levels for each stage. The limestone is capped by a resistant sandstone that protects the underlying cave from surface erosion while at the same time providing allogenic input for many domepits and vadose canyons. The rock is also poorly jointed, which means groundwater migrates for long distances on separate bedding planes before a route can be found to drop to the next lower layer of limestone. All these geologic features, plus inspired and diligent cave exploration, have produced the world's longest cave.

The special case caves formed by mixed or thermal waters tend to be more controlled by local structural features such as joints, bedding planes, and faults because they form mostly independent of the surface geomorphology. Jointing in particular is important in most of these cave types because the conditions controlling cave development do not allow any joint to out-compete any of its neighbors. The result is that many of these special case caves are network mazes (Wind and Jewel Caves). If the jointing is poor relative to the other pathways in the rock (such as pores), spongework mazes result (Carlsbad Caverns and Lechuguilla Cave).

Dissolutional Sculpturing of Caves

Few caves are made up only of featureless, bare rock walls, as seen in mines, subways, and storm sewers. In addition to mineral coatings, sediments, and breakdown, dissolution caves have a wide variety of dissolutional sculpturings created by the water that carved the cave passage to begin with. These dissolutional sculpturings, called "speleogens," provide clues to how the cave passage formed and changed through time. Some of the more common speleogens are discussed below.

Anastomoses are tiny networks of tubes and openings found in joint, fault, and bedding planes. The tubes are almost circular in cross section, and connect and re-connect in a maze-like manner. The tubes are rarely large enough to enter. They are most common along bedding planes, where they can be looked into from the side, or are exposed when collapse along a bedding plane shows their complex, interconnected pattern. They can range from a few, scattered tubes in rock to situations in which the bedding plane is mostly tube and the bulk of the rock is gone. Some cave geologists believe they represent the initial stage of cave development, but others feel they reflect flood and drain episodes, perhaps relating to the transition of the cave passage from always full of water to only seasonally full of water.

Spongework is a highly complicated system of tiny holes, tubes, and interconnected cavities found on cave walls that can resemble Swiss cheese. The name "boneyard" has been used where the holes are large enough to enter because of the resemblance to bone structure. Even when not human-sized, the spongework can penetrate the cave wall for many meters. It seems to be formed by very chemically active groundwater, such as in mixed water caves, where initial rock porosity is high and jointing is weak. Spongework mazes seem to be spongework on a grand scale.

Pendants are smooth bedrock pillars hanging from the cave ceiling and from ledges. They are part of the original bedrock material left behind by solution, not a secondary mineral deposit like a stalactite. They form in highly jointed areas, as residual bedrock from anastomoses, because their tip is protected by an insoluble layer (like a chert nodule), or because of random patterns of water flow. They are generally regarded as phreatic features, forming when the portion of the passage they occupy was under water.

Floor slots are narrow, solutionally enlarged cracks in the floor. They can be quite deep and long, and may be large enough to permit exploration. They can represent original phreatic solution along a joint or fault that failed to widen as the upper part of the passage did, flood water enlargement of a joint not utilized during initial cave formation, the start of a vadose canyon, or a crack produced by initial collapse processes that has been modified by solution.

Ceiling channels are what appear to be upside-down streambeds in the roof of passages. They often appear to hold a constant level, beginning as the main cave roof descends and disappearing as the roof lifts. There are three main ways they are thought to have formed. Some feel that they represent the initial horizon of cave development, with subsequent enlargement of the passage immediately below. Others feel that they originate by a processes called "paragenesis," in which excess sediment blocks the passage floor, protecting the floor from dissolution and forcing the cave stream to dissolve upwards. A minority feel they represent a floodwater feature, or pathway of entrained air in the cave stream. In passages almost full of sediment or water, ceiling channels may be the only avenue for continued exploration.

Horizontal wall grooves in cave walls are formed by the cave stream cutting its way laterally into the cave wall. In horizontal rocks, this can be nothing more than solution along a favored bedding plane or layer. They can result from perching of the stream on sediments so that the stream cuts into the wall, or they can be from migration of the cave stream from side to side in a passage under vadose conditions. In Clearwater Cave in Mulu, they have been followed for thousands of meters of passage and are not adequately explained.

Incised meanders are the result of the chaotic migration path of an underfit vadose stream in a larger passage (Figure 5). As the stream migrates in its flow, it carves into the cave floor, producing a narrow canyon. This canyon may undercut the cave wall, forming meander loops that leave and rejoin the main passage. In many cases, the vadose flow departs the larger passage for good, and can provide an important way to locate more cave.

Wall and ceiling pockets are holes and depressions dissolved into cave walls and ceilings. Unlike spongework, they are usually widely spaced and don't connect to other pockets. They may be carved into a featureless rock surface, or may follow a joint or other fracture. For some reason, dissolution has been more active where they are found. Explanations have centered around floodwaters enlarging minor wall and ceiling irregularities (joints are especially susceptible to this), mixing of diffuse water leaving the wall rock and encountering the cave stream (once again joints are useful as pathways), collection of air pockets and bubbles, and even the biological activities of bats. Ceiling pockets have been called "bell holes" for their similarity in shape to the inside of a bell (minus the clapper). They are noted for their smooth shape and lack of vertical features associated with descending vadose water. Pockets along joints in walls have been called "joint spurs."

Potholes are bell hole-like structures in passage floors. While some could be formed the way bell holes do, they are cylindrical in shape. Most are thought to be sediment or rock mills carved into the cave floor by the turbulent flow of water setting particles into circular motion against the floor. They are found in settings with coarse sediment and other floor erosion features associated with turbulent flow in surface streams.

Scallops are asymmetrical cuspate pockets formed on exposed bedrock surfaces of cave walls, floors and ceilings. They form by turbulent water flow, which produces counterflow eddies against the rock. These eddies dissolve the scallops so that they are steep on the upstream side and tangential to the rock on the downstream side. They range in size from a centimeter up to a meter. The faster the water flow, the more turbulence and the greater number of small eddies. The slower the flow, fewer eddies of a larger size form . The scallop therefore tells us two things in a cave passage: the direction of water flow (steep side of scallop is upstream) and the velocity of water flow (faster flow means smaller scallops). A ten-centimeter scallop means a velocity of 30 centimeters/second, whereas a one-meter scallop indicates a flow velocity of one centimeter per second. In dry, abandoned passages, scallops allow the explorer to determine water flow rate and direction in the past.

Vadose grooves are vertical incisions into cave walls produced by descending vadose water. The grooves are very straight and semicircular in plan.

They are common in domepits and other areas where vadose water coming from the surface is still not yet saturated with calcite. Like the domepits, the make effective use of a minimal amount of water and can form very fast. They are a clear indication of past vadose conditions when found in a passage with no current vadose input.

Cave Sediments

Caves become filled with material originating from inside the cave or with materials which have been transported from someplace else. The most important of these are breakdown and clastic sediments, the latter having both local and distant sources.

Breakdown is a residual pile of bedrock fragments that results from the failure of cavern roofs and walls. Failure of massive beds along bedding planes or failure of whole sequences of beds at once give rise to block breakdown. Failure of single, thinner beds yields slab breakdown. Small shards and fragments that have not separated along bedding planes constitute chip breakdown. Block and slab breakdowns often break along joints or other pre-existing structural weaknesses. It is possible to analyze roof failure by the mechanics of fixed and cantilever beams. For any given thickness of bedding, there will be a maximum span (passage width) beyond which the ceiling bed will not support its own weight. A passage 30 meters wide would typically require a meter thick bed for the roof to support its own weight. The bedding thickness provides a limit to the width of cave passages. Caves in folded rocks are more susceptible to breakdown. In the ceilings of strike passages in dipping beds, the bedding plane forms one plane of weakness, the perpendicular joint another, and long, triangular prisms of rock easily detach themselves from the ceiling. This type of breakdown is common in caves in folded limestone and gives rise to a characteristic triangular cross section. There are several processes that trigger breakdown. Some are: (1) initial draining of the cave with resultant loss of buoyant support; (2) undercutting of walls by free-surface streams that later

Cave Minerals		
Name	Formula	Mode of Occurrence
Carbonate Minerals		
Calcite	$CaCO_3$	Flowstone, dripstone, pool deposits, helectites, and many other forms
Aragonite	$CaCO_3$	Anthodites, flowstone, and dripstone
Magnesite	$MgCO_3$	Rare, moonmilk and wall crusts
Dolomite	$CaMg(CO_3)_2$	Rare, mostly crusts and crystal coatings
Huntite	$CaMg_3(CO_3)_4$	Moonmilk
Hydromagnesite	$Mg_5(CO_3)_4(OH)_2 \cdot 4H_2O$	Moonmilk
Evaporite Minerals		
Gypsum	$CaSO_4 \cdot 2H_2O$	Flowers, crusts, crystals, dripstone
Epsomite	$MgSO_4 \cdot 7H_2O$	Flowers, crusts, dripstone
Mirabilite	$NaSO_4 \cdot 10H_2O$	Flowers, crusts, dripstone
Celestite	$SrSO_4$	Rare, crusts
Halite	$NaCl$	Flowers, crusts
Phosphate and Nitrate Minerals		
Hydroxyapatite	$Ca_5(PO_4)_3(OH)$	Reaction zone between dripstone and guano
Whitlockite	$Ca_3(PO_4)_2$	Reaction of guano with limestone
Brushite	$CaHPO_4 \cdot 2H_2O$	Reaction of guano with limestone
Nitrocalcite	$Ca(NO_3)_2 \cdot 4H_2O$	Dispersed in cave soils
Nitre	KNO_3	Nitre moss, dispersed in cave soils
Oxide and Hydrate Minerals		
Ice	H_2O	Permanent deposits in alpine caves
Goethite	$FeO(OH)$	Crusts and coatings

Table 3 A listing of cave minerals.

make use of the open passages; (3) action of surface waters weakening roofs in the later stages of the cave's history when the land surface is lowered; (4) action of vertical shafts which may remove parts of walls and other breakdown which may be supporting the roof; (5) wedging and chemical attack by minerals, mainly sulfates, forming in the bedrock; (7) frost wedging near entrances; and (8) effects of floodwater enlargement of joints, faults and bedding planes, de-stablizing the cave passage.

Clastic sediments are of two main types: weathering detritus and transported or fluvial sediments.

Weathering detritus is the residual material left behind when the limestone walls are dissolved. The main mineral constituent is quartz. Quartz occurs as chert nodules common in many limestones, silicified fossil fragments, and grains of quartz sand. Indeed, examination of a number of fills reveals that the bulk of what cavers call "mud" is actually quartz. Clay minerals—kaolinite, montmorillonite, and illite—occur but are a smaller fraction of the bulk sediment.

Broadly, there are two ways in which insoluble materials can be transported into a cave depositional site: horizontally and vertically. The infiltrates are clastic materials transported vertically under the direct influence of gravity with or without the aid of flowing water. Soils in karst regions are washed, piped, or slumped into open crevices and sinkholes. They are eventually discharged into the cavern system without much chemical modification. Solution crevices, chimneys, and vertical shafts reach through the cavernous bedrock and break through to the surface. Fragments of overlying bedrocks and surface debris fall down these openings to become part of the infiltrate sediment. Cave entrances are also sites of intense erosion because of frost pry and freezing and thawing of the rocks and soils upslope. Horizontal entrances usually lead to the top of an entrance talus cone of varying height down which one must descend to the cave passage. Entrance talus materials are a mixture of breakdown and infiltrated debris. The infiltrates are exceptionally important sediments because they contain most of the fossil and archaeological remains. Animals fall down sinkholes and become buried in the accumulating sediment. The gradual accumulation of entrance talus buries the camp sites of primeval peoples.

Fluvial sediments (stream-borne deposits) which may be transported through filled pipes as well as in open channels, make up the greatest part of most cavern sediments. They are derived from many sources. Some are re-worked weathering detritus, some have been derived from rocks higher in the stratigraphic column, and some have been transported from non-karstic border lands by sinking streams. The material usually consists of stream-rounded rock fragments, sand, silt, and clay. The finer grain-size material cannot usually be distinguished from weathering detritus or the infiltrates without extensive analyses. The composition and grain size merely reflect the character of the surrounding bedrock and the load-carrying capacity of the cavern streams. In many cases, sandstone, cobble, and boulder fills occur in thickness of tens of meters.

Fluvial sediments occur in stratigraphic sequence and these strata are sometimes exposed where later free surface streams in the cave cut through them. The Appalachian sequence is frequently one of silts, sands, and gravels in various combination, but the topmost bed is often a fine clay reflecting quieter water conditions as the passage filled with sediment. It would be pleasing to think that the complex sedimentary record in many caves could be used to decipher the Pleistocene history of the region. Unfortunately, attempts that have been made have not come to any useful conclusions. A careful examination of the clastic sediments of a single passage in the Mammoth Cave System of Kentucky showed that the section changed continuously. Individual beds could not be traced very far.

Organic debris is the droppings of birds and bats which in some caves make up a distinct stratigraphic sequence and has in addition a distinct phosphate mineralogy where the leaching solutions interact with the limestone wall rock. Guano caves are common in the southwest, in the Caribbean and in South America.

Cave Minerals and Speleothems

Cave Minerals

Perhaps the most attractive features of caves are their mineral deposits. In the constant environment of the cave, mineralization processes can proceed uninterrupted over long periods of time. The result is a wide variety of mineral features known as "speleothems." Minerals are naturally-occurring chemical compounds of specified chemical composition and crystal structure. Nearly 3,000 such compounds have been identified in the earth (and a few on the moon). Of these, perhaps 80 or 90 occur in caves. However, many of the cave minerals require very special conditions for their formation. The chemistry of limestone caves is really rather simple with only a few metallic elements (calcium, magnesium, sodium, strontium, and iron) occurring commonly and only a few anions (carbonate, sulfate, phosphate, and hydroxide) available for the cations to combine with. As a result only a few minerals are expected to form in the "normal" cave environment. Nineteen of these are listed in Table 3. Many of the minerals even on this restricted list are not very common and only

Figure 7—A group of helectites. (photo Paul Stevens)

three—calcite, gypsum, and aragonite—account for most of the speleothems seen by cavers.

Speleothems

Mineral-depositing solutions move vertically through the vadose zone under the influence of gravity. The mineral deposits left behind by dripping or flowing water, therefore, tend to take on shapes in which the gravitational control of the solution is much in evidence. Each mineral, however, has a characteristic growth habit. Certain crystal forms are preferred above others and certain crystal directions grow faster than others. Modification in the chemistry of the solution or in the rate of deposition can modify the habit or can change the relative rate of growth in different crystallographic directions. Thus there is a competition between shapes guided by the flow path of the solution and shapes guided by the particular mineral and its crystallization habit. This gives rise to two broad classes of speleothems: dripstone and flowstone forms, and erratic forms. Within the context of these basic mechanisms, there is an immense and indeed continuous variety of shapes for the travertine (calcium carbonate) deposits depending on the vagaries of exact flow path, flow rate, chemical characteristics of the water, and relative humidity and carbon dioxide pressure of the cave atmosphere.

Because caves, particularly commercial caves, derive much of their charm from speleothems, these deposits have gained many fanciful names. Rather complete descriptions of speleothems may be found in Hill and Forti's (1986) guide to cave minerals. We use here a two-level system of classification and speak of the "form" of a speleothem as the shape that can be distinguished by growth habit or depositional mechanism. "Styles" are variants of the forms and can be described by adjectial modifiers in as much detail and complexity as seems useful. In this system a stalactite is a form, whereas a soda straw stalactite refers to a specific style.

A listing of the most common speleothem forms is given below:
A. Dripstone and Flowstone Forms (gravity controlled)
   1. Stalactites
   2. Stalagmites
   3. Draperies
   4. Flowstone sheets
B. Erratic Forms (crystal growth controlled)
   1. Shields
   2. Helictites
   3. Botryoidal forms (popcorn, grape, etc.)
   4. Anthodites
   5. Oulopholites (gypsum flowers)
   6. Moonmilk
C. Sub-Aqueous Forms
   1. Rimstone dams
   2. Concretions of various kinds (including cave pearls)
   3. Pool deposits
   4. Crystal linings
Water emerging from joints in cave ceilings hangs there in drops for a short time before the

Figure 8—A beautiful example of a "bacon strip" drapery. The formation is translucent so light shines through showing the structure. (photo David Black)

drops fall to the floor. During the time in which the drop hangs, carbon dioxide is degassed, the solution becomes supersaturated and a small amount of mineral matter is deposited in a ring with a diameter similar to that of the drop. This ring grows downward at constant diameter as more material is deposited until a slender tube of calcite known as a soda straw stalactite is formed. The tube is somewhat porous, and water can seep between grains and along cleavage cracks to deposit minerals on the outside as well. Additional fluid from other joints may stream down the outside of the straw and also build up additional layers.

The natural evolution of the stalactite is from the primary tube to a pendant form. As the stalactite grows, the central canal may become clogged and filled in, but some trace of it usually remains. In cross section, stalactites have a series of concentric rings representing different concentrations of impurities and different rates of growth. They are not annual rings and in spite of several efforts, no good interpretation has been placed on them. Long-term climatic variation in the cave region would be the most probable guess. Many minerals other than calcite occur in stalactite forms; both aragonite and gypsum occur this way.

Stalactites fed by more than one drip point may grown into quite complex shapes. Water flowing over the outside builds up ribs and folds to yield the form known as the drapery. Water that trails along the underside of ledges or of other stalactites may build up a sort of unfolded stalactite in which the growth layers are linear and parallel to the ledge and which is known colloquially as the "bacon strip."

Water dripping to the floor of the cave loses more carbon dioxide, deposits more minerals and builds up the mound-like masses of travertine known as stalagmites. If the cave is not at 100% relative humidity, evaporation will contribute to the $CaCO_3$ deposition also. Stalagmites have no central canal. In longitudinal section they appear to be built up of superimposed caps, thicker in the center and thinning toward the edge as the solution flowing outward from the drip point gradually is depleted in dissolved calcium carbonate. If the drip rate is constant, there will be an equilibrium diameter for the stalagmite determined by the drip rate and the amount of calcium carbonate in solution. Stalagmites are not limited by the amount of weight that can be suspended as stalactites are and can grow to quite large sizes. Many are fed by more than one drip point and can take on more complex shapes, or there can be one large core stalagmite with smaller stalagmites growing on it. Solutions flowing down walls and over ledges deposit masses of travertine with the appearance of a waterfall of rock. These deposits are called flowstone and can be of very large volume.

Figure 9 — A shield from Grand Caverns, Virginia. (photo Paul & Lee Stevens)

Shields are massive plates or slabs of travertine that jut out from cave walls at angles apparently determined by the arrangement of joints. They are rare speleothems but occur in great numbers in some caves such as Grand Caverns, Virginia, and in Lehman Caves, Nevada.

Helictites are smooth-surface stalactitic forms that grow in curved paths instead of hanging vertically. Helictites have a central canal and appear to grow from the tip. They appear to form when flow rates through the canal are too slow to permit the formation of drops and are therefore controlled by the shifting orientation of the fast growth direction of the calcite crystal.

Botryoidal forms are small bead- or knob-like projections from cave walls. Globulite, or cave coral, is a term used for the smaller ones. They are usually of calcite and are layered structures. However, the center of the layering is a small projection or growth point on the wall of the cave. Growth mechanisms are unknown except that they seem to be associated with fast-moving films of water on cave walls.

The term anthodite has been applied to radiating clumps of crystalline aragonite. Typical anthodites grow in tufts of elongate acicular crystals radiating from a common center. Dendtritic growth of individual crystals is common, resulting in a spiky appearance. It is not known how anthodites grow, although their appearance suggests that they must grow from the tip, otherwise the dendritic pattern is difficult to explain. Likewise, there are transitional forms between anthodites and helictites with calcite overgrown on aragonite. Some contain tufts or lumps of moonmilk on the tips of the crystals, suggesting that the magnesium is the last material to precipitate from the evaporating solutions.

gure 10—Gypsum flowers from Cumberland Caverns, Tennessee. (photo Tom Rea)

Oulopholites (gypsum flowers) are a form apparently unique to the sulfate minerals and require the different growth habit of the sulfates. In their most spectacular form, oulopholites consist of petals of gypsum growing outward from a common center. The petals are curved and are made up of bundles of individual gypsum crystals. They have much in common with the anthodites except that growth is almost certainly from the base. The petals of the flowers spread outward because of faster growth at the center of the cluster. This speleothem is best developed in the Mississippian limestone caves of Kentucky and Tennessee.

Concretions are roughly spherical, unattached deposits that occur in pools or shallow basins. Several styles are found of which the smooth, polished variety known as "cave pearls" have received most attention. The other common style is a rough, rather porous structure. Both are layered structures and growth appears to take place around some piece of foreign material that acts as a nucleus. Concretions vary in size from fractions of a centimeter to several centimeters in diameter. The water dripping into the basins in which they form must agitate the water sufficiently to keep the speleothem from becoming cemented to the bottom. Other restrictions on flow rate or chemistry are not known.

Water collecting in pools continues to degas CO_2 from the pool surface. The supersaturated solution deposits calcite on the walls of the pool, sometimes as rough, rather spongy deposits and sometimes as well-developed calcite crystals. A re-markable feature of cave pools is that some of them tend to be self-damming.

Rimstone dams are travertine deposits, usually much thinner than they are high and often with a complex, convoluted pattern. Typical dams are perhaps ten centimeters in height. Dams are known, however, that reach heights of several meters. Calcite also tends to deposit outward over the surface of the pool forming lily pad-like masses.

A few instances are known in which a cave has been completely re-flooded after the excavation of the cave itself. If the re-flooding waters are supersaturated with respect to calcite, the entire cave interior may be lined with crystals. The caves of the Black Hills of South Dakota are particularly noted for crystal lining.

References and Additional Information:

Ford, D.C., and P.W. Williams (1989) *Karst Geomorphology and Hydrology*: Winchester, MA, Unwin Hyman, Inc., 601 pp.

Ford, T.D. and C.H.D. Cullingford (1976) *The Science of Speleology*: New York, Academic Press, 595 pp.

Hill, C.A. and P. Forti (1986) *Cave Minerals of the World*: Huntsville, AL, National Speleological Society, 238 pp.

Jennings, J.N. (1985) *Karst Geomorphology*: New York, Basil Blackwell, Inc., 293 pp.

Moore, G.W. and G.N. Sullivan (1978) *Speleology: The Study of Caves*: Teaneck, NJ, Zephyrus Press, 150 pp.

Palmer, A.N. (1981) *A Geological Guide to Mammoth Cave National Park*: Teaneck, NJ, Zephyrus Press, 196 pp.

Palmer, A.N. (1991) "Origin and Morphology of Limestone Caves": *Geological Society of America Bulletin*, V. 103, pp. 1-25.

Trudgill, S. (1985) *Limestone Geomorphology*: New York, Longman Group, Ltd., 196 pp.

White, W.B. (1976), "The Geology of Caves," in *Geology and Biology of Pennsylvania Caves*, Harrisburg, PA, General Geology Report 66, Fourth Series, Harrisburg, PA, pp 1-71.

White, W.B. (1988) *Geomorphology and Hydrology of Karst Terrains*: New York, Oxford Press, 464 pp.

Chapter 26

AN INTRODUCTION TO BIOSPELEOLOGY

William R. Elliott
NSS 10847
Photographs by Robert W. Mitchell

What Biospeleology Is

Biospeleology, the study of cave-dwelling life, is the full-time pursuit of relatively few professional biologists. However, it has interested many biologists from time to time for various reasons. It is actually a multi-disciplinary science encompassing aspects of zoology, zoogeography, taxonomy, evolutionary biology, ecology, genetics, population biology, physiology, ethology, developmental biology, mycology, and other disciplines. Many of our professional cave biologists developed their interest as young cavers. Others, such as many systematists (people who describe and classify species), became interested in biospeleology through their study of particular animal groups on which they specialize—groups that may be well represented in caves. Thus, a biospeleologist may not be a full-time devotee of the science, but he may have a continuing interest in one or more aspects of it.

One does not have to be a professional biologist to become involved in biospeleology. This chapter will describe how the ordinary caver can, and often does, make a real contribution to the study and conservation of cave life. Observation, documented collections, and photographs of cave life by cavers can be a great help to the professional who is in contact with the caving community.

What Inhabits Caves?

A general terminology has developed among biospeleologists to describe ecological types of cave animals.

A "troglobite" is an animal that is an obligatory cavernicole (cave-dweller), that is, it can only complete its life cycle underground. Most troglobites exhibit varying degrees of depigmentation and eyelessness as a result of many generations of evolution. A few do not appear markedly different from closely-related species that may be found above ground, but are nevertheless limited to caves for biological reasons. Some arthropod groups are entirely eyeless (some millipedes, insects, and arachnids) wherever they are found. Some aquatic troglobites, such as amphipods and isopods, are occasionally found in springs and wells that communicate with cave systems. Such forms are often called "phreatobites" because they inhabit phreatic waters.

Troglobites often display other characteristic adaptations to their habitat such as increased appendage length, greater chemosensory and tactile sensitivity, lowered metabolic rate, greater locomotor and feeding efficiency, and smaller clutch sizes made up of larger eggs.

"Troglophiles" are a second major ecological category. Troglophiles may be found primarily in caves but also in similar habitats such as under rocks, in crevices or burrows, or in soil and leaf litter. Many troglophiles exhibit adaptations that grade into those of troglobites. Some may be incipient troglobites which, though isolated in caves, have not had sufficient evolutionary time to develop an obviously troglobitic appearance. Others are opportunistic species that may be found in caves and similar habitats across entire continents.

"Trogloxenes" (Figure 1) are species that use caves for part of their activities but which are not limited to caves. Examples are cave crickets and bats, which roost and even reproduce in caves but which feed outside, or even certain species that specialize in the twilight zone habitat near the entrance. In many instances the biology of a particular species may be too poorly known to make a sure ecological designation. In such cases the general morphology (form and appearance) of the animal and the habits of its closest relations may serve to make a tentative designation.

Photosynthetic plants, which require sunlight to grow, cannot exist in the total darkness of caves. Their seeds may sprout in darkness but die after

Figure 1—Ceuthophilus *sp, trogloxenic cave cricket.*

using their food reserves. However, the entrance sinks and twilight zones of caves often harbor plants that are rare in the surrounding countryside. The botany of cave entrances is poorly known and may someday provide fruitful work for plant geographers. One might expect to find some relictual (remnant) forms there which have become extinct elsewhere because of climatic changes. Likewise, the bacteria and fungi of caves are poorly known, but they may have some ecological importance since they require no light and are rather common in some cave muds, rotting debris, and animal feces. Troglobites, such as some collembola and millipedes, may graze almost exclusively on bacteria and fungi.

Many animal groups have troglobitic forms. It would be impossible to discuss here the hundreds of cave-adapted species known in North America alone. Undoubtedly, many more species remain to be discovered, especially in the western United States, Mexico, and Central America. Instead, let us take a look at the major taxa (groups) that inhabit caves. A general survey of the world cave fauna may be found in Vandel's *Biospeleology* (1965), but it is already somewhat out-of-date. An excellent introduction to the cave life of North America is Mohr and Poulson's *The Life of the Cave* (1969), which contains many fine photographs.

Almost all major freshwater and terrestrial taxa contain cave-adapted species, and some predominantly marine (saltwater) taxa also have representatives. By far the most important phylum, in caves or elsewhere, is the Arthropoda, which includes arachnids, crustaceans, centipedes, millipedes, and insects. Probably the second most important group is the Vertebrata (troglobitic fishes and salamanders), then the Platyhelminthes (planarians, Figure 2), then a few Mollusca (aquatic and terrestrial snails and even some freshwater clams!). Some large groups have essentially no cave forms: Cnidaria (except for a few freshwater *Hydra*) and Echinodermata (starfishes and their allies, which are all marine). The As-

chelminthes probably have some cave-adapted species in the form of nematodes (roundworms), but it is difficult to distinguish them from common, soil-dwelling nematodes. Some Onychophora (clawed worms) and Annelida (earthworms) are cave-adapted.

Since most significant cave systems are formed in limestone by the action of fresh groundwater, it is not difficult to see why there are few marine groups with troglobites. However, some marine forms have been able to adapt to freshwater conditions and have given rise to troglobites. Good examples are some amphipod and isopod crustaceans and blind fishes of the families Synbranchidae (eel-like) and Brotulidae (catfish-like).

No two caves are exactly alike, so it is difficult to discuss what inhabits a typical cave. For the sake of example, we can imagine an idealized American cave and note what life we would encounter.

The plants in a sink entrance may differ from those of the surrounding area because of the different microclimates. Ferns are commonly found at cave entrances. Certain birds nest at cave entrances: phoebes in some areas and cave swallows in many southwestern caves. Pits in Mexico commonly house swifts and parakeets. Guacharos (oil birds) nest in the dark of some South American caves. Even vultures have been found roosting in some entrances. They have an all too frequent defensive response—vomiting upon the intruder. Contrary to popular belief, snakes are infrequent in cave entrances and are rare in the dark zone. However, certain frogs, toads, and salamanders frequent entrance areas. Depending on the nature of the twilight zone, one may find an abundance of trogloxenic insects and arachnids that exploit this limited habitat, which is all too often ignored by collectors. At this point one often encounters dense populations of trogloxenic harvestmen ("daddylong-legs") and cave crickets on the walls and ceiling. Harvestmen are eight-legged arachnids but they are not spiders. They are non-poisonous and quite harmless, although they can be annoying. In some southwestern caves they form dense, undulating blankets that, when disturbed, fall off the ceiling in masses and onto cavers. There are many species of cave (camel) cricket throughout the United States but most California caves seem to lack them even though there are some camel crickets found above ground there. Some Mexican caves harbor true crickets (Gryllidae), a few of which are eyeless troglobites. Some caves in the northwestern United States have rare grylloblattids, a group similar to both roaches and crickets.

If there is a stream in the cave, you may find eyed crayfishes and amphipods in the twilight zone. During the winter many of the above-mentioned species may be found deeper in the cave where it is warmer.

The zone of total darkness and relatively constant temperature is where one most often sees

Figure 2—Sphalloplana zeschi, *a troglobitic planarian, extending its proboscides for feeding.*

Figure 3—Rhadine subterranea, *a troglobitic carabid beetle, feeding on a cave cricket egg.*

Figure 4— Cambala speobia, *a troglobitic cambalid millipede.*

troglobites. Several families of beetle (Carabidae, Leiodidae, Pselaphidae) have many different troglobitic species throughout the United States (Figure 3). Some are specialized predators on cave cricket eggs or on other arthropods; others are scavengers. Dermestid beetles are common in bat guano (feces), although not strictly cave-limited.

Their larvae feed on dead bats so efficiently that a bat skeleton can be "cleaned" in a few minutes. Incidentally, few troglobites are found in the vicinity of large bat guano deposits—the conditions are usually not right. Guano communities have their own cast of characters, "guanophiles," which may reach incredible densities. Some bat fleas have been known to reach densities of 11,000 per square meter in the vicinity of dying bats, and dermestid larvae, gnats, and pseudoscorpions can also be quite abundant. Some of the large bat caves of the Southwest and Mexico are intriguing ecosystems that deserve more study. However, the heat, stench, flies, and ammonia can be quite disagreeable to any but the most devoted student.

In a more typical food-poor cave, one often finds small troglobitic millipedes feeding on organic detritus. They are harmless and should not be confused

with centipedes. Millipedes (Figure 4) are slow moving and have two pairs of legs on most body segments. Centipedes (Figure 5) are rare in caves, generally are fast moving, and have one pair of long legs on each body segment. They also have poison mouthparts (but no poison leg claws, as commonly believed), but most are too small to inflict a bite on a person. Some groups of millipedes and centipedes are naturally eyeless whether they inhabit caves or not. The cave forms of many parts of North America are poorly known.

Arachnids are a class of eight-legged arthropod. Many families of the Order Araneae (spiders) have troglophilic and troglobitic species: Agelenidae, Leptonetidae, Nesticidae (Figure 6), Pholcidae, Telemidae, and even a few tarantulas of the family Dipluridae. Spiders, like most arachnids, prey on other arthropods and are important members of most cave ecosystems. We have mentioned trogloxenic harvestmen, and there are troglobitic ones as well (Figure 7). Harvestmen (Order Phalangida) can be distinguished from spiders by their lack of a constricted waist between the prosoma (anterior part of the body) and opisthosoma (abdomen). While trogloxenic harvestmen are often scavengers, many

Figure 5—*A geophilomorph centipede.*

Figure 6—Nesticus *sp, troglobitic spider.*

troglobitic ones seem to be predators on microarthropods, such as collembola. The scorpions have few truly troglobitic forms—several species are known from Mexico. Pseudoscorpions (Figure 8) form an order separate from scorpions. They are minute forms that have the claw-like pedipalps of a scorpion, but no tail and sting. Some forms are adapted to bat guano communities, others are troglobites. All are predators. There undoubtedly are many unknown species of troglobitic mites. Even the best known mite family in caves, the Rhagidiidae, has been studied only recently in North America. Some cave rhagidiids are among the giants of the mite world: up to two millimeters body length with legs almost twice the length of the body. Even so, they are so tiny that they have sometimes been found sitting on the surface film of quiet water. They, too, are predators. In the tropics there are cave forms from other, less commonly known arachnid orders: Schizomida, Palpigradi, Amblypygi, and Ricinulei. Until about 1968, the Ricinulei were thought so rare that just about every specimen that had ever been collected (a few dozen) could be accounted for. Abundant populations of several species of these reddish,

Figure 7—Texella mulaiki, a troglobitic harvestman.

Figure 8—A troglobitic pseudoscorpion.

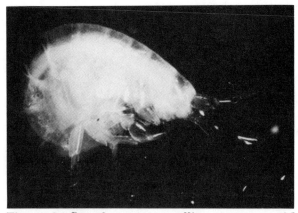

Figure 9—Stygobromus russelli, a crangonyctid amphipod.

tick-like creatures have been discovered in Mexican caves. Ticks themselves, which are closer to mites, have no troglobitic forms, but are common in bat caves.

The large and complex Class Crustacea has many troglobitic species, mostly in the orders Decapoda, Amphipoda, and Isopoda. There are a few among the more primitive orders Copepoda, Ostracoda, Thermosbaenacea, Speleograephacea, and Mysidacea. Many American caves have troglobites of the amphipod genus *Stygobromus* (Figure 9). These small, aquatic creatures look like shrimp with the tail bent forward under the body. They are scavenger/predators and, as with most cave-adapted crustaceans, the exoskeleton is so thin and colorless that the internal organs often can be seen. Decapods are represented by atyid shrimp (which are found in the southeastern United States, Yucatan, Cuba, and Puerto Rico), palaemonid shrimp (Figure 10) (Texas, Florida, the Antilles, and Mexico), crayfish (midwestern and southeastern United States and parts of Mexico), and even a blind land crab of the genus *Typhlopseudothelphusa* from Mexico and Guatemala. Three isopod families are common in American caves. Cirolanid isopods (Figure 11) are all aquatic and mostly tropical (one species occurs in Virginia, another in Texas, and several in Mexico). Cirolanids are generally elliptical and dome-shaped and usually crawl on the bottom, but occasionally swim if disturbed. Asellid isopods are also aquatic, crawling forms, but they look like centipedes, being long and narrow. There are many species of asellids in caves across the United States. Some are over a centimeter long while others are tiny and cling to pieces of wood or the undersides of rocks. Trichoniscid isopods look more like the "pillbug" isopods familiar to most people. Many white, eyeless species of the genera *Brackenridgia* (Figure 12) and *Miktonsicus* are found in North America. Some are aquatic, some terrestrial, and many seem capable of an amphibious existence. Grayish, trogloxenic forms of the pillbug, Armadillidiidae, are often found in entrance areas.

Figure 10—Palaemonetes antrorum, *a pala-emonid shrimp.*

Figure 11—Speocirolana pelaezi, *a cirolanid isopod.*

Figure 12—Brackenridgia bridgesi, *a trichoniscid isopod.*

North America has many different species of blind cave fish while Europe has none. The family Amblyopsidae has four cave species distributed from Alabama to Indiana and Kentucky to Oklahoma. Amblyopsis and Typhlichthys are the more common genera; Speoplatyrhinus is known from one cave in Alabama. These fish are among the more highly cave-adapted vertebrates in the world. In Texas two blind catfish species are known from deep artesian wells near San Antonio (they have never been found in accessible caves). In Mexico there are five families of fish having troglobitic forms—the number of species is currently in doubt and may range from six to eight or more. Cave fish in the United States generally have small populations and should not be collected unless for very good reasons. In parts of Mexico, blind cave fish of the genus Astyanax are so astronomically abundant that some cavers feel it is all right to take a few home for their aquaria. At the worst, this is merely a bad example to set and it is difficult to make a strong case against such collecting, except that it is against Mexican law to collect without a permit.

On the evolutionary scale, the highest group to contain troglobites is the Amphibia. No frogs are troglobitic, only a few salamanders. Texas has the majority. five described species and about 35 known populations of the genera *Eurycea* and *Typhlomolge* (Figure 13). Like most troglobitic salamanders, they retain their gills and live in water all their lives, a "neotenic" condition. The Ozark blind salamander, *Typhlotriton spelaeus* occurs in the Ozarks but is not an advanced troglobite. The juveniles live at cave entrances and have functional eyes

Figure 13—Typhlomolge rathbuni, *the famous blind salamander from San Marcos, Texas.*

and some pigment. The adult loses its gills and penetrates deeper into the cave, losing some pigment and eye function. If kept in the light, the retina still degenerates but the eyelids do not fuse as usual. The genus *Gyrinophilus* has two troglobitic species: one from Tennessee that is neotenic, and one from West Virginia that undergoes metamorphosis. In Florida and Georgia there is a troglobitic, neotenic salamander, *Haideotriton wallacei*. The only other troglobitic salamander in the world is the famous *Proteus anguinus*, a neotenic form from southeastern Europe.

Bats (Order Chiroptera) are the only true flying mammals and form an important component of many cave ecosystems. Of the sixteen families, three occur in the United States:

1. Pyllostomatidae (Leaf-nosed bats) — Mainly tropical in distribution; five species range into the southwestern United States. All are cave bats and three are nectar feeders. All are migratory.
2. Vespertilionidae — World-wide distribution; most hibernate; 12 of the 29 United States species use caves. Common cave forms are *Myotis Lucifugus, M. velifer, M. sodalis, Eptesicus fuscus,* and *Plecotus townsendii*.
3. Molossidae — Distributed from the tropics into southern United States; two of the six species use caves. *Tadarida brasiliensis mexicana* is the most common bat in southwestern caves and migrates to Mexico.

About half of these forty species utilize caves in some way at some time — for day or night roosting, hibernation, or reproduction. Most of our bats are insectivorous. Summer colonies of *Tadarida brasiliensis mexicana* number in the millions in some southwestern caves. On their nightly forays, bats devour many tons of insects and are one of our best natural controls of pests. Over the past 20 years our bat populations have undergone an alarming decline. Disturbance by humans probably has affected many species, but there is good evidence that insecticide poisoning (via insects) is a major cause. Biologists have largely stopped banding bats as this too has been suspected as a minor cause of mortality.

As one moves into Mexico, the number and diversity of bats increases dramatically. The family Desmodontidae is composed of three species of true vampires. *Desmodus rotundus*, the most common vampire, inhabits many caves. Its guano is familiar to many cavers as a dark, molasses-like fluid which may harbor many tiny beetles.

A General Ethic for Collecting

For many years the National Speoeological Society has had a general rule against cavers disturbing or collecting cave life. This rule often takes the form: "Do not collect cave life except under specific direc-

tion of a scientist" (e.g., see Moore and Sullivan, 1978). Many biospeleologists would probably agree that this rule is a bit too strict and needs elaboration. What the National Speleological Society should discourage, of course, is the unnecessary disturbance of cave life, especially if it is for no scientific or conservationist gain. Thus, personal collections of cave animals as mere curiosities should be frowned upon unless obtained under special circumstances. For instance, certain Mexican cave fish (Astyanax) can be purchased from aquarium shops and have been bred from a small beginning stock that was collected decades ago. The cave ecosystem from which they were taken (Cueva Chica in San Luis Potosi) was not adversely affected and thrives to this day.

Over the years, cavers in all parts of the country have aided biospeleologists by making small collections of cave animals wherever they have explored new caves or studied known caves that were poorly known biologically. Such collections are frequently sent to biospeleologists who have ongoing research projects on certain regions or animal groups. For example, much of what is known about the vast and diverse cave faunas of Texas and Mexico would still be unknown if none of the members of the Texas Speleological Association and the Association for Mexican Cave Studies had made routine collections whenever they explored and mapped. Even the most staunch conservationist might agree that we cannot adequately protect cave life until we know what is living in the caves. There must be published scientific information on the cave fauna of any region before one can really begin to see what is there to protect. Moreover, such scientific documentation is necessary before legal action can be pursued to good effect, say in the protection of a possibly threatened or endangered species. The cave fauna of many regions is too poorly known to yet say what is endangered.

At one extreme some might equate the collecting of a cave animal with breaking and removing a stalactite. This viewpoint does not take into account the enormous amount of scientific information that even one specimen of an unknown species can contain or the fact that living things can reproduce themselves, unlike speleothems. Although some species of cave animal may have very small populations and thus be endangered by collecting, the popular notion that all cave populations are small and vulnerable is unsupported by hard evidence. Cave species are most often endangered by the loss of habitat and pollution, not by small-scale collecting. To quote James Reddell (1976), a leading American biospeleologist, ". . . the type of collecting that cavers do will in no way endanger the cave forms they may find or interfere significantly with the cave ecology."

No general rule for collecting will apply in all situations. The amateur collector should not collect in caves that have been well-studied or ecologically damaged, unless at the specific request of a scientist who knows the situation and asks for specific numbers of a certain species. If the caver is in serious doubt about the conditions, he should not collect, but he should make observations and notes. No collections should be made unless the caver already knows a scientist who will take the collections and put them to good use. This is not exactly the "supervision" in the rule of old.

In some instances, just visiting certain bat caves can be harmful when the bats are hibernating during the winter or giving birth in the spring. Over the years bat biologists and cavers have identified certain caves that should be considered "off-limits," at least for part of the year. No doubt many more such caves will be identified in the future. Accidentally stirring up bats during their hibernation may cause them to deplete their fat reserves, which may mean death or reduced reproductive capacity later on. The collecting of bats by amateurs should be discouraged in most cases, especially since some bats carry rabies. Most cavers are thoughtful conservationists and can apply their own informed reasoning ability to each situation.

How to Collect

The simplest collecting kit one can carry into a cave is a one or two-ounce screw-cap jar containing 70 to 80% ethyl or isopropyl alcohol. Isopropyl (rubbing) alcohol is cheap and can be bought in most drug and grocery stores. Baby food jars work nicely if they have screw lids (snap lids should be avoided). Most animals can be preserved in alcohol, but formaldehyde is preferred for fish, frogs, salamanders, and earthworms. Drugstore formaldehyde is usually 40% and should be mixed one part to ten parts water. Small plastic baby bottles are best for formaldehyde (the lid should be taped shut). Planarians (aquatic flatworms) are best taken alive and air mailed immediately in some original cave water in an insulated container to a specialist.

Collecting tools are not absolutely necessary. Most arthropods can be picked up with light finger pressure. Crickets require quick aim and a firm grasp, or they can be trapped under the cupped hand and then brushed into the jar. For very small insects you can wet your finger with alcohol, touch the animal gently, and then stick your finger back into the alcohol to wash off the insect. A fine paintbrush is useful for microarthropods, insects in small crevices, and for picking up planarians off the surface film of pools. Most tweezers and forceps are too stiff and will only crush the specimens. The author makes very light, flimsy forceps by cutting them out with scissors from

a flattened aluminum drink can, in paper-doll fashion. Such forceps often require rebending to keep the tips aligned, but they can be used on all but the tiniest and largest of insects. Small insects on rocks or sticks can be tapped over or dipped into the jar. Creatures on the ceiling can be persuaded to leap into the jar. One should be careful not to crush the specimen or break legs, antennae, or tails. These appendages are often necessary for species identification. Earthworms should be killed in alcohol. This requires only a few seconds, then the worm is removed, straightened by rolling it like a string of clay in the hand or on the thigh, then placed in diluted formaldehyde.

A small, inexpensive aquarium dip net is good for most aquatic collecting and will easily fit into a cave pack or pocket. Wrap it in a plastic bag to prevent tearing the netting. Tea strainers also make good nets. Many aquatic forms will be on the bottom or under rocks but can be shooed into open water where they can be netted.

The single jar technique represents a minimal effort but better scientific information is obtained by taking several jars and using each in a different habitat in the same cave: entrance area, guano deposit, organic detritus, etc. Also, it is best to put larger specimens (such as large crickets, beetles, millipedes, and spiders) in a different jar than small specimens, which are often damaged by the larger ones kicking and squirming.

Usually, two or three specimens of each larger species and a dozen or so of the smaller ones will be enough for the specialist to identify. Often the collector will have insufficient time to collect that many anyway. Larger numbers should be collected only at the specific request of a qualified biologist.

At the end of the collecting trip, preferably as soon as you leave the cave, a small collecting label should be put inside each jar. The label should be on strong paper, in pencil (most inks will fade), and should have the following information:

1. Name and location of the cave, including county (municipality, if in Mexico), state, and other locating information such as direction and distance from the county seat or prominent town, topographic map coordinates, cave survey number, etc.
2. Date of collection (spell out the month or use a Roman numeral).
3. Collector's name.
4. Habitat where collected, temperature if known, and so on.

It is at this point that some collectors ruin their own efforts. A collection with doubtful or missing data is useless and may have to be discarded by the biologist who receives it. Obviously, one should never put specimens from different caves in the same jar.

The habit of taking field notes, even on pleasure caving trips, should be encouraged. Observations on

Figure 14—Pseudosinella violenta, *a collembolan or springtail.*

water and air temperatures, humidity, species associations, prime collecting areas, density of animals, hydrologic and meteorologic information, pollution, and the like, can be invaluable later on and should be written down even if collecting is not your interest. Close-up photography of live specimens can be useful, but identification to species usually requires preserved specimens.

All areas of the cave should be checked. The entrance area is too often ignored, but nevertheless contains species of interest to the biospeleologist. Pay particular attention to organic materials such as feces (usually a rich source of collembola, tiny hopping insects shown in Figure 14), rotting vegetation, and thin films of mud and feces on flowstone. Even litter should be examined (I once found a very rare beetle under a moldy match box). Many tiny arthropods, such as beetles, pseudoscorpions, and diplurans live under rocks. Spend at least a few minutes turning over rocks in each new area, especially if they are imbedded in mud (put them back if this defaces the floor). Look on the bottom of the rock and in the hole and be prepared to move fast as these secretive little guys will scurry away before you know it. A more thorough account of equipment and techniques may be found in Cooper and Poulson (1979).

Much valuable collecting is done by cavers while they are mapping or exploring. There are many times on a caving trip when someone is waiting for someone else—while the sketchman is trying to catch up, while the novice is struggling up the rope, or while the photographer is setting up that big room shot. You may be surprised to find what is living under you. In fact, you may have crushed it and may as well collect it anyway, assuming you know a biologist to send it to.

After The Trip

The collection should be sent off to the biologist with whom you are working as soon as possible. However, you should first make a list of all the collections and send it in a letter to the biologist, keeping a copy for your files. Make sure the lids are on tight (taping them is a good idea). Pad the jars with foam or crumpled paper and pack it all tightly in a strong box or mailing tube. Tape the box securely and wrap it in strong paper. This can be mailed by third class. The biologist should notify you when he has received the package. If he has not, you can ask the postal service to trace it.

Most biologists keep a good correspondence going with their collectors and are happy to send back identifications and interesting information on what was collected. When the information is published, they are glad to furnish collectors with copies of their articles. Addresses of biospeleologists who can help you get your collections to the right specialists are given at the end of this chapter.

Conserving Cave Life

There are several things that we can do in our own caving activities to conserve cave life:
1. Never dump carbide in a cave! It is poisonous. Carry all your trash out with you.
2. On the other hand, it is usually best to leave someone else's old organic litter (wood, paper, food, feces) in the dark zone of the cave, as it may be providing food and shelter to cave-adapted animals. Cave clean-up campaigns are becoming more popular and we should be thankful, but the thrill of ridding a cave of man-made trash should not blind us to the possibility that it already may have become part of the cave ecosystem. If such materials are removed, they should be thoroughly examined for animals, which should then be released in a similar habitat in the cave or collected for study.
3. Cave gates, if they are necessary, should allow access by bats and other normal cave visitors. See Hunt and Stitt (1975) and Tuttle (1977). More bat caves will need to be identified as "off-limits" during critical times of the year. This is especially true for the Gray Bat, *Myotis grisescens*, the Indiana Bat, *Myotis sodalis*, and the Virginia Big-eared Bat, *Plecotus townsendii virginianus*, all endangered species.

Every year more and more caves are polluted or destroyed by trash dumping, land development, quarrying, and dam building. The loss of habitat and food resources that results from these activities is much more threatening to cave life than the most irresponsible collecting. To counteract this regrettable situation, many cavers have joined together in study groups, regional and state cave surveys, and conservation task forces. These groups and you can make a real contribution to saving our caves and cave life by:
1. Studying the caves and their contents and documenting what is found in scientific bulletins and journals.

2. Attending public hearings held by government agencies on land use policies.

3. Petitioning government agencies and politicians in a non-abrasive but forthright and well-informed manner to rectify intolerable situations.

4. Seeking publicity for particularly dire situations by writing articles for national magazines or communicating with large news media of good repute.

5. Buying land and caves for nature preserves, or supporting organizations like the National Speleological Society and the Nature Conservancy that do just that.

Cavers tend to be passive conservationists, that is, they conserve by not doing certain things. Cavers also tend to be excessively frugal. But it is not too late to change our ways and support active conservation as well. Whether we like it or not, economic power can make a difference.

The Biology Section of the National Speleological Society

The Biology Section of the National Speleological Society meets at least once a year (at the National Speleological Society convention) and hosts educational talks and scientific symposia on cave biology. It elects officers and publishes The North American Biospeleology Newsletter several times a year. The North American Biospeleology Newsletter is an excellent source of information on current cave biology happenings in North America and the world. Members' names, addresses, and interests are published, and a running bibliography of scientific papers is offered with each issue. Membership is open to all interested persons and the current (1992) dues are $5.00 a year. Back issues are available. The officers will handle inquiries on specialists to work with and other matters. Consult the NSS Members Manual for names and addresses of current officers. The current editor is Dr. Daniel Fong, Department of Biology, The American University, 4400 Massachusetts Avenue NW, Washington, DC 20016-8007.

The following biospeleologists are willing to assist serious collectors in sorting problem materials for distribution and in providing advice and addresses:

East and Southeast
Dr. John R. Holsinger
Department of Biology
Old Dominion University
Norfolk, VA 23529

Southwest and California
Dr. William R. Elliott
12102 Grimsley Drive
Austin, TX 78759

West and Pacific
Rod Crawford
University of Washington
Burke Museum (DB-10)
Seattle, WA 98195

Midwest
Dr. Horton H. Hobbs III
Department of Biology
Wittenberg University
Springfield, OH 45501

Hawai'i
Dr. Francis G. Howarth
Bishop Museum
PO Box 19000A
Honolulu, HI 96817-0916

Mexico and Central America
Mr. James R. Reddell
Texas Memorial Museum
2400 Trinity Street
Austin, TX 78705

References

Barbour, R.W. and W.H. Davis (1969) — *Bats of America*: Univ. Press, Lexington, KY, 286 pp, 20pl.

Cooper, J.E. and T.L. Poulson (1979) — *A Guide for Biological Collecting in Caves*, Caving Information Series #7801, National Speleological Society, Huntsville, AL, 14 pp.

Hunt, G., and R.R. Stitt (1975) — *Cave Gating, A Handbook*: National Speleological Society, Huntsville, AL, 42 pp.

Mohr, C.E. and T.L. Poulson (1969) — *The Life of the Cave*: McGraw-Hill Book Co., New York, NY, 232 pp.

Moore, G.W. and G.N. Sullivan (1978) — *Speleology, the Study of Caves*: Zephyrus Press, Inc., Teaneck, NJ, 150 pp.

Reddell, J.R. (1976) — "Biological Collecting Made Easy": *Texas Caver*, 21(3):40-46.

Tuttle, M.D. (1977) — "Gating As A Means Of Protecting Cave-Dwelling Bats," pp. 72-82; In T. Aley and D. Rhodes (Eds), *National Cave Management Symposium Proceedings, Mountain View, AR, 1976*: Speleobooks, Albuquerque, NM, 106 pp. Reprinted in: *NSS News*, 35:175-180.

Vandel, A. (1965) — *Biospeleology, the Biology of Cavernicolous Animals*: Pergamon Press, NY, 524 pp.

Chapter 27

ARCHAEOLOGY IN CAVES

George M. Crothers
NSS 24150

Introduction

Archaeology and caves are sometimes thought of synonymously. However, few archaeologists work in cave sites and even fewer are familiar with the deep cave environment. Most archaeological materials in caves occur in that zone of twilight near the cave entrance or vestibule known to have been frequently inhabited by prehistoric people throughout the world. Occasionally, the term cave is also misused by archaeologists to refer to what is actually a natural rock shelter or bluff overhang.

However, this is not to say that some of the most spectacular archaeological sites in the world are not found within the cave environment. The French and Spanish painted caves of Upper Paleolithic age (17,000 to 12,000 years ago) are some of the earliest known forms of art in the world. Although many such sites are found in the Perigord, Pyrenees, and Cantabrian mountains, two of the more famous are Altamira in Santander Province, northern Spain, and Lascaux in the Dordogne valley of southwest France. Lifelike representations of animals, including bison, red deer, ox, and horses, rendered with pigments of red iron oxide and black manganese dioxide, are the most common figures adorning the walls and ceilings of these prehistoric galleries. While archaeologists and anthropologists may debate the meaning of these figures, their context in the cave environment indicates that as early as 17,000 years ago Paleolithic age humans were familiar with the cave environment and apparently ritualized the setting.

In southern Mexico and Central America where the Classic Maya civilization arose (A.D. 300 to 900), caves were important as reliable sources of water. In the karst regions of the northern Yucatán Peninsula, surface runoff sinks almost immediately into a labyrinth of solutional caverns. The lowland Maya heavily relied upon this subsurface water supply to support their great civilization. At sites such as Bolonch'en in Campeche, the Maya descended 450 feet via an extensive series of ladders and through tortuous passages to retrieve water from several underground pools. Caves were also used in ritual contexts. Perhaps the most famous is the sacred cenote of Chichén Itzá, a Post Classic site with a major occupation between A.D. 1000 and 1250. A cenote is a sink or vertical shaft complex with an opening to the surface. The Maya often used these vertical shafts as ceremonial places to deposit bodies and sacrificial artifacts. Some scholars believe that

the bodies were also sacrifices. The sacred cenote of Chichén Itzá is well known not only for the large number of bodies found in it but also for the impressive array of jade, gold, and copper artifacts.

In North America the world's longest cave, the Mammoth Cave System in Kentucky, was extensively explored prehistorically. Between 1000 B.C. and A.D. 500 Native Americans routinely entered this and numerous other caves in the mid-latitude regions of the eastern United States and systematically mined them for a variety of materials, such as chert or flint, argonite, gypsum, and possibly other sulfate minerals occurring with gypsum (for example mirabilite and epsomite). Mammoth and Salts caves were extensively mined for gypsum and selenite by prehistoric cavers who left great quantities of perishable artifacts that have been preserved in the stable atmosphere: artifacts such as gourd and squash bowls, woven slippers or foot gear, woven bags, and cordage of various kinds. Also, over the years, a number of "mummies" or desiccated human bodies have been discovered in these caves. Most were probably intentionally placed in the cave, but at least in one case, a prehistoric miner was killed in Mammoth Cave when he undermined a large boulder while digging for selenite crystals and was crushed before he could escape.

Within the field of paleoanthropology, the study of human origins and evolution, caves have yielded many important hominid (meaning human-like) fossils. The caves of Zhoukoudian (Choukoutien), southwest of Beijing, China, are famous for the discovery of "Peking Man," fossil remains of Homo erectus, dating 400,000 to 500,000 years ago. The Zhoukoudian fossils represent over 40 individuals, and at the time of their discovery in the 1920s and 1930s they represented the largest collection ever made of a single fossil population of hominids. The Zhoukoudian hominids that inhabited these caves were also evidently skilled hunters, bringing their kills, which included red deer and a diversity of animals, back to the cave to be butchered. Remains of other hominid activities found in the cave include tools and debris from making stone, bone, and possibly wood artifacts; debris from preparing vegetable foods; broken ostrich egg shells which may have been containers; and evidence of the ability to control fire if not the outright technology and knowledge to make fire at will.

Several small caves in the Transvaal region of South Africa, such as Sterkfontein, Makapansgat, and Swartkrans, have yielded numerous and important fossil remains of our earliest bipedal (meaning to walk erect on the hind limbs) hominid ancestors known as australopithecines. The fossil remains from these caves date between 2.5 and 1 million years ago. Although australopithecines never actually inhabited these small caves, their remains washed or fell into the caves as they filled with sediment or collapsed. Small pit caves such as these are important because they act as natural traps for the animals that inhabit the surrounding area, providing not only bone beds for paleontological study, but also a means to reconstruct past environments and study how those environments have changed through time.

It is ironic, then, that the history of archaeology is replete with famous archaeological cave sites, but so few archaeologists are cavers or even routinely investigate caves for archaeological remains. This is because most archaeological cave sites have been discovered by cavers, explorers, miners and others who make it their business or avocation to search out and explore caves. The archaeologist is the dependent character in this relationship; dependent in the sense that cavers make most of the discoveries and in the sense that most archaeologists rely upon cavers for their safety, whether it be on belay climbing a cable ladder, use of caving equipment and lighting, or simply because they have little sense of direction underground. Although the author enjoys chimneying a high canyon passage, appreciates a soft, sandy floor in a long crawlway, and has gone out of his way to learn vertical techniques to avoid ever using a cable ladder again, he is an archaeologist first and a caver second.

On the other hand, while most archaeologists are naive about the cave environment, many cavers do not understand or appreciate what modern archaeology is or the kinds of questions archaeologists try to answer. This chapter has three goals. First is to explain briefly the objectives of modern archaeology and how it relates to its parent discipline, anthropology, using examples to illustrate the points. Second, the type of remains one might expect to encounter will be briefly characterized, paying special attention to cave archaeology in eastern North America. Third, a few suggestions are presented about what should be done and how you should proceed on that one day in your underground exploits when you make the cave archaeology find of the century or simply discover something unusual and are not sure whether it is archaeological or natural.

Extensive citations are not used in the text, but obviously the author has been influenced by many previous works. At the end of this chapter you will find a list of references and suggested readings. Many have been consulted to keep the facts in this chapter straight and others are good starting points for those who are interested in additional information on cave archaeology. Some of these are technical and others are more general or adventure oriented, thus the bibliography is separated into two lists accordingly.

The Conduct of Archaeology

Archaeology is the scientific study of the remains of past human societies from an anthropological viewpoint. In the broadest sense, anthropology is the study of humankind, both the physical or biological aspects and the social or cultural aspects of human existence. Because humans are social as well as biological beings, anthropology and archaeology are more properly called social sciences. The scientific process is the slow accumulation of observations, attempting to explain the patterns occurring in those observations with hypotheses, testing those hypotheses against future observations, and building theory that provides a greater understanding of the phenomena under study, enabling the investigators to make new, higher-level observations. The most crutial skills an archaeologist must perfect are observation and description. It is the hope of anthropologists and archaeologists that by studying past and present human behavior, we may contribute to a better understanding of the present and future course of humankind.

It should not be surprising that humans prehistorically—as they did historically and as we do today—conceived of caves in a variety of contexts with a variety of uses. Each of these uses reflects a different meaning, purpose, and material consequence of that use. As an example, think of some uses for caves now or in the recent past. A farmer might use a cave for the storage of food stuffs. The farmer's use of the cave is practical—the constant, cool temperature of the cave is ideally suited for use as a natural root cellar. In some smaller towns, dance floors were built in local caverns to allow people to escape the summer heat and to provide a social outlet for the community.

The patrons' use of such caves is social. Religious services have been held within caves and it is not unknown for a couple who met on the dance floor to conduct their nuptials in a cave. Caves are widely associated with themes of darkness, the unknown, the mysterious—a natural setting to invoke reverence or obedience in ceremonial or religious settings. There is probably no greater use of caves presently than as tourist attractions. Use of the tourist cave is social, recreational, and economic.

Already we can think of utilitarian, social or recreational, religious, and economic uses of caves. Each use has implications for the types of remains that may be found there. The farmer's cave may contain iron barrel hoops, broken mason jars, and stoneware. The dance floor will require a large number of nails and other building materials in its construction. The dance hall patrons will likely lose numerous personal effects over the years. The tourist cave will probably contain artificial lighting and it is likely that the passages will be modified to accommodate walking.

A single cave may also be used for a variety of purposes through time. A cave mined for saltpetre during the War of 1812 may have been used for dances in the 1930s and today be a show cave. As society and technology changes, people's concept of fashion, fad, and popular culture is redefined. Chest freezers have replaced root cellars, the dance hall in a cave can not compete with the local disco, and a new interstate may bypasses the local tourist cave drawing travellers instead into a nearby theme park.

It is the archaeologist's task to infer the past uses of a site from the remains that survive. Of course, for historic uses of caves, written records may exist, old-timers may be able to recollect past uses. It is easier to identify an artifact when similar items are still commonly used. The archaeologist's key to reconstructing past uses of a site and how those uses have changed is the context in which those remains are found.

Context is a simple but crucial concept for the archaeologist. The value that an archaeologist sees in an artifact is in its context not its aesthetic appeal. A Mayan water jar may be an object of beauty and craftsmanship, but understanding that certain jars were used to collect "virgin" water dripping from the ceilings of caves and had a very important role in Mayan ceremonial life provides a more complete understanding of what it was like to be an ancient Mayan citizen. Uncontaminated water dripping from the ceiling had much more significance than water collected from the ground. The Maya went to great lengths to place water jars in isolated places within the caves and apparently important rituals were held in connection with this water supply. Large numbers of water jars were ceremonially destroyed in these contexts by the Maya, a practice that probably relates to the importance even today of using *zuhuy ha* or uncontaminated water and *zuhuy* vessels, that is, unused vessels, for each new ceremony (Thompson 1959).

Studying artifacts in their context, that is, where they are found, is the archaeologists' job. Part of what makes archaeology difficult is trying to determine whether an artifact, when it is found, is in its original context or has been moved and or altered by one or more processes. Only by carefully observing its association with other artifacts and recording the details of its location can the archaeologist begin reconstructing the past. Once an artifact is excavated or has been removed from its context, that information is destroyed and can never be regained. That is why archaeologist go to elaborate, sometimes tedious, ends to record as much information as possible about the context of an artifact.

It is one thing to interpret the historic use of caves when written and oral accounts of that use exist, or in the case of the Maya, where indigenous populations still practice forms of ancient ceremonies and quite another to reconstruct the uses of caves by long-gone members of extinct societies. Here, archaeological context becomes even more important. There is no written record of the native North Americans prior to the arrival of Europeans. In most of North America, the native inhabitants were removed from their lands and the continuity between past and present practices was destroyed.

It has only been recently that a more complete picture of the long and varied prehistoric use of caves in eastern North America has begun to emerge. A small number of archaeologists has been systematically recording and studying deep cave sites over the last 20 years from which this picture emerges. This includes the work of Patty Jo Watson working in the caves of Kentucky and Tennessee, Charles H. Faulkner working in Tennessee and Virginia, and Patrick and Cheryl Munson working in Indiana and Kentucky. Several good overviews of this work include Faulkner and Willey (1989) and Watson (1985, 1986).

Archaeological Remains in Caves of the Eastern United States

There is very good evidence that humans have inhabited North and South America beginning about 12,000 to 15,000 years ago. There is some controversial evidence that humans may have been on the two continents by 35,000 years ago, but only time and more discoveries will determine whether these claims are substantiated.

But clearly, by 12,000 B.P.[1] humans inhabited most of the New World. These early inhabitants were of Asiatic origin, crossing from Siberia into Alaska by way of a land bridge across the Bering Straits during glacial advances when the ocean's water level was significantly lower than it is today. These nomadic hunters may have simply been following herds of game or traveling along the coast line, completely unaware that they had entered a new continent. However, within a relatively short period of time (perhaps within a thousand years), this migration had reached the southern tip of South America.

---

[1] B.P. stands for Before Present, a convention used by archaeologists with the advent of radiocarbon dating. Present is calculated as 1950, the standard set by radiocarbon laboratories for consistency. To convert radiocarbon dates to the Christian calendar subtract the B.P. date from 1950. Negative numbers would be read B.C. and positive numbers, A.D. For example, a radiocarbon date of 4,500 B.P. would be: $1950 - 4500 = -2550$ or 2550 B.C.

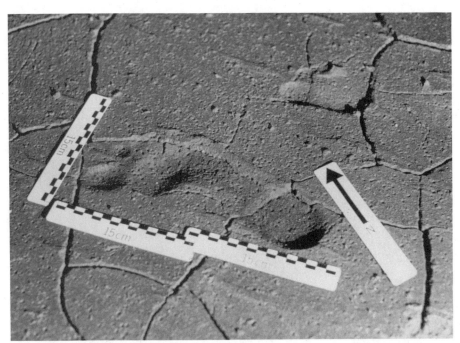

Figure 1—Aboriginal footprint preserved in the soft mud of a cave floor. Such evidence of prehistoric human visitation is extremely delicate, but in some cave contexts may be preserved several thousand years. (photo Patty Jo Watson)

cave in eastern North America is approximately 4,600 years B.P. (2650 B.C.). In a remote passage in a cave in north central Tennessee, a series of 272 complete footprints were discovered by cavers as they were mapping the passage. The prints preserved in the still pliable mud floor, together with a sparse trail of cane torch charcoal and smudges on the cave walls, comprise the only evidence of prehistoric activity in this cave.

Anthropologist Louise Robbins determined, based on dimensions and morphology of the prints, that nine individuals had been present, at least two of whom may have been female and one an adolescent (Robbins *et al.* 1981). Close examination of the superposition of individual prints indicated to her that at least two different trips were made through the passage. This cave is remarkable, not only for the fragile evidence of aboriginal caving trips re-

Various ideas remain in the popular press that groups of humans, whether they were the Lost Tribes of Israel or Celtic voyagers, traveled from the Old World to the New and left their marks, or ancient writings, upon rocks, cave walls, and the like. Most of these ideas are perpetuated by nonarchaeologists, their findings are poorly documented, and most can be explained as natural phenomena or as forgeries. There is no good evidence, except for the establishment of a short-lived Viking settlement on the Newfoundland coast in the 9th or 10th century, that any Mediterranean or European people ever reached the New World until Columbus' voyage.

While there is good evidence of humans inhabiting the continent by 12,000 years B.P., including the use of rock shelters and cave entrances as habitation sites, the earliest firm radiocarbon dates for prehistoric exploration of a

Figure 2—Portion of a bottle gourd (Lagenaria siceraria) *from Big Bone Cave, Tennessee, probably used in mining selenite. The gourd has been mended with a cross stitch using 2-ply cordage. (photo George Crothers)*

corded in its soft clay floor, but also because it unequivocally conveys the skill of these prehistoric cavers. On two occasions small parties of aboriginal explorers, composed of men, women, and adolescents, penetrated a remote section of the cave, not rediscovered until the mid-1970s; explored in a rather casual way to the end of the passage; and returned. It is possible that caves such as this are indicative of routine prehistoric exploration of deep cave environments. But the record of such activity is only occasionally preserved and rarely recognized before it is obliterated.

A number of other caves in Tennessee and Kentucky have revealed evidence of early exploration, including footprints and torch charcoal, with radiocarbon dates around 4,000 years B.P. However, there does not appear to be any activity, other than exploration, associated with these sites. Beginning about 3,000 years B.P. (1050 B.C.) and lasting until approximately 1,500 years B.P. (A.D. 450) a new use for caves is evident in the archaeological record. The mining of high quality flint from a cave in Tennessee; the extensive mining of gypsum crust, selenite, and satin spar from Mammoth and Salts caves, Kentucky, and Big Bone Cave, Tennessee; and the mining of an aragonite column in Wyandotte Cave, Indiana, all date to this time.

A number of fancy artifacts, such as platform pipes and gorgets, have been microscopically identified as being made of Wyandotte Cave aragonite, and found at a number of sites in Indiana, Illinois, Iowa, Ohio, and Tennessee (Tankersley *et al.* 1990). Artifacts made of Wyandotte Cave aragonite were probably high prestige items, traded throughout the Midwest.

Gypsum in its various forms—wall crusts, selenite, and satin spar—is not stable outside the cave environment and will break down under wet conditions. Hence it is not surprising that gypsum is rarely recovered in an archaeological context outside the cave environment. Either the crystals themselves or crushed gypsum in powder form, which will make white pigment or paint, must have been highly prized given the extensive quantity of minerals mined from Mammoth, Salts, and Big Bone caves. It is also likely

Figure 3—A pair of woven slipper fragments found in their original context as left by the prehistoric caver in Big Bone Cave, Tennessee. (photo George Crothers)

that gypsum was a valuable substance traded throughout the Midwest. Although the mining of these minerals from the cave may have been routine or rather systematic, the value placed on these commodities for prestigious or ceremonial uses may have been very high.

Most prehistoric mining in caves appears to have ceased by A.D. 500. Two new uses of caves began to appear toward the later end of this period and continued in various areas until 1600 A.D. One is the use of caves for burial chambers or burial pits. The second is the use of caves as galleries for drawing geometric designs, abstract figures, animals, and various other motifs in the soft mud coating on walls or incised into the limestone.

Burial caves appear to be of two types. The first consists of simple horizontal caves in which bodies have been laid out and sometimes covered with clay. This practice appears to have been more common in the Tennessee-Alabama-Georgia (TAG) region during the Middle Woodland period, which dates from 200 B.C. to A.D. 500. The practice of laying bodies out in an extended position often accompanied with elaborate grave goods has been well defined for the Copena culture of northern Alabama (Walthall and DeJarnette, 1974).

The practice of dropping bodies into vertical pits appears to have been widespread but is poorly documented. A number of pit caves containing prehistoric human remains have been found ranging from Maryland and Virginia to Texas. However, the greatest number of these sites is found in southwestern Vir-

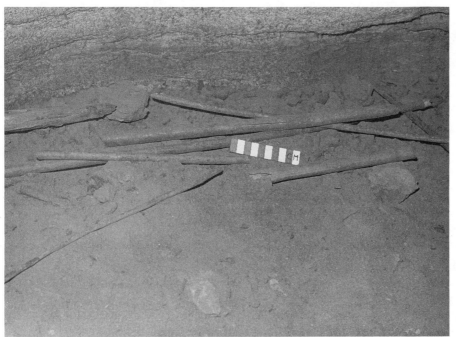

Figure 4—A scatter of cane (Arundinaria gigantea) *torch debris, typical of prehistoric cave exploration in dry caves. (photo George Crothers)*

3,000 years B.P. and continuing until 1,500 years B.P. mining of various materials appears to have been widespread. Toward the end of the period of mining and continuing probably until the time of contact with European explorers, a number of regional uses of caves developed. This includes the Copena burial caves in northern Alabama; the burial pit caves, particularly in southwestern Virginia; and the late prehistoric decorated caves such as Mud Glyph Cave in Tennessee.

While we now have an outline of changing cave use through time for the eastern United States, many gaps and details of this record remain to be completed. Unfortunately, only a small number of archaeologists can devote their efforts to studying archaeological cave sites. Today, most archaeology is associated with development and construction projects. Archaeologists are racing to stay ahead of the bulldozers and earth movers that are building subdivisions, strip mining, logging, laying roads, renovating urban areas, and carrying out numerous other projects that alter the land and disturb or destroy the archaeological records of past societies. Fortunately, most cave-rich areas have been spared development, and for at least the near future cavers will continue to be in the forefront of discovering archaeological cave sites.

ginia. They appear to date from A.D. 900 to 1600. Only a few limited archaeological studies have been made of these caves and many more of them have been looted beyond meaningful study. It appears that large numbers of bodies were dropped or thrown into these caves. Artifacts—including shell and copper beads, ornaments, and smoking pipes—often accompany the bodies. The use of these pit caves is not unlike the Mayan use of the sacred cenote, but their origins are probably independent.

The use of caves as galleries for decoration or drawing is also a late prehistoric phenomeon, dating between A.D. 900 and 1600. Most of the sites have been found in Tennessee, of which the most famous is Mud Glyph Cave (Faulkner ed., 1986), but a few are known from Virginia and Kentucky. We can only speculate as to the meaning of these figures, or of the act of drawing these figures on the cave walls. Hunting magic, narratives, or spiritual communion are all plausible explanations. Like the Paleolithic painted caves of Europe, the cave environment may have been believed to be particularly conducive to ritual or ceremonial activities.

In summary, the earliest evidence of exploration in the deep cave environment in eastern North America dates to approximately 4,600 to 4,000 years B.P. It is not clear why there is an 8,000-year lag between human entry into the continent and exploration of the large number of caves found in the east. It is possible that evidence of any activity prior to 4,600 years B.P., due to its scarcity and its fragile nature, has not been preserved. However, by

The Treatment of Archaeological Remains in Caves

It is quite possible that a caver, believing he or she has entered a virgin passage, may find, with careful observation, that prehistoric explorers were there hundreds or even thousands of years before. The evidence may be obscure: the prints of bare feet in mud or dust, occasional scatters of charcoal from their cane or stick-bundle torches, charcoal smudges on the walls or ceilings where a torch was accidentally or purposely struck against the rock to remove excess embers, or faint drawings incised into mud or etched into the limestone walls. There is also a possibility that a caver in a passage that is well traveled may find, with close observation, that prehistoric remains are still present only a few feet from the beaten path. However, the evidence may be hidden, trampled by years of traffic, kicked or fallen into the crevices between breakdown blocks, and covered by modern trash.

There are a few precautions you can take to avoid disturbing archaeological materials, and a few signs you can look for that may alert one to the possibility of archaeological remains in a deep cave environment. If archaeological materials are to remain in good context in a cave environment they must be in relatively inactive hydrologic zones, that is in dry upper level passages or in hydrologically abandoned caves. Dry caves in limestone capped with impermeable rocks, such as sandstone or shale, may also preserve perishable material.

Figure 5—Stoke marks from a prehistoric torch bundle commonly found in both wet and dry caves explored by aboriginal cavers. (photo Patty Jo Watson)

If you should be so fortunate as to discover virgin passage, or are entering passages that have seen little traffic, then take a few extra precautions, particularly if the cave is known to have prehistoric remains in other passages. Archaeological evidence such as footprints or drawings incised in mud are extremely delicate. Passing through a passage even one time may obliterate a record of past events that has existed for thousands of years. Be observant. In the tortoise and hare approach to moving through a cave containing fragile items of any sort, the tortoise will eventually achieve greater rewards.

Prehistoric cavers used a variety of plant materials for torches, but in those latitudes (south of the Kentucky-Indiana border) where river cane grows it seems to have been the preferred torch fuel. Weed stalks and small tree shoots were also commonly used. At Wyandotte Cave, Indiana, a region where cane is not common, strips of shagbark hickory bark were used as torches. During the course of experiments made in Salts Cave, Kentucky, it was learned that a bundle of five to seven canes tied with plant fibers provides an adequate and reliable source of light (Ehman, 1966). Experiments with burning cane torches have shown that characteristic stoke marks are produced on the cave walls when the burning end of the torch is tapped on or jammed into the rock. This action serves to readjust the burning ends in relation to each other and removes excess cinders. It also leaves a trail of charcoal on the floor or ledges. These characteristic torch marks are commonly found in caves that have been explored prehistorically.

Charred material may enter caves in a number of ways, particularly as water born deposits. However, torch charcoal can usually be distinguished from other naturally occurring deposits. First, if the material is river cane there is a good possibility that it is archaeological. The characteristic morphology of cane is often clearly evident even after burning. Second, the charcoal will often be associated with stoke marks on the ceilings or walls of the cave. Third, the scatter of charcoal should form a consistent trail through the cave. If you observe these characteristics it is likely that you are following in the footsteps of prehistoric cavers.

Archaeological material in dry caves should normally be more easily identified. Textile artifacts, gourd or squash fruits, and unburned torch material may be preserved in certain cave environments. However, many large, dry caves have also been intensively used in historic times. The mining of saltpeter has probably had a greater impact upon these sites than any other single activity. This is true for both Mammoth Cave, Kentucky, and for Big Bone Cave, Tennessee. Prehistoric archaeological material surviving in these caves is often severely damaged or destroyed by saltpeter mining and other historic activities. However, areas beyond the primary saltpeter mining may contain archaeological deposits in good context. This is fortunately the case for both Mammoth and

Big Bone caves. A great deal of information has been recorded for these caves despite decades of intense historic activity.

The talus cone at the base of a vertical pit is usually a hydrologically active environment. Water washing debris in from the surface will continue to build the talus cone and redeposit existing material down slope. Human remains dropped into this environment will be significantly altered and dispersed through the talus. In addition, other animals may fall or be discarded into these pits. Therefore, it requires a rather detailed knowledge of human osteology to distinguish human from other animal bones in these situations.

The discovery of human remains in a cave creates several additional problems. In most states human burials, including prehistoric burials, are protected by cemetery laws. Removing or altering a burial without the proper clearance may be considered a felony. Native American burial rights are a sensitive issue and all human burial remains should be treated with respect. If you should encounter human remains in a cave, and you do not know whether they are recent or prehistoric, you may also need to contact local law enforcement agencies and forensic specialists. In any event, do not remove the remains. If they are in danger of being destroyed, or are in the process of being looted, contact the land owner and the local law enforcement agency immediately.

Petroglyph sites are fairly common in many parts of the United States. Petroglyph sites in caves are less common, but more are being reported. Particularly rare and delicate are the mud-glyph caves, in which prehistoric drawings are incised into the mud coating on a wall or into the floor. Like footprints in the mud, they can be obliterated in a few careless moments. Authenticating and recording such discoveries require that the site be in very good condition.

In general, archaeological remains in a cave should be treated like all material in a cave—leave nothing but cautiously placed footprints, take nothing but pictures. This also includes historic remains, such as those from saltpeter mining and other historic uses of caves. If you believe you have discovered something of archaeological interest, preserve it by leaving it where you find it. If you believe you have entered a very sensitive archaeological area such as a footprint passage, stop. Record enough information that you or someone else can find their way to that spot in the cave. Drawings or photographs of the objects may be helpful. Keep your discovery to yourself until you can contact the appropriate authorities and steps can be taken to protect the site.

Remember, you may have difficulty finding an archaeologist who is experienced in working in caves. However, you should attempt to interest the nearest professional archaeologist in your find. The local university with an anthropology department, or a museum with an archaeologist on the staff, is a good place to start. Do not exaggerate your find, but a well documented discovery is more likely to pique the professional archaeologist's interest. If you fail to get satisfaction from local professionals and still believe you have found something important, try contacting the National Speleological Society. They can direct you to a member who specializes in cave archaeology such as the author or the people mentioned at the beginning of this chapter.

Summary

Archaeology is a scientific discipline in which the subject matter is limited and irreplaceable. Human beings and their ancestors have been walking erect, using tools, and leaving their marks upon this planet for 2.5 million years, although written history has recorded only parts of the last 5,000 years. This leaves an immense span of time for the archaeologist to work in, but knowledge of this time span shrinks every time a site is destroyed before it can be studied.

Cave archaeology in eastern North America has grown considerably in knowledge and practice over the last 20 years. Sites in this region are as impressive as the better known archaeological cave sites of Europe and the Yucatán. The prehistoric inhabitants of eastern North America were some of the most accomplished cavers the ancient world has ever known.

It is likely that if you cave long enough you will see, if not discover, many of the archaeological remains described in this chapter. It is the conscientious caver's responsibility to help preserve those remains for future study and for future cavers to see.

Bibliography
General Interest and Adventure

Crothers, George M. (1983) "Archaeological Investigations in Sand Cave, Kentucky." *NSS Bulletin,* 45:19-33.

Dawkins, W. Boyd (1973) *Cave Huntinq, Researches on the Evidence of Caves Respecting the Early Inhabitants of Europe.* Reprinted Zephyrus Press, Teaneck. Originally published 1874, MacMillan, London.

Faulkner, Charles and P. Willey (1989) "Cave Archaeology in the Midsouth." In *Caves and Caving in TAG: A Guidebook for the 1989 Convention of the National Speleological Society,* edited by William O. Putnam, National Speleological Society, Huntsville, Alabama.

Faulkner, Charles H. (1988) "Painters of the 'Dark Zone.'" *Archaeology,* 41(2):30-38.

Mercer, Henry C. (1975) *The Hill-Caves of Yucatán*. Reprinted University of Oklahoma Press, Norman. Originally published 1896, Lippincott, Philadelphia.

Pond, Alonzo W. (1937) "Lost John of Mummy Ledge." *Natural History* 39:176-184.

Schwartz, Douglas W. (1960) "Prehistoric Man in Mammoth Cave." *Scientific American, 203:130-140*.

Watson, Patty Jo (1966) "Prehistoric Miners of Salts Cave, Kentucky." *Archaeology, 19:237-243*.

———— (1985) "Archeology." In *Caves and Karst of Kentucky*, edited by Percy H. Dougherty. Special Publication 12, Series XI. Kentucky Geological Survey, University of Kentucky, Lexington.

Bibliography
Technical Interest

Ehman, Michael F. (1966) "Cane Torches as Cave Illumination." *NSS News,* 24(3):34-36.

Faulkner, Charles H., Editor (1986) *The Prehistoric Native American Art of Mud Glyph Cave*. University of Tennessee Press, Knoxville.

Faulkner, Charles H. (1988) "A Study of Seven Southeastern Glyph Caves." *North American Archaeologist* 9:223-246.

Faulkner, Charles H., Bill Deane, and Howard H. Earnest Jr. (1984) "A Mississippian Period Ritual Cave in Tennessee." *American Antiquity,* 49:350-361.

Munson, Patrick J. and Cheryl Ann Munson (1990) *The Prehistoric and Early Historic Archaeology of Wyandotte Cave and Other Caves in Southern Indiana*. Prehistoric Research Series, Vol. VII, No. 1, Indiana Historical Society, Indianapolis.

Robbins, Louise M., Ronald C. Wilson, and Patty Jo Watson (1981) "Paleontology and Archeology of Jaguar Cave, Tennessee." *Proceedinqs of the Eighth International Congress of Speleology, 1:377-380*.

Tankersley, Kenneth B., Cheryl Ann Munson, Patrick J. Munson, Nelson R. Shaffer and R. K. Leininger (1990) "The Mineralogy of Wyandotte Cave Aragonite, Indiana, and its Archaeological Significance." In *Archaeological Geology of North America*. Geological Society of America, Centennial Special Publication, Volume 4.

Thompson, J. E. S. (1959) "The Role of Caves in the Maya Culture." *Mitteilungen aus dem Museum f. Völkerkunde in Hamburg,* 25:122-129.

Walthall, John A. and David L. DeJarnette (1974) "Copena Burial Caves." *Journal of Alabama Archaeology,* 20:1- 59.

Watson, Patty Jo, Editor (1969) The Prehistory of Salts Cave, Kentucky. Report of Investigations No. 16. Illinois State Museum, Springfield.

———— (1974) *Archaeoloqy of the Mammoth Cave Area*. Academic, New York.

Watson, Patty Jo (1986) "Prehistoric Cavers of the Eastern Woodlands." *The Prehistoric Native American Art of Mud Glyph Cave*, edited by Charles H. Faulkner, pp. 109-116. University of Tennessee Press, Knoxville.

Willey, P., George Crothers and Charles H. Faulkner (1988) "Aboriginal Skeletons and Petroglyphs in Officer Cave, Tennessee." *Tennessee Anthropologist,* 13:51-75.

Appendices

The Miners Castle and Miners Castle Cave at Pictured Rocks National Lakeshore in Lake Superior, Michigan. (photo Tom Rea)

Appendix A

SUGGESTED FURTHER READING

Most of the chapters in this book include references the authors have chosen to more fully cover their subject. The books listed here are more general and will be interesting reading for anyone fascinated by caves. The editor has resisted the temptation to place these books in categories because too many of them fit more than one.

Some of these books are out of print and will have to be found in libraries or in friends' collections. One or two of the vendors listed in Appendix D carry out-of-print books. Most of the books that are still in print can be obtained from the National Speleological Society Bookstore or other cave equipment vendors who offer books.

There are thousands of cave books, both in and out of print. Those presented here have been opinionatedly selected to give a broad coverage of the subject for the serious beginner.

Adventure of Caving
David R. McClurg, 332 pages, 1986. A guide for beginning and advanced cavers, covering safety and hazards, conservation, personal gear, horizontal techniques, rigging, and vertical caving.

American Caves and Caving
William R. Halliday MD, 348 pages, 1974. A guide to caving covering types of caves, caving equipment, communications, rescue, and much more.

Atlas of the Great Caves of the World
Paul Courbon, Claude Chabert, Peter Bosted, Karen Lindsley, (English edition) 369 pages, 1989. Maps and brief descriptions of major caves worldwide. Originally published in French in 1986.

Cave Minerals of the World
Carol Hill and Paolo Forti, 283 pages, 1986. A description of cave minerals from all over the world with over 100 photographs and a bibliography with over 2,000 references.

The Caves Beyond
Joe Lawrence Jr and Roger W. Brucker, 290 pages, 1975 (reprint—originally published in 1955). The story of the 1954 week-long exploration of Crystal Cave, Kentucky, the first such venture in the United States.

Caves of the Organ Cave Plateau
Paul J. Stevens (ed), 200 pages, 1988. Detailed descriptions and maps of the Organ Cave System, West Virginia.

Caving in America
Paul H. Damon Sr (ed), 445 pages, 1991. The story of the National Speleological Society from its founding in 1941 through its 50th year, 1991, including a special illustrated history of cave exploration.

Celebrated American Caverns
Horace C. Hovey, 1970 (reprint—originally published in 1896) A reprint of a long out of print book; a fascinating survey of 19th century caves.

Cumberland Caverns
Larry E. Matthews, 317 pages, 1989. The story of the discovery and exploration of Cumberland Caverns, Tennessee.

Depths of the Earth
William R. Halliday MD, 432 pages, 1976. Stories of American caving and a brief account of the history of caving in America.

Discovery at Rio Camuy
Russell and Jeanne Gurnee, 1974. The fascinating story of the discovery and exploration of a major cave system in Puerto Rico.

Exploring American Caves
Franklin Folsom, 280 pages, 1956. A general book touching on the geology and biology of caves, human use of caves, history of caving, and how to get started in caving. A good book that presented the state-of-the-art in the 1950s.

Exploring Caves
David McClurg, 287 pages, 1980. Covers conservation, safety, finding caves, personal gear, ropes, vertical techniques, and equipment.

Fieldbook for Boys and Men
Boy Scouts of America, various dates, reprinted regularly. Covers techniques for living comfortably in the field. The Fieldbook is not just for kids. If you like to camp and hike, you need it.

Geomorphology and Hydrology of Karst Terrains

William B. White, 464 pages, 1988. The chemistry of karst waters, the process of sedimentary in-filling, the origin of caves, and the evolution of karst systems down through geologic time.

Ghar Parau

D. Johnson, 1973. The story of the British expedition to the "big one" in Iran in 1872-73. The cave is 3,000 feet deep with 26 pitches.

The Grand Kentucky Junction

Patricia P. Crowther, et al, 96 pages, 1984. The story of the connection between the Flint Ridge Cave System and Mammoth Cave to form the longest known cave in the world as told in the words of each of the seven participants on the historic connection trip.

The Gurnee Guide to American Caves

Russell & Jeanne Gurnee, a guide to show caves in the United States open to the public. Includes descriptions of the caves and directions for finding each one.

The Hill Caves of Yucatán

H.C. Mercer, 1975 (reprint—originally published in 1896). Searching for evidence of human activity in Central American caves.

The Jewel Cave Adventure

Herb and Jan Conn, 240 pages, 1977. The fascinating story of two people exploring and mapping what is now the second longest cave in the United States.

Journey to the Center of the Earth

Jules Verne, 1864, fiction. This is a classic, full of nonsense, but every caver should read it!

Karst Landforms

Marjorie M. Sweeting (ed), 448 pages, 1981. A world-wide review of karst, not only of landforms, but also water tracing, carbonate solution chemistry, karst hydrology, and types of karst.

Lechuguilla—Jewel of the Underground

Michael Ray Taylor (ed), 144 pages, 1991. A photo tour of Lechuguilla Cave, New Mexico.

The Life of the Cave

Charles E. Mohr, and Thomas L. Poulson, 232 pages, 1966. A popular book devoted to cave life with many fine photographs and illustrations.

Listening in the Dark

D.R. Griffin, 1958. Acoustics and sonar used by bats to avoid bumping into cave walls and each other.

The Longest Cave

Roger W. Brucker and Richard A. Watson, 312 pages, 1976. The story of the events leading to the connection of the Flint Ridge Cave System to Mammoth Cave.

Manual of U.S. Cave Rescue Techniques

Steve Hudson (ed), (second edition) 260 pages, 1981. A compendium of the latest cave rescue techniques compiled from many years of review of actual and mock rescue situations.

On Rope

Allen Padgett and Bruce Smith, 341 pages, 1987. North American vertical rope techniques for caving, search and rescue, and mountaineering.

The Science of Speleology

T.S. Ford and C.H.D. Cullingford (eds), 593 pages, 1976. Chapters on surveying, chemistry of cave waters, cave minerals, geomorphology, fauna and flora, and computer use in speleology.

Shibumi

Trevanian, 374 pages, 1979, fiction. Not really a cave book but a spy thriller which has some fantastic and authentic caving adventures woven into the story.

Speleology, The Study of Caves

George W. Moore and G. Nicholas Sullivan, 150 pages, 1978. An introduction to the science of speleology for the layman.

Trapped!

Robert K. Murray and Roger W. Brucker, 335 pages, 1979. The story of the 1925 attempted rescue of Floyd Collins from Sand Cave, Kentucky.

Under Plowman's Floor

Richard A. Watson, 224 pages, 1978, fiction. A story about a man who does far-out solo caving and the motivation behind his actions.

Venturing Underground

Ben Lyon, 1983. A generally excellent British book. Contains some curious opinions on American vertical techniques.

LEGAL FORMS AND RELEASES

Chapter 19 author, Joel Stevenson, accumulated this collection of sample forms. He wishes to thank Jay Clark of the Texas Bar, Burt Allen of the Middle Ozark Lower Earth Society, and Russell H. Gurnee of the National Speleological Foundation for contributing some of the releases which are included in this Appendix.

Notice

Although the materials contained in this Appendix B are specifically exempted from the copyright of this book, utilization of these documents without the advice of an attorney is at the risk of the user.

Reasonable protection from potential liability can only be achieved through consultation with an attorney licenced to practice in your jurisdiction. The documents in this appendix may or may not be effective in your jurisdiction at the time you decide to use them.

DANGER!!

THIS CAVE HAS NUMEROUS UNMARKED VERTICAL PITS. FOOTING IS TREACHEROUS. UNSTABLE ROCK IS PRESENT. THE CAVE IS SUBJECT TO SUDDEN FLOODING.

ENTRY INTO THIS CAVE PRESENTS DANGER OF DEATH OR SERIOUS INJURY FROM THESE AND OTHER HAZARDS.

ENTRY INTO THIS CAVE IS FORBIDDEN WITHOUT PRIOR EXECUTION OF A LIABILITY RELEASE!

ENTRY INTO THIS CAVE CONSTITUTES ASSUMPTION OF THE RISK OF INJURY OR DEATH!

Warning Sign

Any specific dangers which are not presented by the particular cave should be deleted from the actual sign. The sign should be posted so as to be observable and readily readable but care should be taken that the sign is not subject to removal or to being defaced or obliterated.

No warning sign, liability release, or other legal device can constitute absolute insulation from liability. They can only serve to lessen the probability of an action being successful if brought. Obviously, the more that such legal devices do tend to lessen the probability of success, the less attractive are actions for the recovery of damages.

RELEASE

I, the undersigned, do hereby release _____

_____ ,
its officers, agents, or servants or others from any and all liability, claims, demands, actions, and causes of action whatsoever, arising out of or relating to any loss, damage, or injury, including death, that may be sustained by the undersigned while at or enroute to or from any expedition or project under supervision by or in connection with caving.

The undersigned being duly aware of the risks and hazards inherent in caving or in participation in caving, does hereby elect voluntarily to participate knowing of said dangers.

This release shall be binding upon the distributees, heirs, next-of-kin, executors, and administrators of the undersigned and is given in consideration of the undersigned being allowed to participate in caving activities in which the released entities identified above are involved.

In WITNESS WHEREOF, the undersigned has hereto voluntarily affixed his signature.

Date	Name	Address	Telephone (incl. Area Code)

RELEASE AND WAIVER

(county), (state)
(date)

In consideration of the granting of permission to
_____ to enter upon premises known
as _____ located at
_____, and owned or controlled
by _____, for the purpose
of exploring underground holes, caves, crevices, and passageways,
the undersigned acknowledges that such exploration may be inherently dangerous and assumes all risks, known and unknown, which
may arise from such exploration and hereby waives any and all
losses, claims, or liabilities which I or my heirs may have for any
and all losses and damage which may occur to my person or property
while engaged in such exploration and further do hereby release
and hold harmless the owner, _____,
agents and employees, and heirs from such claims or liabilities.

I have read this release and understand all its terms. I execute it
voluntarily and with full knowledge of its significance.

_____
(signature)
(Parent or Guardian if minor)

AFFIDAVIT OF COMPETENCY AND ASSUMPTION OF RISK; AGREEMENT AND DEFINITION OF RELATIONSHIP OF PARTIES; RELEASE FROM LIABILITY; AND INDEMNITY AGREEMENT

1. General. This instrument constitutes both an agreement between parties and an agreed stipulation of facts which relate to the relationship and agreement of the parties hereto. Should any word, phrase, statement, or provision hereof be determined, as a matter of law, ineffectual to carry out the intent of the parties as expressed herein, such item shall be deemed severable and the remainder of this instrument shall remain in full force and effect.

a. Parties are identified herein as masculine singular, whether one or more, male or female, individual or corporate.

b. Provision is made for acknowledgement if same shall be both desired and convenient; no presumption shall arise by virtue of a lack of acknowledgement.

c. All lists are included as examples and not as limitations.

d. This instrument shall have, to the greatest extent allowed by law, both retroactive and prospective effect, and shall be deemed in effect at any time User has been or will be upon Owner's premises. Prospective effect may be withdrawn by either party by writing delivered in person or by mail to the address endorsed hereon.

e. Parties. For purposes of this instrument, the following definitions are agreed:

(1) "Owner" — The holder of any part of any manner of right, title, or interest in the referenced premises and any agent acting for any owner in connection with this instrument, whether or not any such persons are specifically named herein. It is the intention of the parties that in the event of mistake as to an agent's authority, or of any aspect of ownership, or the crossing of boundaries of third persons by User, the benefits herein given to Owner shall extend to all persons, known or unknown at the execution of this instrument, who hold any manner of right in the premises entered by User, and all agents of such persons, provided only that any such person acquiesce in User's presence upon the premises.

(2) "User" — The undersigned recreational user of Owner's premises. (Note: While one person may execute this instrument on behalf of all Owners, each User should individually sign, since one User may have no legal right to bind another User.)

f. Premises. This instrument shall be effective with respect to all lands of Owner entered by User. The parties may elect to endorse hereon an approximate description of such lands, and should note hereon any lands of Owner which are excepted from this instrument (i.e., lands upon which User has no permission to enter).

g. If this instrument is executed by a parent, guardian, or spouse of any User, or any other person having any family or support relationship to any User, such person, whether or not a User in his own right, agrees to the terms and conditions of this instrument with respect to any cause of action which might arise regarding the User with whom he has such relationship, whether such cause be independent or representative, and shall include, inter alia, any cause for loss of support or services, consortium, out of pocket expenses, wrongful death, or any other matter arising from the presence of User upon Owner's premises.

h. The parties are aware that the laws of the State may protect landowners from liability and encourage landowners to make their property available for recreational use. The parties feel that existing laws may be inadequate to fully protect the landowner, and it is therefore one purpose of this instrument to add to all existing statutory and common law protection of Owner the additional protections, assurances, and agreements contained herein.

2. User is interested in the exploration of caves and other geological features, primarily for recreation, and in the search for such features previously unknown. In connection therewith, User desires to enter upon the premises of the Owner. It is understood that this instrument is executed by User in solicitation of Owner's permission for User to enter upon, for User's own purposes, the premises of Owner. It is agreed that owner's grant of such permission constitutes good and valuable consideration for the assurances, benefits, and protections herein given to Owner. User warrants that he has no cause of action against Owner from User's previous presence upon Owner's premises and specifically releases Owner from any liability which might at any time be alleged to arise from such previous presence.

3. Owner agrees:

a. Bare permission to enter his premises is hereby granted to User without representation or warranty whatever.

b. No admission charge of any kind is required of User.

c. He will refrain from willful or malicious injury to User.

4. User agrees and warrants:

a. He is physically and mentally sound, and thoroughly qualified and experienced in caving, climbing, diving, and all other activities which he will attempt upon the premises and User is in a position superior to that of Owner in knowing and evaluating User's condition, ability, and judgement, to include that of other Users concurrently upon the premises.

b. Caving, climbing, diving, and all other activities which User may attempt upon the premises are inherently dangerous. Among others, such dangers may include unsafe footing, loose and falling material, flooding, entrapment in constricted areas, unsafe air and gasses, disease from organisms or harmful substances, and loss of direction. Such dangers are often aggravated by poor visibility, fatigue, hypothermia, and negligence of companions. Caves, bluff lines, and other areas are often modified by human activity and thus made more unstable and dangerous than same would be in their natural states. Often, unsafe conditions are not detected until it is too late. USER VOLUNTARILY EXPOSES HIMSELF to these and other dangers, and VOLUNTARILY ASSUMES ALL RISKS of injury in such environment.

c. He will use reasonable care to prevent fires, avoid litter, insure that gates are left as he finds them, and avoid unnecessary disturbance of livestock and damage to crops. He will not damage, deface, alter, or remove and natural feature or any of Owner's property in the absence of Owner's specific permission to do so.

d. Owner shall incur no liability whatever for any effect of mining operations or any other modification of the premises which may have been made or may be made by anyone, whether same be known by Owner or not. User assumes the risk even of the presence of live explosives or other harmful substances upon the premises.

e. User will at all times be upon the premises as a bare licensee.

(1) No voluntary act of Owner, as for example any act done for the safety, comfort, or convenience of User, shall alter the relationship of the parties or create any other basis for liability whatever.

(2) No voluntary act of User, as for example providing Owner with information, maps, photographs, or other materials, shall alter the relationship of the parties, be deemed a form of admission charge, or otherwise create any basis of liability whatever.

f. The undersigned User for himself, his heirs, assigns, and personal representatives, hereby releases Owner (to include, as aforesaid), his heirs, assigns, successors, and personal representatives, from all liability for any injury, death, loss, or damage to person or property of the undersigned User (and any person he represents or is acting for), while he or such property shall be upon Owner's premises, whether or not such injury, death, or loss or damage shall have been proximately caused by negligence of Owner, negligence of third persons, or condition of the premises.

g. User further binds himself, his heirs, assigns, and personal representatives to repay to Owner, his heirs, assigns, successors, or personal representatives any sum of money (including, but not limited to, fees of attorneys and expert witnesses) that Owner might reasonably expend in the avoidance or defense of any manner of claim arising in any way from User's presence upon Owner's premises (save and except willful or malicious acts or omissions). If allowed by law, User will pay to Owner double damages, which is to say, twice the total of all amounts expended as set forth in this paragraph.

5. It is stipulated by the parties hereto that in the event of any legal action between the parties, this instrument may be entered into evidence by either party and the entire contents hereof made available to the trier of fact in such action.

6. Be it remembered, this instrument has been prepared by cave explorers (Users), and not by any Owner, for the purpose of landowner protection as a means of obtaining access to caves and related features, which are more and more often closed by Owners in self defense against a litigious society. Whereas Users preparing this instrument desire to do everything possible to keep caves and related features open to their use, this instrument may be widely distributed, and provided to Owners. The fact, therefore, that an Owner may provide this form as a condition precedent to the grant of permission to enter shall be interpreted in light of the fact that this form of instrument has been prepared by Users, and actively promoted and encouraged by Users. Each undersigned User adopts and ratifies this form of instrument as his own, mindful that had he objected to any provision hereof, he would have been free to propose his own form.

I HAVE CAREFULLY READ THIS INSTRUMENT AND UNDERSTAND ITS CONTENTS. I have received a copy or do not request one.

I now hereunto set my hand as my own free act this _____ day of _____, 19_____

_____   _____   _____
          (signature)   (address)   (status)

_____   (Owner, User, Witness)
         (printed name)

RELEASE AND COVENANT NOT TO SUE

THIS AGREEMENT is made and entered into on this the _____ day of
_____, 19_____ by and between _____,
said Party being hereinafter referred to as Property Owner, and an informal association
of joint venturers calling themselves _____ Expedition, said Party
being hereinafter referred to as The Expedition.

The purpose of this Agreement is to release the Property Owner from any and all
liability whatsoever for any injury, including damage to property or death which may
hereinafter result to any participant in the expedition as a result of such member
engaging in the exploration of any cave located upon property owned in whole or in part,
by the Property Owner. This release shall apply not only to any injury incurred while
actually exploring any cave, but also to any injury which may be incurred while any
member of The Expedition is on the property of the Property Owner for any reason
related to the exploration of such cave, including but not limited to, going to such caves,
returning from such caves, or engaging in topographical surveys of the surface of the
property of the Property Owner. It is the intention of the Parties to this Agreement that
the Property Owner shall be fully and completely protected from any potential liability
which may arise out of the activities of the expedition and this document is executed to
effect that purpose.

The consideration for this Agreement is the mutual promises and covenants contained
herein. Those mutual promises and covenants are specifically; on the part of the
Property Owner that the expedition shall be allowed access to the caves located upon
the Property Owner's property, whether such caves are now known or are hereinafter
discovered, and whether such caves are connected to now known caves or are unconnec-
ted and independently existing caves, and; on the part of The Expedition that the
Property Owner shall be completely absolved of all liability for injury as is herein set
out. The Expedition agrees with the Property Owner that as a condition precedent to
any Expedition member entering on to the property of Property Owner that such
member will be require to fully and completely release Property Owner from any and
all liability for injury and that such shall be signified by such member signing an
acceptance of this Release.

The terms of this Release are as follows: All participants in the activities of The
Expedition are engaged in a joint venture together, to-wit: the exploration of
_____ Cave and of related and adjoining caves. In order to
afford the Property Owner, the same protection from possible liability now enjoyed by
the members of The Expedition as between themselves, it is hereby agreed between The
Expedition and the Property Owner that The Expedition and the Property Owner are
themselves engaged in the joint venture of exploring said caves. It is understood and
agreed by the Parties that the only contribution made by the Property Owner to the
joint venture between Property Owner and The Expedition is that the Property Owner
shall, at such reasonable times as the Parties may agree between them, grant permission
to The Expedition to enter upon the property of Property Owner for the purpose of
exploring caves as above set out. It is specifically understood and agreed that Property
Owner shall incur no liability of any kind or nature as a result of his status as a joint

venturer with The Expedition and that the only benefits to Property Owner contemplated by the Parties are the continuing exploration of caves owned by Property Owner and the Release from Liability which results from Property Owner's status as a joint venturer. In addition to the Release from Liability which results from Property Owners status as a joint venturer with The Expedition and completely independent thereof, The Expedition and each member thereof do hereby themselves completely, fully, and absolutely release Property Owner and his successors and assigns from any and all liability whatsoever whether for property damage, personal injury, disfigurement, death, or otherwise, when such injury shall have resulted, in whole or in part, from any activity of the individual member or The Expedition upon or about the property of the Property Owner as a result of any activities of expedition relating to the things and matters hereinabove contemplated. It is understood and agreed by the Parties that the terms of this Release shall also apply to and protect employees of Property Owner. The Expedition, and each member thereof additionally by these presents do covenant with Property Owner that they, collectively and individually, shall institute no legal action against Property Owner as a result of any injury as that term has been hereinbefore employed in this Release. This Release is executed by each individual member of The Expedition on behalf of themselves individually and their heirs, successors, and assigns, to the end that this Release shall totally, completely, and finally release Property Owner from any liability whatsoever as is herein contemplated.

This document may be revoked only by a written instrument signed by the revoking party and delivered to the other Party. If either Party shall orally give notice of intention to revoke, then and in that event, it shall be the absolute duty of the other Party to accept written notice of revocation. Any revocation shall be prospective only and shall in no way impair the effect of this Release and Covenant not to Sue as to any events which have taken place. If there shall be any subsequent aggravation of injury received prior to any revocation of this Release, then this Release shall apply to such aggravation, it being the intention of the Parties that Property Owner be protected from liability in all events whatsoever.

Before any member of The Expedition shall enter onto the property of Property Owner, members shall sign an acceptance of this Release and Covenant not to Sue, and said signed acceptance shall be delivered to an agent of Property Owner by a member of The Expedition.

This document shall be governed by the Laws of the State of _____.

This Agreement is executed and entered into on the day and date first above written by:

_____
Property Owner

_____
Authorized Representative, _____ Expedition,
An Informal Association of Venurers

ACCEPTANCE OF TERMS OF RELEASE OF LIABILITY

THE UNDERSIGNED, each being a member of the _____ Expedition, an Informal Association of Joint Venturers, do hereby represent that I have read the Release of Liability and Covenant not to Sue heretofore entered into between the _____ Expedition and _____, owner of the property upon which I shall enter for the purpose of cave exploration. I do hereby accept and ratify all the terms and conditions of said Release of Liability, and on behalf of myself, my assigns, my heirs, and my executors, do hereby adopt said Agreement and fully and completely Release _____ from any and all liability as is contemplated in the Release immediately above referred to.

This the _____ day of _____, 19_____.

_____   _____

_____   _____

_____   _____

_____   _____

_____   _____

_____   _____

_____   _____

_____   _____

_____   _____

_____   _____

ACKNOWLEDGEMENT

State of _____)
) SS.
County of _____)

Be it remembered, on this day came before me, the undersigned, a Notary Public within and for the aforesaid State and County,

_____

_____

_____

to me well known as parties to the above and foregoing instrument, and being first duly sworn, each acknowledged that he had executed the same for the consideration and purposes therein mentioned and set forth, and that the facts stated therein were true and correct.

Witness my hand and Notorial Seal this the _____ day of _____, 19_____.

_____
Notary Public

_____
Printed Signature

My commission expires _____

Acknowledgement

This acknowledgement can be used with any of the preceeding instruments when either or both of the parties want the instrument acknowledged before a Notary Public. The form may vary slightly from state to state.

If an Acknowledgement is to be used, the parties should not sign any of the instruments until they are in the presence of the Notary.

GLOSSARY OF ACROYNYMS
AND TERMS USED IN CAVING

Acronyms

AAAS—American Association for the Advancement of Science. The NSS is an affiliate member of AAAS.

ACA—*American Caving Accidents*. A series of publications of the NSS describing accidents in caves.

ACCA—American Cave Conservation Association. An organization devoted to the protection of caves, located in Horse Cave, Kentucky.

ACS—Alabama Cave Survey. An NSS Survey.

AGI—American Geological Institute. The NSS is a member of the AGI.

ANSI—American National Standards Institute. A federal agency that sets standards for materials and safety.

AMCS—Association for Mexican Cave Studies. A group of cavers who explore Mexican caves.

ARA—Arizona Regional Association. An NSS region.

AS—Associate Member. An NSS membership category.

ASHA—American Spelean History Association. An NSS Section.

ASTM—American Society for Testing and Materials.

AUAG—Andrews University Area Grotto. An NSS chapter.

AVL—Audio Visual Library. An NSS committee which collects programs on cave-related subjects and makes them available for circulation to members through the NSS office.

AVP—Administrative Vice President. One of the NSS officers.

BCI—Bat Conservation International. A worldwide membership organization devoted to protection of bats, located at the University of Texas, Austin, TX. The NSS is a sustaining member of BCI.

BCRA—British Cave Research Institute.

BIG—Bloomington Indiana Grotto. An NSS chapter.

BLM—Bureau of Land Management. A government agency.

BOG—Board of Governors. The governing body of the NSS composed of twelve directors elected by the members and four officers elected by the directors.

B & B—Bob & Bob. Equipment supplier.

CAVES—Council of Appalachian Volunteers Engaged in Speleology. An NSS region.

CAVERS—Charlotte Cumberland Area Vertical Exploration Recreational Society. An NSS chapter.

CB—Citizens' Band (Radio). A low powered radio, operating in the 27-MHz band, for which no licence is required.

CCI—Cave Conservation International. An organization of cavers concerned with cave conservation and protection, located in southwestern Virginia.

CCNP—Carlsbad Caverns National Park.

CCV—Cave Conservancy of the Virginias. An advisory board to the Governor of Virginia on cave-related matters, located in Richmond, VA.

CIG—Central Indiana Grotto. An NSS chapter.

CIS—*Caving Information Series*. A series of articles published separately by the NSS describing the latest information in various cave-related fields.

CKCS—Central Kentucky Cave Survey. An NSS Survey.

CKKC—Central Kentucky Karst Coalition.

CM—Certificate of Merit. An award given to a member by the NSS for an outstanding specific accomplishment.

CMI—Colorado Mountain Industries. Equipment manufacturer.

COG—Congress of Grottos. An advisory board to the BOG composed of elected representatives of all IOs.
—Central Ohio Grotto. An NSS chapter.
—Central Oklahoma Grotto. An NSS chapter.

CPS—Cave Photography Section. An NSS Section.

CRF—Cave Research Foundation. An organization of cavers united primarily for the scientific exploration and study of caves.

CTF—Conservation Task Force. An NSS activity which works on a specific cave conservation problem. Reports to the chairman of the Conservation Committee.

DASS—Dayton Area Speleological Society. An NSS chapter.

DCG—District of Columbia Grotto. An NSS chapter.
—Dogwood City Grotto. An NSS chapter.

DUG—Detroit Urban Grotto. An NSS chapter.

EC—Executive Committee. The officers of an organization, either the NSS or a grotto.

EMG—Evansville Metropolitan Grotto. An NSS chapter.

EMT—Emergency Medical Technician.

EVP—Executive Vice President. One of the NSS officers.

FA—Family Associate. An NSS membership category.

FCRPA—Federal Cave Resources Protection Act.

FE—Fellow. An award given to a member by the NSS for service to speleology or the Society.

FL—Family Life. An NSS membership category.

FR—Family Regular. An NSS membership category.

FS—Family Sustaining. An NSS membership category.

FSS—Florida Speleological Survey. An NSS chapter.

FUN—Fairfax Underground Network. An NSS chapter.

GCG—Greater Cincinnati Grotto. An NSS chapter.

GEO^2—The newsletter of the Geology and Geography Section of the NSS.

GROSS—Greater Randolph Organization for Speleological Science. An NSS chapter.

HM—Honorary Member. An award given to an individual by the NSS. One of the Society's two highest Awards.

ICS—International Congress of Speleology. A convention of cavers from around the world organized every four years by one of the organizations belonging to the UIS.

—Indiana Cave Survey.

IKC—Indiana Karst Conservancy. An NSS conservancy.

IN—Institutional Member. An NSS membership category.

IO—Internal Organization. An organization which is part of the NSS: chapters (grottos), regions, sections, or surveys.

LCP—Lechuguilla Cave Project.

LM—Life Member. An NSS membership category.

MAR—Mid-Appalachian Region. An NSS region.

MCNP—Mammoth Cave National Park.

MIG—Michigan Interlakes Grotto. An NSS chapter.

MKC—Michigan Karst Conservancy. An independant conservancy.

MOU—Memorandum of Understanding.

MRA—Mountain Rescue Association.

MSS—Missouri Speleological Survey.

MVG—Miami Valley Grotto. An NSS chapter.

MVOR—Mississippi Valley Ozark Region. An NSS region.

—A convention sponsored by the MVOR twice each year.

NASAR—National Association for Search and Rescue.

NCA—Northwest Caving Association. An NSS region.

—National Caves Association. An organization of show cave owners.

NCR—North Country Region. An NSS region.

NCRC—National Cave Rescue Commission. An NSS organization which coordinates cave rescue resources and training.

NCRI—Northwest Cave Research Institute.

NIG—Northern Indiana Grotto. An NSS chapter.

NOLS—National Outdoor Leadership School.

NPS—National Park Service. A government agency.

NRO—Northeastern Regional Organization. An NSS region.

NSF—National Speleological Foundation. An organization which manages investments for cave related organizations or activities.

NSS—National Speleological Society.

OS—William J. Stephenson Award for Outstanding Service. An award given to a member by the NSS. One of the Society's two highest Awards.

OTR—Old Timers Reunion. A cavers meeting held each Labor Day weekend in West Virginia. See TRA.

OVR—Ohio Valley Region. An NSS region.

PMI—Pigeon Mountain Industries. A caving rope manufacturer.

POWIE—Prince of Wales Island [Alaska] Expedition. A group of cavers exploring caves and pits on Prince of Wales Island.

PSC—Potomac Speleological Club. An independant caving club.

RAC—Research Advisory Committee. An NSS committee which coordinates grants and advice for scientific investigation.

RASS—Richmond Area Speleological Society. An NSS chapter.

RM—Regular Member. An NSS Membership Category.

SAR—Search and Rescue.

S-T—Secretary-Treasurer. One of the NSS officers.

SD—*Speleo Digest* An annual series of publications of the NSS compiling information from various IO newsletters.

SERA—Southeastern Regional Association. An NSS region.

SFBC—San Francisco Bay Chapter. An NSS chapter.

SMC—Seattle Manufacturing Corporation, a manufacturer of climbing hardware.

SRT—Single Rope Technique.

SSA—Speleological Society of America. A national caving organization founded in the 1970s which no longer exists.

STC—Safety and Techniques Committee. An NSS committee which promotes safe caving.

SU—Sustaining Member. An NSS membership category.

TAG—Tennessee, Alabama, Georgia. A popular caving area.

TBAG—Tampa Bay Area Grotto. An NSS chapter.

TNC—The Nature Conservancy. A cave owner.

TRA—The Robertson Association. The organization that sponsors the Old Timers Reunion. See OTR.

TSA—Texas Speleological Association. An NSS region.

TSS—Texas Speleological Survey. An NSS Survey.

UIS—*Union Internationale de Spéléologie* (French). International Speleological Union. An international organization of caving organizations. The NSS is the U.S. member of the UIS.

USFS—United States Forest Service. Slang, see USDA-FS.

VAR—Virginia Appalachian Region. An NSS region.

UIAA—Union of International Alpine Associations. Organization that sets standards for climbing and mountaineering.

USGS—United States Geological Survey. A government agency that publishes topographic maps and geological reports.

USDA-FS—U.S. Department of Agriculture—Forest Service.

WUSS—Wittenburg University Speleological Society. An NSS chapter.

WVACS—West Virginia Association for Cave Studies. An organization devoted to collecting data on West Virginia caves.

Caving Terms.

aa—lava with a cindery texture. Usually does not contain lava tubes. See pahoehoe.

anastomoses—tiny networks of tubes and openings found in joint, fault, and bedding planes.

anthodite—radiating clumps of crystalline aragonite. Tufts of crystals radiate from a common center, resulting in a spiky appearance.

aquifer—a water bearing stratum of rock, sand, or gravel, that yields water to a well or spring.

aragonite—a mineral of calcium carbonate, $CaCO_3$, like calcite but of a different crystal form and higher specific gravity.

ascender—a mechanical device with a cam that grips a rope when downward pressure is applied to the device.

bang—any explosive substance.

bedding plane—a surface in a rock unit that separates individual layers or beds of rock.

belay—a safety rope tied to a climber that is played out or taken in by a second person (the belayer) as the climber moves. The purpose of the belay is to catch the climber in the event of a fall.

bell hole—See ceiling pocket.

boneyard—spongework with passageways large enough to enter. See spongework.

booty—virgin passage. See virgin passage.

botryoid—small bead- or knob-like projections from cave walls. They are usually of calcite.

bounce—to go down a pit or drop and come right back up. See yo-yo.

boxwork—intersecting mineral blades projecting from the walls or ceiling of a cave. Can be composed of calcite, gypsum, limonite, silica, or other minerals.

brake bar—a round bar about $2\frac{1}{2} \times \frac{3}{4}$ inches that is placed on a rappel rack or carabiners so that a rope can be threaded through the rack or carabiners for rappelling.

breakdown—rock slabs, blocks, or chips on the floor of a cave that have fallen from the walls or ceiling.

cable ladder—a ladder made of two parallel cables with metal rungs held in place on the cables by metal ferrules crimped to the cables.

calcite—a mineral composed of calcium carbonate, $CaCO_3$; the main mineral composing most common speleothems in limestone.

calcite raft—a thin layer of crystalline carbonate material that floats on the surface of a still cave pool.

carabiner—an oval of steel or aluminum with a movable spring-loaded gate on one side. A carabiner is used in many ways to attach ropes or slings to other objects (see locking carabiner).

carbide—calcium carbide, CaC_2, a grey material that reacts with water to produce acetylene gas and calcium hydroxide.

carbide lamp—a lamp that produces light by burning acetylene gas produced from carbide and water. See Chapter 2.

cave—a naturally formed void in the earth, generally large enough for a man to enter. It is not necessary for a cave to have an opening to the surface.

cave coral—a botryoidal form that resembles coral. See botryoid.

cave pearl—a small, round calcite concretion that has formed in a shallow cave pool or floor depression.

cave system—a series of connecting caves or caves in an area that had been connected at one time.

caver—a person who explores caves in a safe manner while showing respect for the cave, other cavers, the land above the cave, and the cave owner. See spelunker.

cavern—a large cave.

ceiling pocket—a hole or depression dissolved into cave ceilings noted for its smooth shape and lack of vertical features associated with descending vadose water.

cenote—(Spanish) a deep sinkhole in limestone having a pool at the bottom, found especially in Yucatán.

chert—a hard mineral composed of silica, usually light-cream or grey to black in color.

chert nodule—a nodule of chert usually found embedded in the cave wall, ceiling, or floor.

Clog—a British company that manufactures climbing hardware.

column—a speleothem formed when a stalagmite and a stalactite grow together.

commercial cave—a show cave.

contour line—a line drawn on a topographic map such that if it were drawn on the ground would be everywhere at the same elevation above sea level.

crawlway—a cave passage small enough to require a caver to traverse on hands and knees or squeeze through on his back or belly.

dendritic—a branching pattern resembling a tree.

dip—the slope of a bedding plane, expressed as the angle between a straight line along the bed and a horizontal line in the same direction. See strike.

dolomite—a rock or mineral composed of calcium magnesium carbonate, $CaMg(CO_3)_2$.

doline—a broad sinkhole.

dome—a high shaft in a room or passage when seen from below.

dome-pit—a high shaft when seen from near the middle so some of the shaft extends above the viewer and some extends below.

double brake bars—a rappel device of two carabiners with a brake bar on each one connected together by a third carabiner or a metal ring.

electric lamp—in the context of caving, generally a helmet-mounted headpiece (bulb, reflector, and lens) with a wire running to a battery carried elsewhere on the person. See Chapter 3.

etrier—(a-tree-a) a short, flimsy ladder made of webbing, rope, or metal rungs used by cavers primarily to negotiate difficult lips.

figure 8—A rappelling device that looks like an eight.
—a useful knot that looks similar to an eight.

flagging tape—thin plastic ribbon of any color about 1½ inches wide used for marking survey stations, trails, etc.

flowstone—mineral deposits that have accumulated as water slowly seeps over a wall or floor of a cave.

formation(s)—a rock unit with distinct characteristics within a sequence of rocks.
—a term for mineral deposits in caves. See speleothem.

frostwork—an aragonite anthodite with radiating, needle-like form.

Gibbs—a cam-type mechanical ascending device made in the United States.

gorget—an ornamental collar.

grotto—an internal organization of the National Speleological Society made up of individuals who reside in the same general locality. A chapter.
—a small cave or chamber.

guano—a material found on the floor of bat caves made up of the excrement of the bats. A rich fertilizer.

gypsum—a common cave mineral composed of hydrous calcium sulphate, $CaSO_4 \cdot 2H_2O$.

gypsum flower—a fibrous speleothem of sulfate that radiates out in "petals" from a common base.

gypsum needle—a sulphate speleothem having the shape of a needle that grows from gypsiferous cave soils.

hachure—a tick mark drawn perpendicular to a contour line to show the down direction. Hachures always point down slope.

helectite—a smooth-surface stalactitic form that grows in curved paths instead of hanging vertically.

hot-seat rappel—an old method of rappelling with the rope running under one leg and up across the opposite shoulder, controlled with a hand. The friction of the rope on the buttocks creates a lot of heat, hence the name.

hypogenic cave—A cave that forms as a result of water rising from deep within the earth.

hypothermia—a dangerous condition caused by wet and cold. A common complication of a cave accident or of not dressing properly for the cave. Can kill if not handled properly.

joint—a fracture in a series of rock units, generally at an angle to the bedding planes.

jumar—a spring loaded cam-type mechanical ascending device made in Switzerland.

karst—a terrain where the topography is formed by the dissolving of rock, usually limestone or gypsum, and is characterized by solutional surface features, subterranean drainage, and caves.

kernmantle—a type of rope construction consisting of a core of parallel bunches of fibers contained in a tightly woven protective sheath.

knots—various methods of securing or tying ropes or webbing material together.

lava tube—a cave formed by the crusting over of the surface of a flowing stream of molten lava, similar to a skin of ice on a frozen river.

limestone—a grey-blue rock composed of calcium carbonate, $CaCO_3$.

locking carabiner—a carabiner with a sleeve which can be fixed over the opening in the gate in such a way that the gate cannot open.

loess – a homogeneous deposit of mostly silt, usually deposited by wind.

lubber line – the line on the compass that is used to aim it.

marble – a metamorphosed form of limestone – limestone that has been subjected to heat and pressure.

mechanical ascender – term used to specify the use of a mechanical device instead of an ascender knot for climbing up a rope.

middens – accumulations of animal droppings, other than guano; may be solidified.

moonmilk – a white, semi-liquid material which is sometimes seen flowing down cave walls or dripping onto speleothems or the floor. Usually consists of the mineral hydromagnesite.

newsletter – in the context of caving, a publication of a caving club concerning caves, caving, and club activities.

neat line – the line that forms the border of the map portion of a map sheet.

NSS Bulletin – a journal published by the National Speleological Society containing articles of scientific interest.

NSS News – the monthly publication of the National Speleological Society containing articles of caving interest, society news, advertisements, and other items of interest to cavers.

onyx – a banded flowstone, travertine.

oulopholite – a gypsum flower.

pahoehoe – lava with a smooth or billowy texture in which lava tubes are found. See aa.

pallette – a shield.

pendants – smooth bedrock pillars hanging from the cave ceiling and from ledges. They are part of the original bedrock material left behind by solution.

Petzl – A French manufacturer of caving and climbing equipment.

pH – the acid content of water is usually measured in pH units. Water with a pH of less than 7.0 is called acidic and water with a pH greater than 7.0 is called alkaline.

pit – a shaft in a cave when seen from above or an open-air shaft that serves as the entrance to a cave.

pit cave – a cave that must be entered through a pit, usually requiring vertical techniques to descend and ascend.

piton – a flat, spike-like device with an eye in the end driven into cracks in the rock to hold a carabiner to form a rope anchor.

popcorn – a botryoidal form resembling popcorn. See botryoid.

potholes – bell hole-like structures in passage floors.

prusiking – the art of climbing a standing line using Prusik knots.

Prusik knot – a knot tied by looping a smaller diameter rope around a larger standing line that has the property of sliding with no load on the knot, but will hold when it is loaded. Invented by Dr. Karl Prusik in 1931.

pseudokarst – a terrain that appears similar to karst but which was formed by a mechanism different from solution.

quadrangle – in the context of caving, a topographic map sheet.

radon – an elemental radioactive gas formed from the radioactive decay of uranium naturally found in bedrock.

raft – see calcite raft.

rappel – the art of descending a rope using some sort of friction between the rope and the rappeller to control the rate of descent.

rappel rack – a long U-shaped steel bar that holds several brake bars and is used for rappelling.

rappel spool – an early device used for rappelling that consists of a spool on which the rope can be wrapped around several times.

region – in the context of caving, an Internal Organization of the National Speleological Society made up of grottos or other organizations in a common caving area.

regional – a meeting or convention sponsored by a region.

rimstone dam – a wall-shaped calcite deposit that impounds, or formerly impounded, pools of water.

scallops – oval hollows formed on walls and streambeds by flowing water. These hollows have an asymmetric cross section and can be used to determine the direction of water flow.

scoop – to enter a passage first, especially in new discoveries.

scooter – a person who leaves a pit cave without helping to derig the rope.

section – in the context of caving, a society wide internal organization of the National Speleological Society made up of individuals with a particular interest in caving such as photography, vertical caving, etc.

selenite needle – see gypsum needle.

shaft – a vertical cave passage, a pit.

shield – a massive plate or slab of travertine that juts out from the cave wall at an angle apparently determined by the arrangement of joints.

show cave – a cave that is open to the public.

single rope techniques – methods of ascending and descending a single fixed rope.

sinkhole – a depression in the ground caused by solution of the underlying rock or collapse of the roof of an underlying cavern.

sinking stream – a stream that disappears underground, usually in a depression. See swallow hole.

soda straw—a thin hollow stalactite resembling a sipping straw. It grows from the tip by water flowing down the inside.

sótano—(Spanish) a pit.

Speleo Digest—an annual publication of the National Speleological Society that is a collection of articles selected from internal organization newsletters.

speleogen—a cave feature produced by the removal of bedrock such as ceiling pockets or scallops.

speleogenesis—the process by which a cave forms.

speleothem—a secondary mineral deposit formed in caves such as stalactites and stalagmites. See formation.

spelunker—a term usually used by non-cavers to mean a caver. Originally coined as a term to describe cavers but it fell out of favor with cavers as it was picked up by the media to describe all kinds of people who went into caves.

spongework—a highly complicated system of tiny holes, tubes, and interconnected cavities found on cave walls that can resemble Swiss cheese.

squeeze—in the context of caving, a very tight passageway.

stalactite—a speleothem of cylindrical or conical shape hanging from a ceiling or ledge resembling icicles. (Note that there is no "g" sound in the word "stalactite.").

stalagmite—a speleothem of cylindrical or conical shape rising from a floor or ledge.

standing line—a rope that is suspended vertically and used for ascending or descending. That part of the rope that is standing free and not attached to the anchor.

stoping—the upward migration of the ceiling of a passage or room by the action of slabs falling.

strath—a bedrock bench formed by erosion.

stratigraphic column—a graphic means of representing the various rock types of an area of geologic interest.

stratigraphic sequence—the vertical sequence of rock types in an area of geologic interest.

strike—a horizontal line on a bedding-plane surface at right angles to the direction of maximum or true dip at any point. See dip.

suck hole—a colloquial term for a small swallow hole in the bed of a stream that pirates water from the stream.

sump—a place where the ceiling of a passage drops to and below the water level, leaving no air space, with the cave passage continuing under water. Often called a "syphon."

swallet—a swallow hole.

swallow hole—a place where a stream sinks in limestone terrain, usually in a closed depression.

syphon—in the context of caving, a sump.

talus—a sloping mass of rock, dirt, and debris at the base of a drop. A pile of jumbled rocks.

topo map—a topographic map.

topographic map—A map that, in addition to other information, shows the landform by the use of "contour lines," lines representing equal elevations on the earth's surface.

travertine—calcium carbonate which is deposited from ground water in a series of flowstone dams—any flowstone or dripstone deposit.

troglobite—an animal that is fully adapted to life in total darkness and can only live underground.

troglophile—an animal that may live underground but may also be found on the surface.

trogloxene—an animal that visits caves for a part of their activities.

vermiculations—irregular and discontinuous deposits of mud, clay, or other material.

vertical caver—a caver who enjoys and is competent doing vertical caving.

vertical caving—caving that includes the necessity of ascending and descending by the use of rope.

virgin passage—a cave passage (or entire cave) that has not previously been entered, a new discovery.

vug—a small cavity in a rock or vein. May or may not be lined with crystals.

water table—the top or highest level of ground water in a given area. Below this level cave passages may be flooded.

webbing—flat or tubular nylon strapping.

yo-yo—to go down a pit or drop and come right back up. See bounce. A person who does so.

SOURCES OF EQUIPMENT AND BOOKS

This is a basic list of mail order firms that specialize in caving equipment and books. Most of them will send you a catalog upon request. If you're in a hurry (and have a credit card) most suppliers are happy to accept phone orders.

A good place to locate beginning caving equipment is the army-navy or surplus stores found in almost every town. These are a good source of cave packs, camping equipment, and other small items useful to cavers. Inexpensive clothing suitable for caving can be obtained at second-hand stores such as these operated by Goodwill Industries or the Salvation Army.

For more specialized gear like carbide lamps, recommended hard hats, and most vertical equipment the caving suppliers shown here are probably your best bet.

Adventure 92
3661 Annelle Road
Murfreesboro, TN 37130
(615) 890-3948

caving and climbing equipment
"Your Rope Connection"

Blue Water Ltd.
209 Lovvorn Rd
Carrollton, GA 30117

caving rope and vertical equipment

Bob & Bob
PO Box 441
Lewisburg, WV 24901
(304) 772-5049
(304) 772-3074
fax: (304) 772-3076

caving and climbing equipment and books
"Cavers Serving Cavers"

Cave Books
5222 Eastland Dr
New Carlisle, OH 45344

caving books and publications of the
Cave Research Foundation

Custom Cave Gear
PO Box 7351
Charlottesville, VA 22906

vertical cave gear, Simmons roller

Doug Feakes
RR 1 Box 118C
Falcon, MO 65470
(417) 668-7724

fine caving jewelry

Gibbs Products
2608 East 3820 South
Salt Lake City, UT 84109
(801) 272-8354

ascenders
"When Your Life is on the Line"

Inner Mountain Outfitters
102 Travis Circle
Seaford, VA 23696-2412
(804) 898-2809

caving, climbing, and rescue equipment

NSS Bookstore
2813 Cave Avenue
Huntsville, AL 35810-4421
(205) 852-1300
fax: (205) 851-9241

caving books, novelties, and symbolic devices
discount to NSS members

Outdoor Ventures
Myer Distributing
73 East Epler Avenue
Indianapolis, IN 46227
(317) 784-1255

millitary surplus, caving and camping
equipment, and topographic maps

PMI
PO Box 803
Lafayette, GA 30728
(800) 282-7673

caving rope, rescue supplies, vertical
equipment, and Petzl gear.
"A Passion for Caving,
A Commitment to Safety."

Seal Skins
Dave Strickland
14050 Allisonville Road
Noblesville, IN 46060
(317) 773-1878

$1/16$-inch wet suits

Speleobooks
Emily Davis Mobley
PO Box 10
Schoharie, NY 12157
(518) 295-7978

cave and bat books, prints, and ephemera

The Speleoshoppe
Ian Ellis
PO Box 297
Fairdale, KY 40118
(502) 367-6292
orders: (800) 626-5877

caving and climbing equipment and books

Speleo Technologies, Inc.
Doug Dotson
PO Box 293
Frostburg, MD 21532

SMAPS cave surveying software

SSP Wilderness
PO Box 36
Petaluma, CA 94953
(800) 772-5948
fax: (707) 763-2856

sleeping bags, packs, tents, climbing equipment

U.S. Geological Survey
Distribution Branch
Building 41
Box 25286 Federal Center
Denver, CO 80225

topographic and geological maps and reports
state index maps free on request

INDEX

H

I

J

K

L

M